PINERY BOYS

T0289329

Languages and Folklore of the Upper Midwest

JOSEPH SALMONS and JAMES P. LEARY, *Series Editors*

Published in collaboration with the Center for the
Study of Upper Midwestern Cultures at the
University of Wisconsin–Madison

Folksongs of Another America: Field Recordings from the Upper Midwest,
1937–1946
JAMES P. LEARY

The Tamburitza Tradition: From the Balkans to the American Midwest
RICHARD MARCH

Wisconsin Talk: Linguistic Diversity in the Badger State
Edited by THOMAS PURNELL, ERIC RAIMY, and
JOSEPH SALMONS

Yooper Talk: Dialect as Identity in Michigan's Upper Peninsula
KATHRYN A. REMLINGER

Pinery Boys: Songs and Songcatching in the Lumberjack Era
Edited by FRANZ RICKABY with GRETCHEN DYKSTRA and
JAMES P. LEARY

PINERY BOYS

*Songs and Songcatching in the
Lumberjack Era*

Edited by
FRANZ RICKABY
with GRETCHEN DYKSTRA
and JAMES P. LEARY

THE UNIVERSITY OF WISCONSIN PRESS

The University of Wisconsin Press
1930 Monroe Street, 3rd Floor
Madison, Wisconsin 53711-2059
uwpress.wisc.edu

3 Henrietta Street, Covent Garden
London WC2E 8LU, United Kingdom
eurospanbookstore.com

Parts 1 and 3 copyright © 2017 by the Board of Regents of the
University of Wisconsin System
Part 2 copyright © 1926 by Harvard University Press
All rights reserved. Except in the case of brief quotations embedded in
critical articles and reviews, no part of this publication may be reproduced,
stored in a retrieval system, transmitted in any format or by any means—
digital, electronic, mechanical, photocopying, recording, or otherwise—
or conveyed via the Internet or a website without written permission of the
University of Wisconsin Press. Rights inquiries should be directed to
rights@uwpress.wisc.edu.

Printed in the United States of America

This book may be available in a digital edition.

Contents

PART THREE—*Forgotten Songs from the Rickaby Manuscripts, by Franz Rickaby and James P. Leary*

Illustrations

PART ONE

Songcatching in the Lumberjack Era

Franz Rickaby,
the Lumberjacks' Songcatcher

An Introduction

JAMES P. LEARY

AMERICAN SONGCATCHERS emerged in the early twentieth century, an era of accelerating industrialization, urbanization, and media-based communication (Spencer 2011). A few, like Carl Sandburg, son of Swedish working-class immigrants, were up-by-the-bootstraps laborers cum intellectuals committed to a social democratic vision exemplified in songs of the people. Most were Anglo-Americans from well-to-do families who mingled nonetheless with common folk: comfortable in genteel parlors and college classrooms, yet grounded in and enthralled by locales wherein such older agrarian/working-class artistic forms as folksongs persisted. Many were decided antiquarians, romantics, connoisseurs, and purists seeking vestigial, rare, and pristine shards of Old World traditions in New World settings. The best, however, viewed folksongs as venerable yet adaptable, valuable evidence of the present as well as the past, bound up with the ongoing lives of singers and workers in real world settings. Franz Rickaby was one of the best.

Pinery Boys: Songs and Songcatching in the Lumberjack Era incorporates, commemorates, contextualizes, and complements Rickaby's *Ballads and Songs of the Shanty-Boy*. Published in 1926 by Harvard University Press but long out of print, Rickaby's book was and remains the foundation for our understanding of North America's Anglophone lumberjack folksongs, song-makers, and singers. Yet folklorists, cultural historians, and folksong aficionados have known only a little about Rickaby's life

3

and almost nothing about the full extent of his folksong work. Hence *Pinery Boys* is presented in three parts. Part One provides an affectionately illuminating genealogical quest and biography by his granddaughter Gretchen Dykstra. Part Two presents Rickaby's original work in a strategically altered sequence. Rather than replicate early twentieth-century editorial practices venerating texts in isolation, we have shifted Rickaby's keen observations on the backgrounds of songs and singers from their back-of-the-book position to serve as headnotes heralding each particular ballad. Part Three testifies to Rickaby's expansive interests in songs from the Upper Midwest's diverse indigenous and immigrant peoples through an annotated selection of culturally significant, regionally grounded songs from his extensive unpublished manuscripts.

Praised by the poet, historian, and singer Carl Sandburg as "the first important and satisfying series of lumberjack songs that has come off a printing press in this country" (*Chicago Daily News*, September 15, 1926), Rickaby's original book was aptly acknowledged in turn by every subsequent significant lumber camp folksong scholar, from Maine to the Upper Midwest, from the Canadian Maritimes through Ontario.[1] G. Malcolm Laws not only drew strongly on Rickaby when assessing "Ballads of Lumberjacks" in his canonical overview of narrative folksongs composed by English-speaking Americans (1964: 146–74) but also serendipitously prompted what, until now, was the only account of Franz Rickaby's short life. In summer 1964 Daniel Greene, who had taken music classes from Rickaby's father in the early 1930s, read Laws's book and wrote to him requesting more information about the lumberjacks' songcatcher. Laws replied that "not much was known about Rickaby, and that modern folklorists wondered why nothing more was heard from him" (Greene 1968: 316). Greene soon discovered the explanation: born in 1889, Franz Rickaby died in 1925, a few months before his book appeared.

Lauded as a landmark, *Ballads and Songs of the Shanty-Boy* was not the first book on the subject. In 1924, as Rickaby was preparing his manuscript, Roland Palmer Gray published *Songs and Ballads of the Maine Lumberjacks*. Gray was chiefly a desk-bound, text-oriented English professor who included no melodies, offered scant comparative notes, revealed nothing about lumberjack singers, and "relied mainly on students and local amateur collectors" (McNeil 1993: 7). One of the latter, Fannie Hardy Eckstorm, soon rose to professional ranks with the publication of her classic *Minstrelsy of Maine* (1927). Ruing her contribution of "at least eight songs" to Gray's collection, Eckstorm referred to him as "a venomous little beggar" in a 1929 letter to fellow ballad scholar Phillips Barry (MacDougall 2001: 18, 26).

Like Gray, Rickaby acquired some songs from local collaborators, but there similarity ceased. His relationships with one and all were uniformly cordial, especially with William Warren Bartlett (1861–1933), who reminisced, "I soon realized he was the right man for the work and turned over to him what I had gathered and offered to give any further assistance possible" (Bartlett n.d.). Born in Presque Isle, Maine, Bartlett arrived in Eau Claire, Wisconsin, with his parents in 1867. A successful building contractor and a dedicated local historian who published an essay on "Logging Camp Diversion and Humor" (1929), Bartlett provided an impressive series of lumber camp photographs for Rickaby's book, as well as contacts with key singers.

In Bartlett's estimation, Rickaby's firsthand interactions with the shanty boys, river drivers, and sawmill hands responsible for the majority of songs in his collection were consistently amicable and effective. "Dressed in a khaki suit and with his fiddle slung over his shoulder he would get together a group of veteran woodsmen and soon had them singing the old logging camp songs. If one could not recall all the words perhaps another could help him out. Soon Mr. Rickaby would catch the air on his fiddle" (Bartlett n.d.).

Giving credit where due in his posthumous publication, Rickaby invoked his "good friend" Otto Rindlisbacher, an accomplished "lumber camp fiddler."[2] His preface praised and thanked Mike Dean—a worker in Michigan and Minnesota lumber camps and the author of a remarkable songster, *Flying Cloud* (1922)—who sang and shared two dozen ballads. Other woods singers were both generous and appropriately acknowledged. Among them: the brothers Fred and Joe Bainter, Albert C. Hannah, Art Milloy, Ed "Arkansaw" Springstad, Hank Underwood, Archie Alcock and Andrew Ross—friends from Rickaby's stint in Charlevoix—and Wausau's W. N. "Billy" Allen, an acquaintance by way of Bartlett.

Rickaby's biographical sketch of Allen, a timber cruiser and poet whose ballads entered oral tradition, is the first treatment of the life and art of a lumber camp song-maker.

An able musician with a fine ear, Rickaby set down tunes for all but a few songs that were received in correspondence. His exemplary notes spanned ballad scholarship and lumber camp settings, situating songs as enduring texts and living performances. A committed populist who had worked laboring jobs aplenty, Rickaby was not satisfied with confining his discoveries to a university press publication. As Dykstra writes, he shared his findings through an eight-part series on "Famous Old Logging Camp Ballads" for the trade journal *American Forests and Forest Life* (1925a–g). He also offered public programs featuring "songs and ballads of the lumber-woods" in Upper Midwestern theaters and at normal schools "where a large number of homes and a great variety of homes are represented" (Rickaby letters to Bartlett, March 30, 1923, and August 8, 1924 in Bartlett 1923–24). By including "Ole from Norway" in *Ballads and Songs of the Shanty-Boy*, Rickaby was the first scholar attentive to the flourishing genre of broken-English "Scandihoovian" dialect songs in the Upper Midwest. And his bold, insightful claim that lumber camp folksongs, in the main, are fundamentally Irish in poetics and performance was fully substantiated by an ensuing half century of scholarship (Ives 1978: 385).

No wonder Rickaby wrote to Bartlett that Gray's book was "very interesting," but "I have his collection beaten quite a distance" (August 8, 1924 in Bartlett 1923–24). Indeed Rickaby ranks alongside such celebrated, innovative songcatching contemporaries as John Lomax, early chronicler of cowboy songs who similarly financed fieldwork with theatrical public lectures (Porterfield 1996), and Robert Winslow Gordon, founder of the Archive of American Folk Song who, like Rickaby, penned a regular column—"Old Songs That Men Have Sung" in the pulp magazine *Adventure*—that attracted a trove of responses from North America's grizzled singing workers (Kodish 1986: 29–44).

A first rank ballad scholar in his era, Rickaby fell short in some areas that have come to be of critical concern to present-day folklorists. He did not make sound recordings. He avoided bawdy songs. He failed to recognize that those he called "the stolid Indian, the quiet, slow-moving, more purposeful Scandinavian" had already begun to mingle, sing, and play music with "the Irishman, the Scotchman, the French-Canadian" in the region's lumber camps. Excepting his introduction's brief mention of Otto Rindlisbacher and the "logging camp fiddler," he neglected the vigorous lumberjack tradition of instrumental dance music. And by focusing on repertoires formed from 1870 to 1900 during what he called a "Golden Age" of lumber camps, river drives, and songs, he missed subsequent songs of Upper Midwestern "timber beasts" committed to the Industrial Workers of the World.

In Rickaby's defense, no other scholar of his era tackled or even fully recognized all of these neglected areas. Only a very few folksong seekers, for example, were making cylinder recordings in the early 1920s (Brady 1999). Bawdy songs, unsought from lumber camp singers before the late 1930s, could not be published legally and were not discussed publicly by folklorists before the 1962 *Journal of American Folklore* special issue on "Folklore and Obscenity" (Leary 2007). Prior to 1938—when Alan Lomax recorded a Wisconsin Ojibwe lumber camp fiddler who interwove indigenous, Quebecois, and Anglo-Celtic repertoires—researchers sought "pure" vestiges of precontact music, ignoring or dismissing emerging creole traditions combining several cultural strains (Leary 1992). It would also be decades before scholars recognized the rich presence of Nordic songs in Upper Midwestern lumber camps (Leary and March 1993). Specialists likewise produced scores of books emphasizing folksongs before Samuel Preston Bayard published the first serious study of American instrumental folk tunes in 1944. And John Greenway's *American Folksongs of Protest*, the first book on militant workers' songs, did not appear until 1953. Even then, the songs of Finnish loggers striking in 1917 against the Virginia and Rainy Lake Lumber Company—the employer of Mike Dean, Rickaby's most prolific singing shanty boy—were not scrutinized until eighty-six years after Rickaby's death (Haynes 1971; Leary and Virtanen 2010).

As one who has pursued all of these neglected areas, I acknowledge Franz Rickaby as the original pathfinder whose blazed trail I've followed again and again. I grew up in Rice Lake, a farming and logging town in northwestern Wisconsin. As a child in the 1950s, I got to know a handful of old-timers who had worked in lumber camps, including Rickaby's friend Otto Rindlisbacher. In the 1960s I worked in the woods, cutting fire lanes and peeling aspen bark for a local mill, and in fall 1972, while pursuing an MA in Folklore at the University of North Carolina, I discovered Rickaby's *Ballads and Songs of the Shanty-Boy*. A few years later, I paid fifty dollars to a rare-book dealer for a used copy. It was the most expensive book I'd ever bought. Since the 1970s I've interviewed scores of working loggers throughout the Upper Midwest and delved into many more archived and published reminiscences. Rickaby's book, correspondence, and manuscript collections continue to yield insights and prompt new research.

Other Upper Midwesterners, writers and musicians especially, have drawn productively on Rickaby's inspirational work. In 1928, three years after Rickaby's death, Luke Sylvester "Lake Shore" Kearney—a former yardmaster for the Lake Shore Railroad in Rhinelander, Wisconsin, and a co-conspirator with Eugene S. Shepard in the creation of an imaginary woods beast—published *The Hodag and Other Tales of the Logging Camps* (*Milwaukee Journal*, May 19, 1955; Kortenhof 2006). Besides the tall tales, anecdotes, and dialect stories signaled by Kearney's title, he included eleven poems from Wausau's lumber camp bard Billy Allen, while offering comments on lumber camp songs and singers paraphrasing Rickaby:

> First came the Irish, French and Scotch, then later the Scandinavians. The Irish gave the tone to the shanty boy literature, as we have it, for their shanty songs and stories smacked of old Erin. Their songs were original, in spite of the fact that they contained more than a hint of Erin's Isle. The tunes to which they set the words, were usually old, familiar Irish airs, which were also reminiscent of the times when many of the men stood watch against the mast, carrying the flavor and tang of the sea. (Kearney 1928: 30)[3]

Just as Kearney relied in part on Rickaby, so too did Otto Rindlisbacher when forming a Wisconsin Lumberjacks troupe for the 1937 National Folk Festival.[4] Knowing tunes aplenty but few songs, he and fellow musicians worked up "Fred Sargent's Shanty Song," "The River in the Pines," and "The Pinery Boy" from the Rickaby canon (Leary 2015: 75–81, 85–87, 89–90).

Most recently, Brian Miller—a native of Bemidji, Minnesota, home to several of Rickaby's singers—has issued a pair of recordings, *Minnesota*

Lumberjack Songs (Miller 2011) and *The Falling of the Pine* (Miller and Gosa 2013). Featuring empathetic performances of a range of Irish and Scottish lumber camp tunes and songs, including eight corralled by Rickaby, Miller published impeccably researched notes on singers and sources brimming with new information.[5] Miller's regionally anchored historical research provides a vital counterweight to the erstwhile imaginative twenty-first-century drift of "The Pinery Boy." Anthologized in a trio of regional folklore collections (Gard and Sorden 1962: 95–96; Peters 1977: 94; Waltz 2008), this Rickaby-collected variant of an English sea ballad, "The Sailor Boy," has been recorded frequently.

In 1941 Iva Rindlisbacher, drawing from Rickaby, performed a plaintive instrumental rendition issued in 1960 on a Library of Congress LP, *Folk Music from Wisconsin*. Sam Eskin featured "The Pinery Boy"—citing the version set down by Rickaby from "Mrs. M. A. Olin of Eau Claire, Wisconsin"—on his 1951 Folkways album, *Sea Shanties and Loggers' Songs*. Art Thieme, long associated with Chicago's Old Town School of Folk Music, drew on Mrs. Olin's rendition, by way of Rickaby, for his 1986 Folk Legacy album, *On the Wilderness Road*. It was paired subsequently with log drive images for a 1998 "Sesquicentennial Minute" produced for the state's anniversary by Wisconsin Public Television. Australian Goth-rocker Nick Cave's doomy, overheated arrangement lops off the sentimental first and last verses of what is otherwise the Olin version for a 2006 double CD compilation, *Rogue's Gallery: Pirate Ballads, Sea Songs, and Chanteys*. And in 2014 the Emperors of Wyoming, a Wisconsin supergroup of rock veterans convened by former Nirvana and Smashing Pumpkins producer Butch Vig, featured "My Sweet Pinery Boy"—"a tragic Wisconsin river ballad from the 19th century"—on their eponymous CD and as a companion music video (https://www.youtube.com/watch?v=FSBbhw806Dw, accessed July 3, 2015).

The neo-Victorian, steam punk, dress-up visuals of Nick Cave's and the Emperors' website, music video, and CD publication swirl toward a contemporary "lumbersexual" hipster fashion maelstrom in urban America, especially in such venerable logging regions as the Pacific Northwest, northern New England, and the Upper Midwest. "He looks like a man of the woods, but works at The Nerdery, programming for a healthy salary and benefits. His backpack carries a MacBook Air, but looks like it should carry a lumberjack's axe. He is the Lumbersexual" (Puzak: 2014). Echoing folklorist Richard Dorson's classic consideration of *America in Legend* (1973), journalist Willa Brown (2014) astutely linked the lumbersexual phenomenon to earlier romantic idealized envy by bourgeois males of their working-class brethren, albeit not the dust-choked miner, mill rat, and linthead, but the cowboy, the sailor, and the lumberjack breathing the free air of the open range, the deep blue sea, and the piney woods.

Will flannel-clad, booted, beard-oiled cosmopolites launch a musical revival and repurposing of shanty-boy songs? Perhaps, perhaps not. Whatever occurs, they and others can look to Rickaby, not as a means to bend bona fide lumberjack songs in service of faux-brawny identity but as the source of deeply rooted insights into the gritty, almost forgotten reality of their singers and makers.

NOTES

1. The major scholars drawing upon Rickaby for their studies of lumber camp folksongs include Eckstorm (1927), Barry (1939), Beck (1941), Doerflinger (1951), Fowke (1970), Ives (1978), Bethke (1981), and Cazden et al. (1983).

2. Born to Swiss immigrant parents, Rindlisbacher (1895–1975) spent most of his life in Rice Lake where he worked in the woods and in sawmills before opening a café/billiard parlor and (following Prohibition) tavern, the Friendly Buckhorn. An accomplished musician and instrument maker who adorned a backbar wall with "The World's Largest Collection of Odd Lumberjack Musical Instruments," Rindlisbacher welcomed lumberjack fiddlers to the Buckhorn (Leary 2015: xiv–xv, 76–77). Perhaps he learned of Rickaby through an account in the *Eau Claire Leader* (July 13, 1923) of the songcatcher's lumber camp song program for an enthusiastic audience in that city's normal school auditorium? Perhaps his wife, Iva, a music instructor for area normal schools, was the connection? On September 12, 1923, Rickaby wrote to William Bartlett that "a fellow in Rice Lake sent me . . . a lot of shantyboy fiddle music. His name is Rindlisbacher" (Bartlett 1923–24).

3. Regarding Rickaby and Bartlett's mutual friend "Mr. William N. Allen better known as Billy Allen and Shan T. Boy," Kearney wrote: "Probably there is no living member of the old 'lumberjack tribe' of the early years who has contributed so much to the song and poetry of the bunkhouse" (Kearney 1928: 5). Allen died the following spring at the age of eighty-five (*Ironwood Daily Globe*, May 9, 1929).

4. Intriguingly, when Rickaby took a job at the University of North Dakota in 1917, he assumed responsibilities for the Dakota Playmakers from the departing founder, Frederick Koch, who went on to form the celebrated Carolina Playmakers at the University of North Carolina–Chapel Hill. Grounding their productions in regional folk and vernacular traditions, the Playmakers followed the folklore-into-fine-art bent of Irish playwrights John Millington Synge and William Butler Yeats. In 1934 one of Koch's Carolina students, Sarah Gertrude Knott, launched the National Folk Festival, a geographically shifting coalition of folklorists and culturally diverse traditional musicians that persists to the present (Williams 2006: 13–15). When Knott sought Wisconsin lumberjack performers for the 1937 National Folk Festival in Chicago, Otto Rindlisbacher answered the call.

5. Three dozen installments of Miller's *Northwoods Songs* blog (http://www.evergreentrad.com/northwoods-songs/, accessed July 3, 2015) augur a new edition of *Flying Cloud*, the songster published in 1922 by Rickaby's major source, Michael Cassius Dean.

SOURCES

Barry, Phillips. 1939. *The Maine Woods Songster*. Cambridge, MA: Harvard University Press.

Bartlett, William Warren. n.d. "Program of Logging Camp Songs." William W. Bartlett Papers, box 5, folder 1. McIntyre Library, University of Wisconsin–Eau Claire.

———. 1923–24. "Correspondence with Franz Rickaby." William W. Bartlett Papers. McIntyre Library, University of Wisconsin–Eau Claire.

———. 1929. "Logging Camp Diversion and Humor." In *History, Tradition and Adventure in the Chippewa Valley*, 232–36. Eau Claire, WI: the author.

Bayard, Samuel Preston, ed. 1944. *Hill Country Tunes: Instrumental Folk Music from Southwestern Pennsylvania*. Philadelphia: American Folklore Society.

Beck, Earl C., ed. 1941. *Songs of the Michigan Lumberjacks*. Ann Arbor: University of Michigan Press.

Bethke, Robert D. 1981. *Adirondack Voices: Woodsmen and Woods Lore*. Urbana: University of Illinois Press.

Brady, Erika. 1999. *A Spiral Way: How the Phonograph Changed Ethnography*. Jackson: University Press of Mississippi.

Brown, Willa. 2014. "Lumbersexuality and Its Discontents." *Atlantic*, December 10. http://www.theatlantic.com/national/archive/2014/12/lumbersexuality-and-its-discontents/383563/.

Cazden, Norman, Herbert Haufrecht, and Norman Studer, eds. 1983. *Folk Songs of the Catskills*. Albany: SUNY Press.

Dean, Michael Cassius, comp. 1922. *Flying Cloud, and One Hundred and Fifty Other Old Time Songs and Ballads of Outdoor Men, Sailors, Lumber Jacks, Soldiers, Men of the Great Lakes, Railroadmen, Miners, Etc.* Virginia, MN: Quickprint.

Doerflinger, William Main. 1951. *Shantymen and Shantyboys: Songs of the Sailor and Lumberman*. New York: Macmillan.

Dorson, Richard M. 1973. *America in Legend: Folklore from the Colonial Period to the Present*. New York: Pantheon Books.

Eckstorm, Fannie Hardy. 1927. *Minstrelsy of Maine: Folk-Songs and Ballads of the Woods and the Coast*. Boston: Houghton Mifflin.

Emperors of Wyoming. 2014. *Emperors of Wyoming*. Liaison Music LM-4024, compact disc.

Eskin, Sam. 1951. *Sea Shanties and Loggers' Songs*. Folkways Records FW02019.

Stratman-Thomas, Helene. 1960. *Folk Music from Wisconsin*. Library of Congress AAFS L55.

Fowke, Edith. 1970. *Lumbering Songs from the Northern Woods*. Austin: University of Texas Press.

Gard, Robert E., and L. G. Sorden. 1962. *Wisconsin Lore, Antics, and Anecdotes of Wisconsin People and Places*. New York: Duell, Sloan, and Pearce.

Gray, Roland Palmer, ed. 1924. *Songs and Ballads of the Maine Lumberjacks*. Cambridge, MA: Harvard University Press.

Greene, Daniel W. 1968. "'Fiddle and I': The Story of Franz Rickaby." *Journal of American Folklore* 81, no. 322:316–36.

Greenway, John. 1953. *American Folksongs of Protest*. Philadelphia: University of Pennsylvania Press.

Haynes, John E. 1971. "Revolt of the Timber Beasts: IWW Lumber Strike in Minnesota." *Minnesota History* 42, no. 5:162–74.

Ives, Edward D. 1978. *Joe Scott: The Woodsman-Songmaker*. Urbana: University of Illinois Press.

Kearney, Lake Shore. 1928. *The Hodag and Other Tales of the Logging Camps*. Wausau, WI.

Kodish, Debora. 1986. *Good Friends and Bad Enemies: Robert Winslow Gordon and the Study of American Folksong*. Urbana: University of Illinois Press.

Kortenhof, Kurt Daniel. 2006. *Long Live the Hodag! The Life and Legacy of Eugene Simeon Shepard, 1854–1923*. 2nd ed. Rhinelander, WI: Hodag Press.

Laws, G. Malcolm. 1964. *Native American Balladry: A Descriptive Study and a Bibliographical Syllabus*. Rev. ed. Philadelphia: American Folklore Society.

Leary, James P. 1992. "Sawdust and Devils: Indian Fiddling in the Western Great Lakes Region." In *Medicine Fiddle*, edited by James P. Leary, 30–35. Bismarck: North Dakota Humanities Council.

———. 2007. "Woodsmen, Shanty Boys, Bawdy Songs, and Folklorists in America's Upper Midwest." *Folklore Historian* 24:41–63.

———. 2015. *Folksongs of Another America: Field Recordings from the Upper Midwest, 1937–1946*. Madison: University of Wisconsin Press; Atlanta: Dust-to-Digital.

Leary, James P., and Richard March. 1993. "Farm, Forest, and Factory: Songs of Midwestern Labor." In *Songs about Work: Essays in Occupational Culture*, edited by Archie Green, 253–86. Bloomington: Indiana University Folklore Institute Special Publications, no. 3.

Leary, James P., and Hilary Joy Virtanen. 2010. *Finnish-American Songs and Tunes, from Mines, Lumber Camps, and Workers' Halls*. Special issue, *Journal of Finnish Studies* 14, no. 1.

MacDougall, Pauleena. 2001. "'Understanding the Hearts of the People': Fannie Hardy Eckstorm and Phillips Barry." *Folklore Historian* 18:17–28.

McNeil, W. K. 1993. "New Introduction" to Franz Rickaby, *Ballads and Songs of the Shanty-Boy*, 1–11. Baltimore: Clearfield.

Miller, Brian. 2011. *Minnesota Lumberjack Songs*. Two Tap Records TTR014, compact disc.

Miller, Brian, and Randy Gosa. 2013. *The Falling of the Pine*. Two Tap Records TTM015, compact disc.

Peters, Harry. 1977. *Folksongs Out of Wisconsin*. Madison: State Historical Society of Wisconsin.

Porterfield, Nolan. 1996. *Last Cavalier: The Life and Times of John A. Lomax, 1867–1948*. Urbana: University of Illinois Press.

Puzak, Tom. 2014. "The Rise of the 'Lumbersexual.'" *GearJunkie*, https://gearjunkie.com/the-rise-of-the-lumbersexual, October 30.

Rickaby, Franz. 1925a. "Famous Old Logging Camp Ballads I: The Jam on Gerry's Rocks." *American Forests and Forest Life* 31:344–45.

———. 1925b. "Famous Old Logging Camp Ballads II: The Little Brown Bulls." *American Forests and Forest Life* 31:398–99.

———. 1925c. "Famous Old Logging Camp Ballads III: The Banks of the Little Eau Pleine." *American Forests and Forest Life* 31:486–87.

———. 1925d. "Famous Old Logging Camp Ballads IV: Jim Whalen." *American Forests and Forest Life* 31:556–57.

———. 1925e. "Famous Old Logging Camp Ballads V: The Shanty-Boy and the Farmer's Son." *American Forests and Forest Life* 31:614–15.

————. 1925f. "Famous Old Logging Camp Ballads VI: Jack Haggerty's Flat River Girl." *American Forests and Forest Life* 31:662–63.

————. 1925g. "Famous Old Logging Camp Ballads VII and VIII: The Shanty-Man's Life and the Shanty-Man's Alphabet." *American Forests and Forest Life* 31:749–51.

Spencer, Scott B. 2011. *The Ballad Collectors of North America: How Gathering Folksongs Transformed Academic Thought and American Identity*. London: Scarecrow Press.

Thieme, Art. 1986. *On the Wilderness Road*. Folk-Legacy Records FSI 105, compact disc.

Waltz, Robert B, comp. and ed. 2008. *The Minnesota Heritage Songbook*. Minneapolis: Robert B. Waltz. https://mnheritagesongbook.net/, accessed July 3, 2015.

Williams, Michael Ann. 2006. *Staging Tradition: John Lair and Sarah Gertrude Knott*. Urbana: University of Illinois Press.

Wilner, Hal, prod. 2006. *Rogue's Gallery: Pirate Ballads, Sea Songs, and Chanteys*. Anti- 86817-2, compact disc.

In Frenzy's Footsteps

A Walk through History with the Grandfather I Never Knew

GRETCHEN DYKSTRA

FRANZ RICKABY strapped a fiddle over his shoulder, threw a ruck-sack on his back, picked up his walking stick, and headed home. It was August 1919. He would travel 917 miles—much of it on foot—from Charlevoix, Michigan, to Grand Forks, North Dakota, where he was a professor of English at the university.

Seeking the songs of the quickly disappearing lumberjacks of the Upper Midwest, Franz called the book he would later write *Ballads and Songs of the Shanty-Boy*. It was published in 1926, months after he died at the age of thirty-five. He left behind his wife, Lillian, who had nick-named him Frenzy, and their four-year-old boy, called Wunk, who would grow up to become my father.

As a child, I knew Rickaby was my grandfather—he was never a secret—but my father was close to his stepfather, Clarence Dykstra, and remem-bered little, if anything, about Franz. I knew about Franz's first long walk through the Upper Midwest, although I never knew it was the first of many and I never connected it to a movement—I am not even sure I realized he walked with a mission in mind, let alone a mission with significance. I had a copy of his book, but I am embarrassed to say I never read it and I certainly never read—until recently—the many let-ters, poems, journals, and articles he wrote that my grandmother kept in her old brown trunk. They show his restless curiosity, something I saw in my father, which I inherited, too.

After several big jobs in New York that brought me some success, thrust me into the limelight, and, at times, rattled my nerves and challenged my confidence, I hungered to change my pace. So from my home base in New York, I—like some footloose ballad collector—have been wandering the Upper Midwest, searching not for songs but for Frenzy, the grandfather I never knew during a time I never experienced to places I have never been.

That summer of 1919 was his first collecting trip. Over the next four years Franz traveled from North Dakota back to Michigan, Wisconsin, and Minnesota, adding to the miles he traveled, the people he met, and the understanding he gathered from—and about—the shanty boys of the Midwest. He was one of a handful of academics, amateur folklorists, and adventurers intent on preserving the ballads that told in music and words the stories of the people who shaped America. His book, considered a classic among folklorists but long since out of print, was the first to memorialize the songs the lumberjacks—called shanty boys in the Midwest—sang in the crude lumber camps throughout the pine forests of the Upper Midwest. But the extreme isolation and footloose lifestyle that gave rise to the songs were disappearing as industrialization and communications galloped along; it was hard to find the songs. "The insistent cry for quantity," he wrote, "the feverish prayer for efficiency, brought machines, massive, grim, powerful, ultra-human creatures of steel; . . . One morning the romance of logging was gone. . . . The age of steel was upon lumbering—the impersonal age, the non-singing age" (88).[1]

It was far easier for me to trace his steps. Airplanes, rental cars, telephones, email, the web, motel chains, money, and time—none of which Rickaby had—made traveling my 9,794 miles a snap. It was not, however, easy to conjure up exactly what he saw, but I was able to piece together what motivated him—including, I believe, his own poor health and his desire to preserve the lives of other people who were dying, too.

---

1. Unless otherwise indicated, Rickaby quotations come directly from his writings with permission from the Wisconsin Historical Society. Where a page number follows a quotation, it refers to a page in this volume.

I also discovered some similarities between us. Occasionally Franz was asked if he was a veteran—after all, he was wandering the countryside, looking as if he might have been down on his luck. Embarrassed by the possibility of appearing frivolous, he sometimes hedged his answer. Likewise when people asked what I was doing I did not tell the whole truth either. I said I was researching the first person to collect the songs of the midwestern lumberjacks, but I did not say he was my grandfather. I thought it might sound self-congratulatory or, worse, cute—like some genealogical hobby. But, as I dug deeper and got to know him and his times better, my hesitation dissipated. I now proudly say I traced history in his footsteps and thank him for the gift he unknowingly gave me.

THE SINGLE AND FOOTLOOSE

I don't know how Franz found Hank Underwood, but Hank was the real deal. A longtime, former shanty boy, he sang many songs for Rickaby

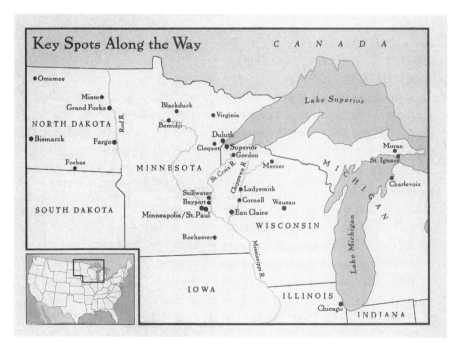

Key spots along the way. (Gretchen Dykstra collection; map by Robert Romagnoli)

when they met on a farm outside Stillwater, Minnesota, not far from Hank's hometown. Born in 1864 along the Saint Croix River, Hank, one of twelve children, became a shanty boy by the time he turned fourteen. He wandered from camp to camp, just as his father had done before him, working odd jobs and making a name for himself with his fine baritone voice. In 1904 Hank, then married, moved with his wife and baby son to Spooner, Wisconsin. A new lumber company had begun operations there, and Hank worked in its camps in northern Wisconsin and Canada, but when Rickaby met him in 1923 Hank was alone—no wife or son. Could they have died in the horrific fire that destroyed all of Spooner in 1910? No, I checked the archives and they are not listed among the dead. Poor Hank. What happened to him? I never answered that question, but the asking took me in an unexpected direction.

Back in the 1880s some counties in the Midwest—with a growing sense of responsibility for their troubled neighbors—purchased farms with government money and sent the poor, the disabled, and the mentally ill to them. These folks lived, worked, and sustained themselves together on the "poor farms." Stillwater had one of the earliest ones in Minnesota. I wondered if that's where poor Hank might have been when Rickaby met him. I went looking for it.

Down county roads over flat farmland the poorhouse is now a slightly worn, unmarked bed-and-breakfast, owned and operated by an Eastern European couple. An ivy-covered, stone building with chipped front stairs, a tiny tin sign next to the front door, and low light upon entrance, the inn welcomes bikers, birdwatchers, hikers, coupon clippers, and occasional exorcists. Right before I arrived, a group of "spiritual releasers" had spent a weekend there, intent on freeing the spirits buried in the eighty unmarked graves hidden in tall grasses behind the inn. Could Hank be buried there? The inn's proprietor gave me the organizer's name and telephone number and I tracked her down by phone.

"If my colleagues at work knew I did this they'd think I was zonked," Tammy, the organizer of the group, joked. "But it's not spooky stuff. I work with the Creator to unleash trapped souls."

Tammy said she'd be happy to try to contact Hank for me. So the next day after work—she's in sales at a large multinational corporation with offices in Eau Claire—she sat at her kitchen table and reached Hank. Their "connection" was weak, but no, she reported, he had not been at the poor farm; he had been living somewhere south of it, maybe back in Bayport, his hometown, she posited. She sensed that someone had been caring for him. Yes, he had often wandered and yes, he remembered Franz. He appreciated Franz's interest in the songs, but sensed Franz was an outsider. Oh, and by the way, please tell her (I guess that would be Hank's wife) I am not a bad person. I did not learn anything I had not already told Tammy—a tendency I have seen in other well-meaning seers—but my search for Hank gave me a taste of the dead ends that Rickaby must have found, too, and it got me to Stillwater, my first time ever to a one-time logging boomtown.

A bustling, well-preserved tourist town with cafés and small shops, Stillwater sits high above a wide elbow in the Saint Croix River, about thirty miles east of Saint Paul. It was an ideal terminal for the logging industry, as logs driven down the river could be stored in the large river bend. By 1880 the town had ten sawmills on both sides of the Saint Croix operating all day every day; four railroad lines brought thirty-five trains a day into town, and dozens of steamships plied the river coming and going from Saint Louis and beyond.

Timber built America, and American lumber barons built Stillwater. Seventeen different wooden staircases wind up the steep hills where Queen Anne, Edwardian, Victorian, French, and Spanish Moroccan mansions reflect the huge wealth that was generated below. In 1890 Stillwater was the richest city per capita in the United States.

Loggers had depleted the New England forests just as demand for lumber soared: The rapacious railroad companies needed hundreds of thousands of feet of wood to extend their rail lines. Those rail lines, in turn, delivered millions of new settlers to prairies and plains where they needed lumber to build their homes, barns, and towns. Entrepreneurs salivated at the thought of millions upon millions of old-growth trees that stood throughout the northern reaches of the Midwest. They lobbied the federal government to "convince" the Sioux and Chippewa Indians to give up their logging rights, which they did, and between 1850 and 1900 the lumber industry came to define northern Michigan, Wisconsin, and Minnesota. It was the golden age of logging. The song below, an ode to a pine tree, says it all:

Into a prairie house he'll make you,
Where the prairie winds will shake you.
There'll be little rest for thee,
O ye noble Big Pine Tree. (167)

The lumber barons might have owned the forests and the mills, but first into the woods were the surveyors. Hired by timber speculators, these "timber cruisers" chopped their way through underbrush and climbed hillsides covered in slippery pine needles to mark off forty acres by forty acres. They counted trees, measured their circumferences, estimated their heights, and calculated the linear feet that each acre would yield. Then, based on their projections, timber companies, owned by men with names like Weyerhaeuser, Kimberly, Clark, and Cornell, bought the land cheap from the government—or swindled the Indians for it.

One timber cruiser made a serious blunder that benefited me. In 1882 he and his small crew mismarked 140 acres of old-growth pines. They mapped the acres as swampland so no lumber company ever bought the land and no trees were ever cut. Today—on a dirt road between Blackduck and Alvwood, Minnesota, in the Chippewa National Forest—the majestic Lost Forty still stand in protected isolation. I could barely see the tops of the towering white and red pine trees that reach ten to fifteen stories tall. Their massive diameters, grown over 350–400 years, dwarf the skinny logs piled on trucks that travel down Minnesota roads today. It was the only time I saw what the shanty boys would have seen. I am not sure Franz ever saw virgin trees. He would have loved them, as he gained his spiritual and physical sustenance from the great outdoors.

Lumber barons made the fortunes and built the mansions, but the lumberjacks did all the work. The sap in soft pine trees does not run in winter, so that's when the shanty boys worked. Six days a week with long hours of exhausting and dangerous work in primitive conditions in extreme isolation in the coldest part of the country, the job attracted the single and footloose; some were the sons of farmers, some fugitives, and some just plain drifters. Others, like Hank Underwood, were the sons of loggers. They were big, brawny, and tough, stinking of sweat and filthy clothes.

"Up and down and across the country he roamed—here today, there tomorrow; chopping, skidding, rolling, hauling, driving great logs that the snarling saws might be fed. The free life called him, the thunder of falling majesties intoxicated him" (86).

With their heavy, laced rubber boots, axes slung over their shoulders, they radiated out before sunrise each morning from crude wooden shanties, spending all day cutting the massive trees by hand. They began at a river's edge and worked their way deeper and deeper into the forests.

They all had specific jobs. The sawyers felled the trees, sometimes as many as twenty a day, crying "Timber!" as the giant trees fell in violent waves, cracking limbs off neighboring trees, crashing to the ground in clouds of dust, sometimes crushing men below. The swampers followed, cutting the branches off the vast pines and clearing paths so the skidders could guide the logs to the skidway where four men—loaders and cant hookers—piled the logs onto the sleighs, tying them down with binders. Teamsters then drove the sleighs, pulled by oxen, over frozen ground to the closest river, where they stacked the logs in precarious piles sometimes 160 feet high, along the shore. There the logs stayed until the ice melted and the spring drive—the equivalent of the cowboys' round-ups—began with the dramatic and often dangerous rolling of the logs from the shore into the river.

Then the shanty boys became raftsmen, directing the logs from wooden rafts on fast-moving, swollen rivers; they navigated around other river rafts, supply barges, and thousands upon thousands of free-floating logs from multiple camps. The most daring and agile of the shanty boys were the birlers. With spikes on the bottom of their shoes and five-foot cant hooks in their hands they teased, tested, and competed with one another as they stood on the logs and twirled them down the rivers with their feet—some boasting they could walk 120 miles on logs without touching water. They dreaded the sharp turns, fallen trees, hidden rocks, or rushing white water that caused logjams and sent rafts in uncontrollable spins and loggers to their deaths.

"Gerry's Rocks," sometimes called "The Jam at Gerry's Rocks," described the death of a young foreman from a logjam. The song became hugely popular—so popular that some shanty boys claimed it was "sung to death" and others parodied it.

When the rest of the shanty-boys these sad tidings came to
hear,
To search for their dead comrades to the river they did steer.
One of these a headless body found, to their sad grief and woe,
Lay cut and mangled on the beach the head of young Monroe.
(114)

When the drives were over, logjams had been survived, and winter
harvests had reached the sawmills, the shanty boys got paid. They earned
anywhere from two to six hundred dollars a season—and they would
blow it in several weeks of wild debauchery in towns invariably lined
with saloons and houses of ill repute. Rickaby first heard "The Festive
Lumberjack" in Bemidji, Minnesota, when someone named Ed "Arkansaw" Springstad sang it for him. Springstad claimed he wrote it in 1900
with a black man, named only Bill.

But here's a proposition, boys: when next we meet in town,
We'll form a combination and we'll mow the forest down.
We then will cash our handsome checks, we'll neither eat nor
sleep,
Nor will we buy a stitch o' clothes while whiskey is so cheap.
(200)

Stillwater had forty saloons in its heyday, but when Rickaby arrived in
1923, nine years after the last log run, the saloons were empty, the wharves
were quiet, and the sawmills closed. The town had shrunk by two-thirds,
and the people who remained vied for far fewer jobs—few, if any, for
aging shanty boys like Hank Underwood. No wonder Hank lived on a
farm. Franz spent two days with Hank, who sang several ballads for him,
including a version of the perennial favorite "Jack Haggerty."

So come all you bold raftsmen with hearts stout and true,
Don't depend on the women, you're beat if you do.
For when you meet one with a dark chestnut curl,
Oh, just remember Jack Haggerty and his Flat River girl.
(111)

The song was native to southern Michigan but became a great favorite among shanty boys, farmers, and young women throughout the Midwest. Many shanty boys claimed to have known Haggerty, including a man from Greenville, Michigan, who described him as a well-dressed man, "not as rough as those other birds . . . a sort of a gentleman lumberjack." Rickaby included three versions of the song in his book, noting how phrases in the songs differed: Jane Tucker in one version became "her mother, Jane, took her" in another. He explained how these changes evolved and, in doing so, clearly defined what a ballad is—beyond its storytelling.

"Getting the swing of the melody of a song, and then bending both melody and words into a satisfactory union, is fundamental in folksong. . . . This may all sound slovenly and unkempt to the conscious artist; but in the realm of popular balladry, until one does it, the ballad is not truly his" (101).

THE GIGANTIC AND MAGNIFICENT FRANZ

Music was bred in Franz's bones. His father, Thomas Lee Rickaby, was the musical son of William Rickaby, an artistic and lovable low-level manager at a coal mine not far from Durham, England. A lay preacher and a good musician, William often railed against the working conditions underground and lost several jobs because of his protests. His personal frustrations and unfulfilled hopes rendered him unreliable, and he drank and gambled, sometimes disappearing for stretches at a time.

The family lived in High Haswell, a short distance from Durham Cathedral, where Thomas, as a boy, heard the boys' choir and watched the installation of the massive pipe organ that filled the church with glorious sound. He became steeped in the music, the hymns, and literature of the Church of England. Many years later Thomas wrote in his journal: "My teacher was a musician of the old school—gifted, but irritable and eccentric . . . who would sleep while I played, waking up and roaring at some key-board misstep. He was not able to sleep much. . . . I learned the anatomy, but not the soul, the lines with no coloring, the material but not the spirit and through fear of his outbursts of disappointment, I learned concentration and care."

This difficult man gave Thomas a strong base from which to grow, and eventually Thomas became the organist at Lanfield before leaving for America in 1887 to visit a friend in Deepwater, Missouri. I do not know if he intended to return to England, but in Deepwater he met Dora Eve Mohrweis, the sixteen-year-old American-born daughter of a German immigrant farmer. They married and he never returned to England.

Drawn to Thomas's unconventionality, Dora was the practical one, proud and determined. A homemaker, she sewed beautifully, painted china, raised animals, preserved food—and slaughtered chickens when necessary and, as an older woman, returned to college to become a teacher and help the family financially.

The young couple first moved to Bentonville, Arkansas, where Thomas became the organist in a Baptist church, but soon they moved to Rogers, Arkansas, north of Fayetteville. Thomas described Rogers as "a slow Southern village [where] pigs and cows fought pedestrians for the use of a few loose board walks." Franz was born there on December 15, 1889—a Sagittarius with the concomitant traits of expansion and excitement.

The Home Missionary Society of the Congregational Church—with money from a wealthy patron in Saint Louis—had founded a boarding school and cultural center in Rogers years before the public high school opened in town. Rogers Academy offered Greek, German, and Latin to its one hundred students, and it hired Thomas to introduce music to the students and the town folks. He organized a coed young people's orchestra and played the violin in a string quartet and cornet in a brass quartet. Believing boys were drawn to horns more than pianos, he started a small military band and lectured about music, telling Franz later, "If you want people to respond to music you can't squeeze piano concertos between talks on weed extermination and new forms of fertilizer."

After spending seven years in Rogers, the family moved several times with four more children born along the way. But tragedy followed them and three of the five children died: Otto at age two, Anton at age eleven, and Elsa at fourteen from an accidental gunshot. Dora Rickaby slipped into deep and recurring depressions, sometimes requiring hospitalization. Thomas remained positive and strong, traits Franz inherited. The family ended up in Springfield, Illinois, where Thomas became the organist for the Presbyterian church. He contributed to *Etude* magazine in Philadelphia, wrote playful compositions, and supplemented his paltry income with private students—a thousand by 1915. Franz described their home life as "distinguished poverty with constant music."

In his sophomore year of high school in Springfield, Franz at age sixteen dropped out and returned to Rogers.

"Which is worse? To do practically nothing or to do nothing practically. . . . I need to learn to do for myself," he wrote to his father.

Known as the Land of the Big Red Apple, the area was covered with orchards. In 1906, the year Franz returned, Rogers shipped more than three million bushels of good apples out of town and threw the bad ones into local cider presses and vinegar distilleries. Franz thought the good people of Rogers looked like apples. Today only two or three blocks of old Rogers remain—the main street runs parallel to a nondescript strip of fast-food restaurants and car dealerships on the way to Bentonville, the headquarters of Walmart. I saw no apple orchards, and the historical society—often the most enthusiastic promoter of small towns—discouraged me from visiting, saying I would see nothing of the old town.

For two and a half years Franz wandered in the Ozarks. He picked apples, planted saplings, worked in ice plants, hauled barrels of apples, and stacked them in warehouses as the growers waited for a good price in some faraway city. He led horses in circles to crush apples in huge shallow bins and stirred them on drying-room floors; he distilled apples into vinegar and baked them into pies. He built henhouses, hog houses, toolhouses, and corncribs; churned butter; and delivered cream. He graded rough and rutted dirt roads, raised barns, and cleaned up after fires. He hauled wood in the winter, mended fences in the spring, and pruned blackberry bushes in the summer. He conducted the First Regimental band of the Arkansas National Guard, playing along with his cornet, and he played his fiddle at dances, sometimes bartering for room and board, sometimes getting paid.

Then he walked, unannounced and unexpected, into his family's house in Springfield on Christmas Eve 1909 and, as a twenty-year-old man, returned to high school. He called these his wander-years, a precursor to his future travels seeking songs.

Sometime during his last two years of high school, Franz met Vachel Lindsay (1879–1931), the complicated, brilliant, and zany son of a Springfield doctor. Lindsay had studied in Chicago and then hustled his poems and drawings in New York, falling in love, falling out of love, meeting and knowing the inventive artists of the day, and haunting urban hangouts. Returning to Springfield after five years away, Lindsay began to give dramatic readings of his poems in the booming, theatrical voice that eventually won him nationwide fame. He published his poems, drawings, made-up maps, and musings in leaflets he distributed free. He wrote about Buddhism, which he practiced; Christianity, which he attacked; Hindi, which he read; Kansas, which he idealized; Johnny Appleseed, whom he revered; and inventive visions of an ideal future. And he spent time with a range of like-minded people, including his former high school English teacher, who introduced him to Franz, her latest star pupil. Franz and Vachel—kindred spirits—became fast friends.

"Lindsay, the poet, proved to me, a boy, that a poet can be a boy and a jolly companion at the same time . . . and that a man can listen to his maturing soul without losing the lightness of his heart or deeding away the ring in his laughter."

Franz took up self-publishing, too, and for a while ran a little vanity press called Pax Printery, producing collections of his own poems in teeny-tiny volumes, which he distributed free of charge to anyone who would take one. Lindsay read all of Franz's poems, sometimes making marginal notes, sometimes drawing minuscule hearts next to the ones he particularly liked, sometimes providing a preface to a volume.

Franz became part of a small group of young people who gathered at the Lindsays' house every two weeks for talk, debate, arguments, and discoveries. The group poured over *McClure's,* which stormed the nation in the late 1890s when printing presses brought the price of magazines down and the ever-expanding network of railroads made their wide distribution possible. With dreamy, four-color covers punctuated by hard-hitting banners promoting articles about fraud and corruption, *McClure's* staff writers, like muckrakers Lincoln Steffens and Ida Tarbell, explored municipal corruption and corporate monopolies, even as the magazine published literature by Willa Cather, Rudyard Kipling, Jack London, and others.

"We read everything from Shaw to Pshaw and shouted until midnight, some still being high school sophomores and very smart-alecky, all but the gigantic and magnificent Franz, who dominated the scene," wrote Lindsay in a memorial to him in 1926.

My Weary Bones Rejoiced

Franz began his first long walk to find ballads in the summer of 1919 from Charlevoix, Michigan, where he was the unlikely caddie master at the tony Chicago Club golf club on the shore of Lake Michigan. Charlevoix was one of those summer resorts that burst on the scene when Americans began to enjoy leisure time. Enabled by increased industrialization and assisted by the growing network of trains and boats, vacationers could reach out-of-the-way places. Groups of friends from cities, churches, and colleges often started compounds in places like Charlevoix. There Chicago Club members enjoyed sailing, tennis, gambling, and tea dances. The club also built, owned, and managed an eighteen-hole golf course that drew elite families with maids and nannies in tow—from Chicago as well as Detroit, Saint Louis, and even New Orleans. When Professor Thompson, the organist at the Knox Conservatory and a summer resident near Charlevoix, heard the golf club needed a caddie master, he recommended Franz.

Hired first in 1913 and returning for seven summers, even after he became an English professor, Franz managed the caddies by day and led a small dance band at night. He earned $150 a month as boss, den leader, teacher, coach, disciplinarian, entertainer, and referee to as many as 120 boys. He instituted and administered a rotation system for the caddies to ensure tips for all, and he kept the idle ones out of trouble with basketball and horseshoes, tugs-of-war and rounds of gloveless boxing; the boys learned all the variations of soft ball, including mushball and one old cat; they threw jackknives in mumblety-peg and played cards and practiced tricks. If they behaved themselves, Franz let them play golf, fool around on the putting green, or go skinny-dipping in the lake, and at the end of every summer he took his happy, motley crew camping somewhere on the lakeshore.

One summer Franz caused quite a stir when he recruited girls as caddies for the first time ever in Charlevoix, maybe anywhere. Fourteen girls enrolled and learned how to carry and balance the bags, flag a hole, hand

Franz, Charlevoix, Michigan, 1913. (Gretchen Dykstra collection)

Caddies from Charlevoix go a'boatin', 1913. (Gretchen Dykstra collection)

the clubs, stand appropriately, use the vocabulary, spot the birds' nests, and keep the score. Franz noted, "It has become fashion to hold the war responsible for all sorts of social and economic phenomena from the increase in hay fever to the high price of bone buttons . . . [but] now when a player turns to see his clubs taken . . . by some wee bit lassie, he no longer shakes his head dubiously . . . and complains about the far reaching and iconoclastic effects of the war."

Franz walked out of Charlevoix on a late August afternoon and over the next three weeks met 224 people, including some who didn't want to talk, didn't know any songs, and didn't know anyone who did. He met generous people and nasty people, and he befriended a man who spat through the cobwebs in his long white beard. He met people eager to hear about the Bolsheviks in North Dakota and some who knew nothing outside their own half-acre. He slept in deserted camps on beds of cedar chips and in dark bunkhouses on grimy straw mattresses. He lodged with farmers and milked their cows and stayed with widows and chopped their wood; he slept on a wooden pallet in a house infested with flies, and luxuriated one night on a mattress soft as a cloud: "The springs were

Children in the cutover, summer 1919. (Gretchen Dykstra collection)

delicious; the covers clean and sweet. My weary bones rejoiced and I turned my Luck around and kissed her."

But he found only two songs. They came from a toothless shanty boy in a small lumber camp about eleven miles outside Allenville, Michigan, in the Upper Peninsula.

"The road was sandy, and ultra-serpentine, having been originally a logging road winding away among the stumps. On all sides I saw the charred and fire-eaten stumps of what must have been magnificent trees, the hauling out of which this road was made. In this stretch I first saw cedar bark roads. A bad sandy stretch is covered with cedar bark, which the traffic chews up and beats into shreds, which ultimately make a fibrous matting which gives wheels the perfect footing."

Franz wasn't the only visitor that evening. A traveling salesman, trying to sell forty-dollar suits to men who didn't need them or want them, had also appeared. The camp manager reckoned Franz would be more popular, and, who knows, he said, maybe the men will even know some songs.

Eight husky, weary, and dirty guys, carrying axes over their shoulders, drifted back into camp and gathered in the chuck shanty. With an iron

Shanties in the cutover, possibly Allenville, Michigan, 1919. (Gretchen Dykstra collection)

knife and fork, a stone plate, and a shallow metal cup, they devoured meat, fried potatoes, and bread and butter with "jelly of doubtful flavor," all washed down with oily tea. "All was served in silence and smell, and devoured in a mad and noisy haste," wrote Franz.

But after dinner, back in the bunk shanty with pipes, cigarettes, and chewing tobacco, the men, sitting on the deacon seat that ran the periphery of the shanty, turned loquacious.

"Most profane bunch of men I ever heard. Reilly had a toothache and another responded, 'Well by _____ I'll never have th' _____, toothache agin, 'cause I ain't gotta _____, _____, _____ tooth in my _____, _____, _____ head. Went down las' time _____, _____ an' had ever' _____, _____ one o' the _____, _____, _____ yanked out by the _____, _____ roots.' The man wasn't mad, Lillian; he was merely conversing."

Franz took out his fiddle and probably played "Missouri Waltz," "Till We Meet Again," and "Beautiful Ohio," popular songs of the day. The men seemed to like the singing or at least one said, "_____, _____,

if I could play a _____, _____ fiddle like that, what the _____,
d'ya think I'd do another _____, _____ thing?"

Then the man with the bad teeth offered to sing "Harry Dunn" and
"Poor Little Joe" and, as the sky went dark, Franz transcribed the music
and the lyrics.

> I once did know a handsome youth whose name was Harry
> Dunn.
> His father was a farmer in the county of Aldun.
> He had everything he wished for, like houses and good
> land,
> But he thought he would like one winter in the woods of
> Michigan. (209)

Deaths like the one Harry Dunn suffered were sadly common among
shanty boys. Working in tough conditions in bad weather on harsh
terrain—high up in trees or way under them—shanty boys were often
cut or poked, crushed under falling trees, or drowned in swirling eddies.
Shanty boys basically worked alone. Unlike sailors and railroad workers
who needed a rhythm to set a pace at work, shanty boys did not. They
sang for entertainment, not to maintain a work rhythm. Their ballads—
defined as songs that tell a story—described the risks they faced as well
as sorrow and loneliness, women and heartache. They sang at night, deep
in the forests as winter winds whipped around the bunk shanties.

Each shanty boy was expected to sing—never repeating a song already
sung that night—or tell his mates a new story. If he couldn't do either,
he'd have to put a pound of tobacco in a box—bought in the company-
owned canteen, the wanigan—and hope for inspiration the next month.
If one shanty boy could sing better than the others and had a good memory, he'd become a precious asset to the lumber camp. Camp managers
often paid a premium to keep a good cook or a strong singer so that the
other shanty boys would not complain or, worse, leave camp, seeking
better grub or livelier diversion.

Some songs—usually the biographical songs or tragic ones—were sung
solo; others, particularly those with choruses, like "The Festive Lumberjack," called for ensemble singing:

He's a wild rip-snortin' devil ever' time he comes to town.
He's a porky, he's a moose-cat, too busy to set down.
But when his silver's registered and his drinks is comin' few,
He's then as tame as other jacks that's met their Waterloo. (200)

And so they sang and they danced and they fiddled and they told tall tales. Paul Bunyan, the mythic giant of lumberjack lore, was born in these shanties.

The Tales Would Grow and Grow

I went looking for Franz in Bemidji, Minnesota, where some people swear the Mississippi River begins. It was there, they say, that the tank that Babe, Paul Bunyan's giant blue ox, was carrying sprang a leak. I thought it would be fun to wade in the mighty Mississippi at the very spot, but several old locals, eating breakfast together at a small café, could not agree on where I might find it. After several minutes of vigorous debate, one old guy turned to me and said, "Lewis and Clark couldn't find the headwaters, but if you do, be sure to let us know."

The Mississippi does, however, feed into Lake Bemidji, where a lively town of thirteen thousand sits on the banks of the large lake. Bemidji has several sandy beaches, a couple of modern hotels, and the best restaurant I experienced on that particular trip. Franz had performed in Bemidji at the normal school and the Civic and Commercial Association. He often found new songs by singing songs he had found before to jog people's memories. So I went searching for the buildings.

I found the normal school; it now houses the administrative offices of Bemidji State University, a tidy campus of five thousand students stretched out along the lakeshore. But I could not find the old Civic and Commercial Association. Neither the historical society in the old train depot nor the modern visitors' center had any record of where the club might have been, nor did the Chamber of Commerce, the successor to the club. But I did meet Bradley Olson.

"You must meet my son," the woman at the chamber said when she heard what I was doing. "Bradley was the first person ever diagnosed with autism in Bemidji," she added with surprising pride. "He knows everything about music. He has a radio program where he plays songs on request and then answers questions when listeners call in. He'll love your project. You must go see him; he might have something for you."

I did meet Bradley. Several miles outside of town, in a small ranch house with an antenna towering over it, I found him at Mix 103, sitting in front of a computer screen in a dark booth. Tall and thin, wiry and bouncy, Bradley jumped when he heard me ask for him.

"Your mother sent me. She said you know everything about music and might be able to tell me about lumberjack songs."

"I don't know any lumberjack songs," he said unequivocally. With a wide and friendly smile, he added quickly, "But I'd like to. If you send me some songs I'll play them. We're a commercial station; we are not a public station. We play hits. That's what makes us commercial. I don't think lumberjack songs are hits. But if you send me some songs I'll try to play them."

Then he paused in his otherwise rapid speech. "But I do know Paul Bunyan songs. Tex Ritter, you know, the Singing Cowboy, he sang 'Paul Bunyan Love,' and Phil Coley from Maine, I know him, too, he sings Paul Bunyan songs, too. I wonder if they are like lumberjack songs? Lumberjack songs. That's interesting."

Paul Bunyan stories—not the songs—have, indeed, shaped our impression of lumberjacks—powerful, independent, fearless, and hearty. Like the shanty-boy songs Rickaby collected, Paul Bunyan stories evolved and changed, but unlike lumberjack songs, Paul Bunyan was a brand new invention, not rooted in British traditions.

Although sometimes contested by the proud people of Maine, most folklorists believe that Paul Bunyan stories began in the lumber camps of the Great Lakes when western expansion was exploding and large-scale achievements, like the destruction of the forests, and physical prowess, like the hardiness of the shanty boys, were the values of the day.

"Paul Bunyan grew up in shanties around the hot stoves of winter, among socks and mittens drying, in the smell of tobacco smoke and the roar of laughter mocking the outside weather," wrote Carl Sandburg.

After supper a shanty boy sitting on the deacon seat would start, often looking to tease a gullible newcomer. The stories could change nightly.

"Remember that winter at Paul Bunyan's camp when the snow was twenty feet deep?"

"You mean the winter the snow was so blue it changed the color of Paul's big ox?" someone might add.

"That great old ox, the one who swatted logs like flies?"

"Yup, that's the one, the ox with no front teeth?"

"Wait a minute, Shorty, what do you mean he had no front teeth? Everyone knows he had three sets of teeth, one lower, one upper, and one extra for chewing spruce trees."

The tales would grow and grow as tall as the white pines the shanty boys would chop down the next day. Then a clever copywriter, W. B. Laughead, got hold of the stories and made them widely popular.

Born in Xenia, Ohio, Laughead worked in Minnesota lumber camps for almost ten years before he was hired to promote the Red River Lumber Company in 1914. His first effort was a pamphlet the size of a postcard with thirty pages of Paul Bunyan stories interwoven among cartoons, photographs, and ads for the lumber; the company began to use the name Paul Bunyan on its letterhead and Bunyan's portrait as its logo. Then in 1922 Laughead wrote, illustrated, and published *The Marvelous Exploits of Paul Bunyan*, inventing the names of Bunyan's sidekicks, from Bill Brimstone and Johnny Inkslinger to Sourdough Sam; he even named Babe, the Blue Ox. Paul Bunyan went viral, and a new edition was released every year for the next twenty years.

I knew some of the stories, but Rickaby knew them better. He was particularly impressed with one collection, published in 1925 by Esther Shepherd, that used "the vernacular of an old woodsman."

"Well, Paul kept a-goin' up the road as hard as he could leg it with his breath comin' out in puffs like the exhaust of an ocean liner. . . . He was goin' so hard he couldn't stop and kept right on goin' over the hill and down dale."

Franz knew the stories, but he never would have seen the eighteen-foot high, two-and-a-half-ton statue of Paul and Babe that Bemidji erected in 1937, starting America's love affair with roadside attractions. I saw them and they made me smile.

THE WANDERING MINSTREL

Unlike Paul Bunyan, preserved primarily by one advertising guy with logging experience, most of the early songcatchers were either wealthy hobbyists or poor academics with wanderlust. Biographies exist for John Lomax, his son Alan, and Cecil Sharpe, but otherwise we do not know much about these cultural preservationists, who they were, and what motivated them. We only know they shared a commitment to preserve the songs of isolated or marginalized people when industrialization changed the world of work and communications changed the nature of culture. We know a few folklorists never left their desks, sending students and volunteers into the field to find songs or relying on the collections of others, but some were adventurous, climbing mountains, scouring docks, or exploring hollows. Some lugged cumbersome recording devices—invented by Thomas Edison—to capture the singing. (The first field recording was done on wax cylinders in 1890 with the Passamaquoddy Indians in Maine.) Others transcribed the lyrics, asking a singer to sing the song over and over and over again. As a musician who could read and write music, Rickaby transcribed both the lyrics and the music—and then, as a performer, turned around and played the songs to entertain others, hoping to spur their memories and thus find more songs. This ability to entertain made him special among his academic peers.

After Franz's first walk in 1919 the University of North Dakota saw a promotional opportunity in his musical talents and friendly ways. The university was founded in 1883 when the territorial legislature passed out goodies to new towns like so many Christmas presents: Bismarck got the capital, Jamestown got the insane asylum, Fargo got the agricultural school, and Grand Forks the university. (During the Flickertail Follies, an annual campus party, Franz thought the insane asylum had come to Grand Forks.)

Initially the "Pioneer University of the Prairies" struggled: funds were scarce, typhoid fever struck, a flood swallowed Grand Forks, and students were hard to come by—only a few hundred young people graduated from high school statewide each year. Most were the children of non-English-speaking Norwegians, German Russians, Swedes, Danes, and Czechs who suffered the brutal winters, oppressive summers, debilitating isolation, and arduous work of farming the prairies. They had little time—or use—for higher education. Even by 1917, when Franz and his new wife, Lillian, arrived in Grand Forks, the college still had to work hard to introduce itself to rural communities and convince farmers of its value. It hoped that Franz could help promote the university.

So, for the year following that first long walk from Charlevoix, the university booked him into towns around the state, advertising the event with a poster of Franz, his fiddle, and his walking stick. Dubbed by some newspapers as the Wandering Minstrel of the Midwest, Franz would catch a train from Grand Forks and then invariably wait—sometimes in the middle of the night—at some distant depot for a connection on a small branch line. He would arrive at some tiny town—like Minto or Omemee—and entertain people at the local opera house or teachers' college. He worked up a lecture, explaining how ballads were nurtured in isolated communities, often among illiterate people who then passed the songs around. He illustrated his lectures with song and explained how the bare and unadorned style of ballads told stories about the singers' lives. He often used "The Shanty-man's Life."

> Oh, a shanty-man's life is a wearisome life, altho' some think it void of care,
> Swinging an axe from morning till night in the midst of the forests so drear. (148)

He always asked if anyone knew any shanty-boy songs and was willing to share them, and then he ended by promoting the value of a liberal arts education. The university paid him $18 per trip, a welcomed addition to the $1,300 annual salary it paid him.

The Rickabys had arrived in North Dakota just a few years after the last buffalo had been killed on the prairies. They both had been imbued by the cosmopolitan flavor of Galesburg, Illinois, where Lillian had spent most of her childhood and both had attended college. A railroad hub with well-established farms and productive factories, Galesburg was founded in 1836 by a small group of families, including Lillian's grandfather, who moved to central Illinois from upstate New York. They went to establish Knox College, where students would receive a classical education and then go forth to preach an end to slavery.

The first families who arrived paid into a pool, which bought the land for the college, afforded them cheap land for their own houses and businesses, and provided their children free attendance at Knox. Given this history, Galesburg had always been a town of homes and households, husbands and wives, with shared values and common history. It had a cohesion and permanence other frontier towns lacked. Compared to Galesburg, the Rickabys expected to find the Wild West in Grand Forks. They were surprised.

Settlers had been slow to move to North Dakota, fearful of Indian raids and the notoriously brutal climate, but when the railroad that crossed North Dakota went bankrupt in 1873 for lack of passengers and freight, things—ironically—began to change for the better. A clever land agent for the railroad convinced a small group of eastern investors to buy the flat, treeless, and fertile land around the railroad tracks and bundle it into huge farms to demonstrate the agricultural potential of the Red River valley.

By 1885 some ninety of these "bonanza" farms existed in North Dakota, each over three thousand acres large. These well-capitalized wheat farms ran like corporations, with multiple foremen, numerous sheds, barns, private elevators, and all the migrant workers, lumber, food, and new machinery money could buy. The bonanza farms did, indeed, demonstrate how fertile the land and lucrative the farming were. Although these farms were eventually broken up and sold off, they changed the perception of North Dakota. It was not just Indian wars, roaming buffalo, brutal winters, and debilitating isolation; it was also a vast expanse of some of the richest soil on flat and stone-free land in the world. The bonanza farms helped feed the fantasies, farming manuals enticed the dreamers, and land prices made the dreams possible.

Between 1878 and 1890 the population of North Dakota grew from 16,000 to 190,000 with some 8.0 million acres of land bought for as little as $1.25 an acre, and another 3.5 million acres distributed free through the Homestead Act. By 1915 there were 600,000 people in North Dakota, mostly small farmers, with rich farms on the fertile land around the Red River valley.

Grand Forks had the resources to become a modern city. With some 12,500 residents, electric lights, trolleys, paved streets, granite sidewalks, municipal water, two main railroad lines and fourteen branch lines, an extensive park system with tennis courts and golf links, and a retail hub that served all of northern North Dakota and Minnesota, it was a busy and active place. With a few talented architects, it had an entire neighborhood built in Victorian, Queen Anne, and Italianate styles and numerous civic, educational, and commercial buildings, including the courthouse, city hall, and the post office, that were grand, some with Beaux Arts details and shiny copper roofs. The city had an elegance beyond anything that existed in Galesburg—eighty acres of downtown Grand Forks are now listed on the National Register of Historic Places.

The Rickabys rented a little gray stucco house on the banks of the English coulee that ran through the campus. Lillian worked part time, off and on, tended her garden, which bled right into the prairies, and cared for a little white dog that Franz had saved from sure death in the university science lab and stuck in Lillian's Christmas stocking. She named him Jiminy Christmas, Jim for short. "Jim gets wound up in his chain and the fraternity boys laugh at him, but they'll sing a different tune when Jim grows up," Franz wrote in his diary.

Franz initially taught English 1 and English 2, dramatic composition, and Chaucer and attended endless university council meetings, "marked by the usual amount of talk and somewhat less achievement." In early 1919, before his first long walk, he proposed a comparative ballad course,

Lillian tends her garden in Grand Forks, 1919. (Gretchen Dykstra collection)

"The Popular Ballad of England and America." "I have become enamored of the ballad," is all he wrote in his diary, but this is how the course catalog described his offering (I do not know why he thought America was "starved" of ballads, but I presume he changed his opinion as he dug deeper and traveled more):

> Two credits: two hours a week, second semester. Open to seniors and graduates, and others by permission. The aims of this course are as follows: to acquaint the student with the Popular Ballad form; to note, where possible, the actual connection between the balladry of England and that of America, and the similarity of conditions which impelled the striking parallels in form and substance; and to note also the variation in circumstances which nourished the ballad in England and starved it in America.

Although sometimes frustrated by the isolation of the academy, the occasional pettiness of the administration, a hint of anti-intellectualism, and the inequality of the pay among professors, the Rickabys loved Grand Forks and enjoyed campus life. Franz played violin in the orchestra, directed and toured—and sometimes appeared—with the Dakota Playmakers, taught Sunday school, chaperoned college dances, invited students to "drop by and hear us eat," published four one-act plays, and even wrote the college fight song.

> It's for you, North Dakota U
> That we sing our sons and daughters true
> Cheering our comrades to victory
> Renewing allegiance to U-N-D
> Your honor we uphold in every conquest
> As your children aye shall do
> And when you hear that cry of ods-zod-zi
> It's for you, North Dakota U!

After a year of his university-sponsored trips, Rickaby then traveled "on his own nerve" for the next three years. He booked himself into halls, civic clubs, or normal schools throughout Minnesota, Michigan, and

Wisconsin. Normal schools—publicly funded postsecondary institutions that trained public school teachers—had been sprouting up in the Midwest since the middle of the nineteenth century. They represented a state's commitment to education, and the buildings themselves often became a town's cultural center. Normal schools, the precursors to state colleges, often drew professors who were close—and committed—to the communities they served. With people attuned to local circumstances, normal schools proved to be fertile hunting grounds for Franz.

To that end he was eager to get to Eau Claire, Wisconsin, in the west central part of the state, right in the middle of the once thickly forested Chippewa valley. There a new normal school had a strong reputation. I was eager to get there, too, because that's where Rickaby met his most loyal collaborator, William Bartlett.

It is said that the Chippewa valley had forty-six *billion* board feet of white pine, one sixth of all such trees west of the Appalachian Mountains. The forests were so thick and the trees so tall no sunlight reached the forest floor. At the confluence of the Chippewa and Eau Claire Rivers, both fed with numerous tributaries, Eau Claire, like Stillwater, became a logging capital. Now it's a city of sixty-six thousand people that does not appear to care much about trees at all. I got lost in a confusion of highways outside of town where neon lights stand instead of pine trees. A branch of the University of Wisconsin bursts with new construction, but only a few trees soften the new buildings. A new park stretches along the riverfront, but only a few saplings dot the walkways. I swear I didn't see one tree planted on the main drag downtown.

Entrepreneurial lumber bosses in Eau Claire carved a twelve-hundred-foot canal linking the Chippewa River to Half Moon Lake, producing a huge holding pond, perfect for storing logs before they were delivered to the mills. By 1879 eight different companies, owning numerous lumber camps and sawmills among them, produced 166 million pieces of lumber annually—and that did not include the millions of shingles and pickets they also turned out. Virtually every job in the Chippewa valley was tied to lumber, from shanty boys to carpenters, engineers and machinists, blacksmiths, shop owners, and a hundred saloon operators. It wasn't called Sawdust City for nothing. Today health care, education, and government are the big employers, not timber.

Franz wrote the president of Eau Claire State Normal School, who invited him to lecture at the college and also introduced him to William Bartlett. A successful contractor in town, Bartlett had a passion for local history. With impressive foresight he amassed a collection of materials about the lumber industry that has few equals. Today it fills many boxes in the university archives.

Bartlett collected everything he could from three large lumber companies, including maps, ledgers, account books, personnel files, leases, receipts, jokes, directories, and photographs—hundreds and hundreds of photographs from forests, lumber camps, and sawmills. He interviewed locals about Indian feuds, fur trading, and lumbering; he wrote and lectured throughout the state and was a tireless—perhaps even compulsive—networker, eager to introduce the history of lumbering in the Chippewa valley to everyone he could.

But most of the early ballad collectors were English professors. They followed the canon set by the legendary Francis James Child, and that tradition was not interested in the life of the singers.

Born in 1825, Child studied Shakespeare and rhetoric in both Boston and Germany and returned to Harvard as a professor, becoming a towering figure in its pantheon. Child, a tiny man with the enthusiasm of a child—who kept a photograph of the folklorists Brothers Grimm on his desk—pored over esoteric documents, pulling them together and making sense of them. He sought to compile, organize, and publish *every* English and Scottish ballad passed down *before* the printing press was introduced in England in 1476. He believed that once ballads were published and became available to many and inextricably changed, they were stripped of their authenticity, becoming "a low kind of art . . . thoroughly despicable and worthless."

Child systematically categorized the ballads, which he considered poetry, into types, such as tragic love, Robin Hood, fairies, elves and water spirits, and historical events. He tracked the ballads over time in all their various forms and then compared and analyzed where words and phrases came from and how they differed; he traced common elements—like "enchanted horns"—and how they were used in the ballads throughout time and through different versions; he critiqued earlier assessments of ballads and questioned the authorship of others; and he analyzed different versions of the same historical events. He had what one scholar calls "the mind-set of a scientist."

Through his exhaustive work he formalized in America the study of popular but—what he believed were—extant ballads. His *English and Scottish Popular Ballads*, published between 1882 and 1898, became the touchstone for future scholars—at least so far as the analysis of text was concerned.

Child was followed by another intellectually formidable Bostonian, George Lyman Kittredge (1860–1941), who studied with Child, adored Child, and succeeded Child as a preeminent English professor at Harvard. A tall, skinny man, he was notoriously strict in his classes, never tolerating tardiness, yawning, or coughing, but he electrified students with everything from "Chaucer and cowboys to Beowulf and ballads," as one former colleague said at his funeral.

Child had analyzed ballads as popular poetry of a past era, worthy of literary study and philological criticism, but Kittredge saw ballads as evolving, alive, and relevant. He taught his English students to know and appreciate the ancient roots of ballads, but he also urged them to find—and value—ballads that were still alive, still sung, and reflecting new realities and new times. He urged his students to leave their desks in the ivory tower and head into the field to find examples of songs. Kittredge is considered the founder of American folksong studies.

"Go and get this material while it can be found. Set down the dates, the names, preserve the words and the music. That's your job," Kittredge implored his students.

His best-known pupil was John Lomax. As a child, Lomax had heard cowboys singing and yodeling in central Texas as they rode past his father's farm along the Chisholm Trail. Lomax studied at the University of Texas and became a professor at Texas A&M before he took a year off in 1906 to study at Harvard with George Kittredge. Remembering the cowboy songs and encouraged by the professor, Lomax went back to Texas to find and preserve the songs. He distributed flyers, sent queries to newspapers, and rode horseback into cowboy camps, and in 1910 he published 112 songs with an introduction by Theodore Roosevelt, who wrote, "a work of real importance to preserve permanently this unwritten ballad literature of the back country and its frontier."

In that book, Lomax broke the rules Child wrote; he did not identify his sources, and he combined variations of some songs—an act of heresy in the Child tradition. Lomax saw similarities between cowboys and medieval knights, but he also vividly showed that new, worthy ballads emerged from isolated populations, just as they had in medieval England. Ballads were not dead.

Lomax also wanted to make the ballads popular—something the scholarly Child did not care about—which is why Lomax changed some of the songs he found. Indeed, "Home on the Range" and "Git Along Little Dogies" would eventually become American classics—and cowboys themselves American icons.

Lomax was not the first American ballad collector—earlier songcatchers had been at work in the Appalachian Mountains, on Indian reservations, and elsewhere—but he was arguably the most influential. Lomax, however, took a long break after the publication of his first book and he did not reappear for twenty years. Then he and his son Alan began their prodigious collecting, starting in southern prisons, supported by the Archive of American Folk Song at the Library of Congress. Folk festivals began to draw hundreds of people, and by the late 1930s a folk revival had begun; by 1955 the Weavers would sell out Carnegie Hall, and their rendition of Leadbelly's "Good Night, Irene" was number one on the hit parade.

While Child organized ballads by topic, Lomax organized them by function and group. He posited that American ballads could be found among miners, sailors, soldiers, railroad workers, Negroes, down-and-outers like prostitutes and prisoners, and lumberjacks. These categories as well as his cowboy songs rippled through the nascent field of ballad collecting.

Franz wrote to Lillian, "What an intoxicating idea to drink of someone else's vibrant culture, to capture the voices, the songs and the spirit of it all. Don't worry, Angel, I will not do anything rash. John Lomax appears to have cowboys under control, but, what a gift he has given us and who knows? Maybe I'll try my hand again at the wandering life."

Help along the Way

Clearly Lomax's early work inspired Rickaby, and Child and Kittredge gave structure to his study, but it was William Bartlett, the amateur cultural historian, with his extensive knowledge of logging and its people, who gave Franz's collection—and the lives of the shanty boys—context and helped differentiate his collection from others.

Bartlett gave Rickaby encouragement, access to his research and photographs, hospitality, friendship, and leads, including one to William "Billy" Allen. Allen, a lifelong bachelor, was eighty years old and living with his sister (who disapproved of his low-life friends) when Rickaby met him in Wausau, Wisconsin. The oldest of eight children from New Brunswick, Canada, Allen had moved to Michigan and then Wisconsin with his family. As a teenager he became an apprentice to a timber cruiser and traveled the country, traipsing through hundreds of acres of uncut forests to scout out potentially valuable timber claims for investors. As a young boy with only three years of schooling, Allen started writing poetry "that wasn't much good" and, as he traveled, he put these poems to tunes he had heard elsewhere and then sang the songs back to lumberjacks. "Several of my poems are sarcastic descriptions of characters and failings of our respectcable [sic] citizens, and I have been threatened with libel suits and shot-guns on several occasions," he wrote Bartlett. "But most of my subjects are dead, so . . . I am . . . safe for the time being." This is a snippet of one of Allen's more sarcastic tunes.

My song is not a song of love; . . .
But 'tis of a hump-backed blow-hard; his name is S. D.
Knowles. (96)

Allen, who called himself Shan T. Boy, was the only author of ballads Rickaby met—at least the only one whose claims Rickaby believed. Although Allen never told others he was a ballad writer—they would not have believed him—on many occasions he heard variations of his songs— songs that Rickaby had heard, too. The singers would tell Allen about the "feller that wrote that song," and the details were invariably wrong. The songs themselves, Allen wrote, were so "murdered, some of them I couldn't tie together with a string."

Scholars and critics on both sides of the Atlantic had been arguing the question of authorship of ballads for several decades. The debate can appear to be a battle over the immaterial, but it went to the heart of what is a ballad. Two factions with numerous permutations existed: the communalists and the individualists. Although not easily summarized—or perhaps even understood—the communalists believed that the history, structure, and narrative of ballads arose from the collective spirit of people and were basically fossils of culture, remnants of dead traditions. The individualists believed that ballads, although rooted in the traditions of the folk, were not mere reflections of a dead effort, but changed and evolved and lived and could, in fact, be products of individual creativity.

Although purported to be a communalist, Professor Kittredge said it did not matter so much if a ballad was composed collectively or individually as long as the song came from the group, drew from the group's traditions, returned to the group, and then passed on, perhaps changed in the process.

Rickaby believed that the anonymity of authorship was the standard in ballads, and writes amusingly that most claims of authorship were yet another "phase of folk expression." (Perhaps that is what Rickaby thought of the Bemidji lumberjack Ed Springstad's claim to have written the drinking song.) But, by studying the tone, humor, imitations, and adaptations of songs Allen showed him, he became convinced that Allen had composed some well-known songs, including the popular "Banks of the Little Eau Pleine"—a song Rickaby believed had a "peculiar composite of humor and pathos." When he sang it to audiences he noticed "a varying reaction, a sort of ebb and flow of emotions." In the tradition of Child, Rickaby traced its structure to an older Irish ballad, "The Lass of Dunmore" and its tune to "Erin's Green Shore."

> Your Johnny was drowned in the Dells.
> They buried him 'neath a scrub Norway,
>   You will never behold him again.
> No stone marks the spot where your raftsman
>   Sleeps far from the Little Eau Pleine. (132–33)

Collecting songs—like the ones from William Allen—required patience, tact, friendliness, energy, and time—lots of time. Finding songs entailed an extraordinary amount of work in a nontechnical, nondigital world and chasing leads every which way. Rickaby gave lectures, performed concerts, attended old-timers' picnics, and planted numerous newspaper articles. When he heard about a likely source—people like William Allen or Hank Underwood—he tracked them down, wrote letters, made a tentative date, and then searched for a venue in the town where he might perform for money to support the trip. He would catch a train—or two—that would invariably run infrequently at peculiar times of the day, walk around the new town—sometimes in snow and cold—find a cheap hotel, meet new people, worry about money, and leave his family, all the while responsible for his students in Grand Forks. It was essential, but it was exhausting. Soon after his winter trip to Bemidji in 1923 Franz wrote Bartlett, "I am afraid that the obligation incurred by me in the proposed trip to Eau Claire is going to be a little more than I can stand, for I am not physically and nervously equal to as much as some men."

In fact, Franz was dying. Since so few biographies of the early song-catchers exist, it is difficult—if not impossible—to understand their individual motivations. But I have come to know, I believe, what inspired and motivated Franz. I think I have found Frenzy.

FRENZY

Many things motivated Franz, I believe. The restlessness of the shanty boys matched the restlessness that Franz inherited from his own father—first expressed when he dropped out of high school and went to the Ozarks. He might not have related to the roughness and vulgarity of the shanty boys, but he obviously related to their wanderlust. He loved the independent life, and his friendship with Vachel Lindsay, the best-known troubadour of his time, must have inspired him, too. Franz, a friendly and outgoing person, was interested in the lives of others and observant of changing circumstances and the impact on people. As a scholar, he had studied Shakespeare and Chaucer, the populists of their days, and he saw the similarities with the ballads of the shanty boys. He knew about Child and Lomax and Kittredge, and they appealed to his sensibilities. Franz met former shanty boys in Charlevoix and found their stories compelling. Franz lived on the frontier, and shanty boys had made it possible for the frontier to be settled. Franz was a musician and so were they; they worked outdoors and nothing sustained Franz more than the beauty of nature. And preserving a dying culture while he himself was dying must also have fueled his intent. As far as I know, he never said or wrote that explicitly, but many poems he wrote alluded to his own death.

> If I should die tonight, I will that ye
> My friends, my all, should not grieve after me.
> Life has been rich, for I have known a friend.
> Earth has been fair, hence at the hour when she
> Receives me back, call not that hour the end.

Franz contracted rheumatic fever while a student at Knox College. In 1912 he had hitched a ride from his home in Springfield to Galesburg, about ninety miles north, and talked himself into the college with fifty dollars in his pocket. He threw himself into everything the college offered, taking a full course load, "slinging hash" at the Horseshoe Café, and playing his fiddle for money at dances. He played violin in the Knox-Galesburg orchestra, sang second bass in the choir at the Central Church, and directed the Knox band. He wrote for the Knox literary magazine and occasionally appeared in plays on campus. He organized evenings in Beecher Chapel, including one in 1914 with his old friend and mentor Vachel Lindsay, who thrilled the audience when he belted out in his high, shrill, emphatic voice, "Booth led boldly with his big bass drum, Are you washed in the blood of the Lamb?"

All these activities—the source of his nickname, Frenzy—wore him down. When he fell sick with a high fever, a sore throat, and chest and joint pain, he never sought medical assistance—not that there was much one could do for rheumatic fever in those days before antibiotics, even if it had been diagnosed. When Lillian Katar, his future wife, first met him, Franz was a junior, already limping and laughing it off.

He would not know—officially—how serious his condition was until April 1917 when the United States went to war. He had been awarded the Chicago Club's Harvard scholarship, thanks to contacts he had made in Charlevoix, and arrived in Cambridge in the fall of 1916 to study for a master's degree in English.

"Angel, I have arrived, no more the worse for wear. . . . Boston seems almost quaint in its oldness next to gritty, industrial Chicago and Harvard is no more grand than the University of Chicago, although, I must

Lillian rides a bicycle,
1917. (Gretchen Dykstra
collection)

say, Widener Library is imposing. You will be glad to know that I have
not yet tripped over my muddy boots as I scramble up its stairs and no
one has laughed at the cornhusk sticking out of my ear."

Franz lived at 1768 Cambridge Street, not far from Harvard Yard, in a
gingerbread Victorian similar to houses in Galesburg. He was lonely at
first, unable to find people who responded to his violin or, perhaps, his
easy-going, positive midwestern style. Lillian called his classmates the la-
di-das. He took long walks alone down by the river, read plays aloud to
himself, and wrote poems he sent home.

> Home from Harvard came the son,
> His face by woe assailed.
> He fell upon his doting sire

Franz at home in Cambridge, Massachusetts, with Lillian on the wall, 1918. (Gretchen Dykstra collection)

And sobbed, "I failed! I failed!"
"Why, so!" the trembling father said,
"What was it? Bible? Greek?
Philosophy or science? Art
Or Anglo-Saxon? Speak!"
Then sprang the old-time briny tear,
That prince of anesthetics.
"O father, I—I flunked the course
Higher Cigarettics!"

His loneliness was abated somewhat when Vachel Lindsay, out on the lecture circuit, came to his rescue and introduced him to the poet Amy Lowell. "She was mild to all who loved God. . . . It was a fair bargain and Franz was on his way, as far as Massachusetts was concerned," wrote Lindsay. "The next time I passed through Boston, Franz [brought] me to a little group of poets where he was the dominant figure."

Franz took five courses, including one on Shakespeare and Chaucer, doing the best in advanced composition. He did not, however, take a class with George Kittredge—to his later regret—but he was aware of him, as he said in a letter to Lillian: "He seems to be a distinguished man, strong and steady as a river, with a robust curiosity. . . . He edits the *Journal of American Folklore*. Maybe next year if we have either an address or an income we might forego a few concert tickets and subscribe to the magazine."

The year was irrevocably and tragically marked by the bloody war in Europe and the growing shift in public opinion about America joining the Allies. Each time the Germans struck another ship in the Atlantic, Americans, even resistant midwesterners, remembered the sinking of the *Lusitania*, and their collective isolationism waned.

In a letter to Lillian, Franz wrote, "The desire to enter the war grows everyday in these parts. Most students support a draft and many have begun voluntary military training. The Harvard Band plays when foreign soldiers come to town; we play when volunteers march and we play near the Navy recruiting station. I have been in uniform for three days running and the mouthpiece on my cornet is getting worn down, but I love watching those men handle the flag, Angel."

When President Woodrow Wilson, unable to withstand the pressure to join the Allies, asked Congress on April 6, 1917, for permission to enter the war against the Germans, Franz immediately applied to join the volunteer ambulance corps. "It's an honorable way for us adventurers to serve, as few adventurers are suited to the discipline of the military."

He successfully completed his master's degree, but the ambulance corps rejected him, substantiating what others had feared before. Again to Lillian:

The war has taken over here, . . . with little studying going on and early degrees being granted to those who enlist. Spirits are high. But, Angel, I have some disappointing news. I wrestled up the necessary references to convince the Ambulance Corps that I am loyal and maybe even capable, but it seems that Lover is not fit enough to join. The doctor asked about my swollen joints and fatigue and those damnable headaches. I told him my knees only hurt when I play Mr. Fiddle too long or dance too enthusiastically or walk too far, but he doubts me. Perhaps you should write him and attest to my dancing prowess in spite of swollen joints. But I could not lie when he asked me about the headaches; I had to tell them that they are sometimes brutal. It seems that nasty fever I had back at Knox might have done some damage to my heart. The doctor is adamant and says I cannot go. I am sorely disappointed, but now we will evidently have each other because of this infirmity of mine.

Rheumatic fever, caused by strep infections, was insidious and incurable in the days before antibiotics. It acted differently in different people. Some shook with the notorious Saint Vitus' dance, but Franz never did. Some developed rashes on their skin or nodules under it, but Franz never did. He was, however, periodically paralyzed by headaches and crippled by joint pain and, cruelest of all, he would seem to get better, and then dive back down into dark and frightening waters.

His first hospitalization came in February 1922, when they were living in Grand Forks. Bundled up in sweaters and heavy boots, socks, and gloves and wrapped in blankets, Franz traveled to Rochester, Minnesota. Lillian accompanied him and stayed a few days before returning home to care for baby Wunk, their two-year-old son.

It must have felt a bit like seeking the Holy Grail, as even in those days the Mayo Clinic was widely respected. They discovered a bustling city with wide streets, department stores and restaurants, ubiquitous taxis, and numerous medical facilities: There were private convalescent homes and sanitariums; hotels with hospital rooms and hotels with operating rooms; Victorian homes with convalescent beds and hotels with convalescent rooms; a mental institution and the original, but now much larger, Saint Mary's Hospital; Worrell, Damon, and Colonial Hospitals; and one grand, five-story building where all the doctors affiliated with the Mayo Clinic had offices. Medicine and doctors, sickness and health, hope and optimism permeated the town. Rochester and the Mayo Clinic were interchangeable.

In August 1883 Dr. William Mayo and his family were living in Rochester, Minnesota, when a powerful tornado slammed through the town. The doctor and his two sons quickly established temporary clinics in the library and dance hall, where they cared for the wounded. After the worst was over, the Catholic nuns in town offered Mayo a proposition: If they raised the money to build a hospital would he provide the medical care? The persistent nuns succeeded, and in 1889 Saint Mary's Hospital opened with twenty-nine beds. Any doctor could send patients to the hospital, but all patients first had to be evaluated by one of the Doctors Mayo—and a unique, well-coordinated medical establishment began.

Only patients who needed surgery stayed at Mayo, and surgery was not used—as it is now—with rheumatic fever. Instead Franz went to the Cascade Sanatorium, run by Dr. J. E. Crewe, the permanent secretary of the Mayo Clinic's Visitors Club and the manager of a private facility for people with kidney and heart disease. A believer in the restorative power of pasteurized milk, Crewe had developed—and written about—a strict buttermilk diet, purported to reverse the fatigue and the wasting that an enlarged heart caused.

Franz stayed six weeks, initially lying totally still, a Herculean victory for a restless soul, and then later sitting upright in a wide-armed rocking chair next to the bedstand with the ever-present tall glass of buttermilk.

"The joint's got a string on us although I can't see why. . . . If I was going to endear myself to anybody, the last thing I'd do would put 'em in bed and feed 'em nothing but Guernsey milk and prunes," he wrote Lillian.

A talkative French Canadian maid swept and dusted each room daily in a pair of high-heeled pumps; a former soldier "radiated a healthy glow, a sort of exhibit for the potency of the milk diet," who, Franz imagined, "unlike British soldiers who went around France as if they owned the place, . . . probably went around as if he didn't give a snap who owned it." There was the portly young man with a carefully trimmed mustache who was "plainly accustomed to the lap of luxury." The neatly dressed nurse, all in white, "had a strength of character and sureness of purpose under a bright vivacity, which was never frivolity." And there was Crewe's young intern, "immaculate, well-tailored and, of course, good looking, brisk in professional matters, but still pretty much of a kid, a typical product of medical school, before experience has gotten in its sobering licks." Later they would all appear in a sweet, one-act play Franz wrote, entitled *The Fever Ward*, which Walter H. Baker in Boston published the following year—one of four plays the house published by Rickaby. (Lillian Rickaby was coauthor of two of the four plays.)

Franz returned to Grand Forks fatter and rested, but his local doctor ordered continued bed rest, so Franz did not teach, produce plays, or go songcatching for the next several months. He fretted about his inactivity as lumber camps kept closing and radios were coming.

Franz and Lillian did not know anyone in Grand Forks who had a radio—they cost a fortune—but everywhere in America radios had become an obsession. In 1920 KDKA in Pittsburgh had broadcast national election results for the first time ever. People with radio receivers within fifty miles of the station received the broadcast. That starting gun set off a mad dash among cities and towns, private companies and universities to build their own broadcasting stations. In just one year the nation went from eight stations to 564. The university in Grand Forks and the agriculture school in Fargo were in a pitched battle to see which institution could build the first station in North Dakota. Lillian was excited to be asked to sing on the university's first broadcast—when it went live—but Franz was worried: "Every step forward on the radio is a mile away from our past."

In fact, when Franz was finally able to get back on the road that summer, the local newspaper in Ladysmith, Wisconsin, ran an article the day he arrived on how to build a radio at home for a pittance.

Radios revolutionized entertainment, bringing diversion and culture and the outside world to people in their homes and shanty boys in their camps. People no longer needed to entertain themselves; music would, perforce, become more commercial—less traditional, less authentic—and the homegrown songs of the lumber camps would be lost and forgotten.

Cutover Land and Tinder Boxes

Franz sensed a creeping commercialism—influences from music halls, popular songwriters, and publishers—when he met Michael Cassius Dean, an "indefatigable dispenser of good fellowship" (83). Mike was living in the Mesabi Iron Range in northern Minnesota, a topographical mishmash of green hills with occasional outcroppings of white stone and towns all covered with red dust. A former shanty boy, he was a night watchman at the Virginia and Rainy Lake Lumber Company in the treeless, hard-edged town of Virginia. He lived alone at the Pine Tree Inn, a two-story boardinghouse where a hundred men slept in shifts in twenty-five bunk beds. Franz joined him there.

"I dare say you would not much like their linens, but songs trip off Mike's tongue like logs over a waterfall so my short rest on a horsehair mattress on a rusted bunk under a moth-eaten blanket is a small price to pay. Anyway the fleas deserve a good supper, too. I am scribbling madly, working hard to catch the melodies," Franz wrote Lillian.

Dean had learned songs at the knee of his Irish-born mother and had heard—and remembered—songs when he visited his father, who worked winters in the lumber camps of upstate New York. When Dean was fifteen, 'round about 1878, he moved to the Midwest and worked on iron boats, in saloons, and in lumber camps, learning to swing an axe and sing the songs. With just one year of schooling, he did his best to write the songs down, and one year before Franz met him, in 1923, Dean printed them all in a songster under the name *Flying Cloud*.

Rickaby thought many of Dean's songs lacked authenticity. And indeed *Flying Cloud* featured several New York City music hall pieces like the David Braham–Edward Harrigan composition, "My Dad's Dinner Pail." Rickaby alluded to other songs "lying in ditches of maudlin parody." I bet Franz would have disliked—and disdained—"The Old Mud Cabin on the Hill," an Irish echoing of a minstrel show song, "The Little Old Log Cabin in the Lane," that Dean included in his songster.

> May God help the emigrant that leaves poor Paddy's land,
> His friends to mourn his absence while he's gone;
> He sails to dear America with heart both sick and sore,
> For those he loves he braves the world alone.
> But if God does spare my life to passage back again,
> To bring my parents out, if living still,
> But if not, please God, I'll meet them all in a better home
> Than the little old mud cabin on the hill.

But Dean had at least twelve songs, which Rickaby found "true and interesting and wonderful" and included "Shanty-Boy" in his future book.

> As I walk'd out one evening just as the sun went down,
> So carelessly I wander'd to a place called Stonei town.
> There I heard two maids conversing as slowly I passed by;
> One said she loved her farmer's son, and the other her
>   shanty-boy. (156)

This song—reminiscent of what Rickaby called a medieval debate song—illustrates the traditional rivalry between shanty boys and farmers—or what many believed was a rivalry. Rickaby explains the rivalry in the note that accompanies the song: "[But] in his innermost being the shanty-boy, unattached and utterly without home except the camps, knew that, although his experience was the larger, it was more costly. . . . The rivalry, barring the action of liquor, was not deep or vital, and did not reach the fatal intensity of that between the cowboy and the sheepherder, or the ranchman and the fence-farmer" (152).

I love that particular note. By exploring the rivalry in sociological and psychological terms and comparing it to other rivalries, Franz gives us another slice of rich American pie, a taste of the shanty boy's soul, and a morsel of Franz's own empathetic spirit, rooted in his direct experience with the shanty boy.

Franz's most vivid image during his wanderings was, sadly, "land sown with stumps." The destruction and detritus of logging—the stumps, the brush, the needles—were wounds on the earth that when healed would produce the rich and fertile farmlands of today—farms with multiple steel silos that tower over immaculate barns and massive machines that

The wounds of the cutover. (Gretchen Dykstra collection)

work endless rows of corn and soybeans. But these rich farms—which Rickaby never saw—did not come easily. It took horses and dynamite and grueling labor to clear the land after the loggers left. Bill Morgan, an old-time railroad buff in Ladysmith, knows one family that took fifteen years to clear just twenty-five acres.

Such cutover land was not only ugly and unwelcoming, it turned the Upper Midwest into a tinderbox, something Franz saw in the summer of 1919. When the shanty boys cut the giant pines, they left behind stumps and branches, scraps and sawdust that made ideal kindling. Sawmills with piles of cut and uncut timber and sawdust everywhere were giant matchboxes. Towns with wooden sidewalks, wooden homes, wooden churches, and wooden stores with sawdust floors could ignite in a flash. Coal-burning trains with embers dropping from their fireboxes and sparks flying from their smokestacks were constant threats; add summer heat, occasional droughts, and autumn breezes, and fires were all too common in the Upper Midwest. Local volunteers—or paid workers—rushed to extinguish fires burning along the tracks. One man near Manistique, Michigan, told Rickaby his rural county spent $3,000 in just one month paying men to fight their fires. (That's $35,000 in current dollars.)

Sometimes the fires were unstoppable and horrific: People hid in wells for safety, others were burned alive; wailing oxen stampeded, fish burned in rivers, birds were blinded, and horses were roasted. A fire could destroy an ancient tree in seconds, acres in minutes, and miles in a matter of hours. The Great Chicago Fire of October 8, 1871, killed three hundred people and destroyed one third of the city, but on that very same day—and long since forgotten—two thousand people were killed and almost four million acres were destroyed in and around Peshtigo, Wisconsin—and over the next two weeks, fires also devastated Port Huron, Lansing, and Holland, Michigan. In 1894 a massive fire destroyed Hinckley, Minnesota; in 1910 a great fire burned throughout Idaho, and one wiped out Spooner, Minnesota. On October 12, 1918, after months of abnormally dry and hot weather, such a calamity hit Cloquet, Minnesota, west of Duluth.

As he traveled, Franz learned about the songs and the lives of the shanty boys, and in Cloquet he saw the consequences of their work. Five major fires, ignited by embers from a train and fanned by high winds and rapid combustion, united and swept through 250,000 acres of woods and cutover land in four counties. The fires killed 453 people and seriously burned several thousands of others; destroyed some 4,000 houses and 6,000 barns; burned sawmills, barns, offices, and millions of feet of cut lumber; killed countless wild animals and tens of thousands of farm animals—all in one day.

The Cloquet fire is now recognized for the cooperation and speed with which the town bounced back. The governor of Minnesota moved quickly, mobilizing a relief commission that sent materials to the town and livestock and seeds to the farmers; the Red Cross opened a temporary hospital that treated—in addition to the victims of the fire—the many who were struck simultaneously with the terrible flu of 1918. It fed survivors and built two-room, tarpaper shacks for residents—some of which still stand today, used for storage in backyards and farmyards. Local committees moved to keep gawkers and profiteers away, and the three lumber companies in town consolidated their operations and gave free wood— and paid leave—to their employees to rebuild their houses. And, perhaps most impressive, the lumber companies quickly developed new products from the "weed trees," the aspens and balsams that grew in burned areas, to ensure future jobs. (Cloquet still produces balsam wood insulation that was begun back then.)

Franz arrived in Cloquet ten months after the fire, and he saw the remains of remarkable loss and the energy fueling a remarkable recovery. The town was lively—"a perfect hive of activity. The buildings have leaped up from ruins and ashes, more beautiful, modern and substantial than before." Two hotels (one with liquor, one without) were open and another was under construction. A theater was operating and a new one was in the works. A new railroad depot was accepting and discharging passengers, and a new library, now the historical society, was under construction. The newspaper was filled with ads for carpenters and contractors; stores and banks occupied temporary buildings along the main street; brick buildings were under construction; a paper mill and a match factory were open, and the one remaining sawmill was busy. But he also saw—and wrote in his journal—what the lumber business was becoming.

"I saw the logs brought in on cars, dumped into the river, run up into the mill. I saw three steam driven and steam operated carriages, the great

Franz and a little greeter, summer 1919. (Gretchen Dykstra collection)

band saws and the lumber sorted, edged, cut into lengths, and carried out where it was graded and piled and hauled away . . . a marvelous triumph of modern machinery, which threw great logs about like toothpicks, and handled the kindling and waste none the less accurately."

And he met the new generation of shanty boys—men who came only for the money and less for the thrill, married men who did not need the camaraderie of the bunkhouse, men who could read and did not sing—and had never heard the songs.

Like a Boat Hauled Up on the Shore

A three-week trip in the summer of 1923 would be Franz's last collecting trip; North Dakota winters had become too much. Endless snow covered fences, wiped out roads, often canceled classes, and sometimes disoriented people. Temperatures twenty-five degrees or below with winds like knives that cut across the treeless prairies were common. Franz and Lillian would hunker down, playing the washboard, reading aloud to one another—stories like Stephen Leacock's "Ministrations of the Reverend Uttermost Dumfarthing"—and Lillian got used to "hugging radiators," but the brutal winters were hard on Franz's health. "These infernal headaches," he said, "they feel like a stick of wood burning at the top end in my brain."

When it became clear that they could not stay, an old friend from Charlevoix, the Reverend John Gardner, urged them to move west. He had moved to Claremont, California, and waxed poetic about an ideal climate and a town full of strong and serious academics. Franz was offered a job as an assistant professor of English at Pomona College, and in the late summer of 1923 the Rickabys moved to Southern California.

Claremont was a revelation to them. With its clear mountain air, it was defined by tidy rows of orange trees stretching along the foothills of the snow-capped, rough-faced San Gabriel Mountains, just north of town. Familiar elm and oak trees stood side by side with exotic palm trees and bony eucalyptus trees. Roses bloomed all year. Citizen committees, modeled after those in New England towns, did everything from pulling out cacti to planting trees to building schools. Small Victorian houses, Spanish haciendas, Arts and Crafts bungalows, and gabled cottages dotted the town. They rented a small, one-story house covered in leafy vines on East Twelfth Street with two messy eucalyptus trees in front and a view of Mount Baldy in the back.

Claremont and Pomona had the intimacy and values of Galesburg and Knox, the intellectual rigor of Harvard, and James Blaisdell, Pomona's president. He had come from Beloit College in Wisconsin, bringing with him a deep respect for scholars, a fondness for students, and a well-articulated vision for a consortium of small colleges that today are some of the best liberal arts colleges in America, with shared libraries and other facilities.

Franz moved quickly, as he had in Grand Forks, to embed himself in college life. In one issue of the student paper three separate stories ran on the front page of various activities Rickaby was leading. He taught his classes and produced and directed plays. Always the cultural anthropologist, he began a special no-credit writers' group for students to write about everyday life on campus, including what they wore, classes they took, slang they used, clubs they joined, dances they held, anything. And Franz joined the Hobo Club, "the most exclusive organization on campus."

The members had all "bummed" at least one thousand miles. They met periodically around a campfire in the center of campus, wearing torn clothes and floppy hats. They cooked slabs of beef and piles of potatoes as they sang ditties and told tales about their travel on foot, on trains, or in boats. One had earned his miles in the American Expeditionary Forces in Europe, one had seen Mexico, others had explored the coasts, and, of course, Franz had walked the Midwest. The only faculty member to have ever joined, Franz was called the *"boes in facultate."*

Meanwhile he worked to finish *Ballads and Songs of the Shanty-Boy* and get it off to Macmillan, which had expressed interest in it. He chose fifty-one ballads and included the lyrics as well as the music for most and several variations for many. At least thirty-seven of the songs were about the shanty boys themselves, but he also included other songs they sang—many from Michael Dean from Virginia, Minnesota, about battles, boxers, and iron ore. Rickaby believed that those songs were another authentic feature of the shanty boys' lives.

Child had included precise notes for all of the 305 ballads—plus another 1,300 variations—in his seminal work, providing extensive historical notes, analysis of the changes in phrases and words, and notes about the subject matter. Lomax—although not the first ballad collector in America, but arguably the best known—had not followed Child's collecting methods; in his first collection Lomax did not include any information on his sources or variations, and sometimes he even combined variations. Neither of them provided the music or sociological context for understanding the lives of the singers. Furthermore, only a few of the collections published before 1930—except Rickaby's—included any music at all. The text was everything.

In addition to the music, Rickaby provided philological background and comparisons, as other collectors did. This note from "The Shantyboy on the Big Eau Claire" illustrates that: "The 'fleet of Sailor Jack's' usually becomes 'a fleet of lumberjacks.' Similarly, 'a suburban pest-house' becomes 'Asa Baldwin's pest-house,' 'a rapids piece' becomes 'a precipice,' and 'grim death' becomes 'old Grimdad'" (158).

But Rickaby was also intent—as others were not—on conveying the lives of the shanty boys throughout the book. In his long introduction, for instance, he comments on the history of logging in America and what it wrought. "In the East, the North, the South, and the far West the trees still fall; for men must still have lumber, even more than ever. But it is now a cold and calculated process" (88).

He included nine vivid photographs from Bartlett's collection, including one he titled from a line in "Jim Porter's Shanty Song": "Arriving at the shanty with cold and with wet feet, pull off your boots, me boys, for supper you must eat." Rickaby wrote underneath that line a brief description of what the reader sees: "An interior view of the bunk shanty, showing the upper and lower bunks, and the deacon seat—in use. The men sitting in the middle are wearing calked rivermen's boots. All wear their trousers 'stagged,' or cut off just below the knee" (176).

He added a glossary of logging terms so that his readers could understand logging jargon, including the go-devil: "*Go-devil.* A stubby, sled-like affair, three or four feet in length, shaped like the letter A with the point turned up. Used in skidding logs, especially large ones" (345; see also illustration on page 171).

And in extensive notes on the individual ballads, he not only traced the differences in language and the source of the stories, if known, and where he heard it and from whom, but he also used the content of the ballad to further explain or comment on the realities of the shanty boys. The note for "Save Your Money When You're Young" is one of many such notes:

> And if you are a married man, I'll tell you what to do,
> Support your wife and family, you're sworn that to do.
> Keep away from all those grog-shops where liquor's kept and
>   sold,
> For all they want is your money, boys. You'll need it when
>   you're old. (144)

"As many an old fellow sang this, or heard it sung, there must have welled up and overflowed within him a poignant but unavailing regret that life for him should have come to this: all the glory and strength of his young manhood gone, his thousands of hard-earned dollars poured periodically into the fathomless tides of dissolute hours" (143).

In the middle of January 1924, when Franz had almost completed the "great book," Harvard released *Songs and Ballads of the Maine Lumberjacks* by Roland Palmer Gray of the University of Maine—a big and undoubtedly worrisome surprise. Gray's introduction included several brief stories about who had given him the songs and insights into how ballads evolved among the lumberjacks, but the book contained no music and the notes were dry. This is Gray's note about "The Jam at Gerry's Rocks":

"This ballad is widely known among lumberjacks. It had its origin in Maine but has travelled far from home. It is in Lomax, *Cowboy Songs*, as 'Foreman Monroe,' pp. 174 ff.; Shoemaker, *North Pennsylvania Minstrelsy*, pp. 72 ff.; *Focus*, IV, 428–429 (from Virginia). It has been found in West Virginia by J. H. Cox; in Michigan by B. L. Jones (*Folk-Lore in Michigan*, p. 4) and by Miss Alma Blount. It has also made its way to Scotland (see Grieg, *Folk-Song of the North-East*, No. CXXXII)."

Franz found the book "well-gotten up and very interesting, but the forest is big enough for the shanty boys . . . [anyway, they are] literary puzzles constructed at a desk. I think I can do better."

And he did. Here is an excerpt from the note that Rickaby wrote to accompany the same song, "Gerry's Rocks," which describes the death of a foreman in a logjam, his boss's giving the dead man's girlfriend his back pay, and his fellow lumberjacks' generous contribution. Rickaby draws, in part, on a well-respected book by Stewart Edward White about midwestern shanty boys, first published in 1901: "One of the most interesting elements in the story, one which appears in all versions, and happily one reflecting a well-authenticated shanty-boy habit, is the subscription presented to the bereaved sweetheart. In actual life this contribution was sent the wife or other dependent; but the practice was common" (113).

But that spring Macmillan rejected Franz's book. They said it was too expensive to reproduce the music. Franz had had his heart set on a trade publisher, hoping that would draw a larger audience and earn him some money, but he refused to sacrifice the music. "American balladry without its 'air' is ineffective," he said, "sometimes even ugly, like a boat hauled up on the shore" (82).

So he wrote to Kittredge asking if Harvard would publish the book. Kittredge, who had already sent Franz "avalanches of bibliographic materials," said they would. Relieved, Franz finished the book and prepared the manuscript—a mammoth and tedious job. Without computers or even Wite-Out, Franz had to type—and presumably retype—each page, standardizing the format and ensuring there were no errors. He handwrote in ink each bar of music and the lyrics on carefully ruled lines. When he made a mistake, he corrected it by rewriting the bars of music and the lyrics on separate paper, cutting them out and carefully pasting them in tidy horizontal strips on the original typed manuscript. On January 2, 1925, Franz sent the completed manuscript to Kittredge with a simple note to the printer: "Make any arrangement you deem advisable." The Houghton Library at Harvard still has—and protects—the original manuscript.

Franz and Lillian celebrated the submission by adding up all the miles he had walked, rails he had ridden, the people he had met, the tunes he had sung, the audiences he had entertained, and the hours he had devoted to the book over the past six years. I wish I had his scorecard, but I don't.

He then wrote several articles for *American Forest and Forest Life* magazine, hoping its readers would be future buyers of his book, and he began to hatch new projects: He wrote Bartlett saying he wanted to explore the logging industry in Oregon and Washington; he tried to convince the Los Angeles radio station to let him sing on-air in the hopes of rustling up some memories of the California loggers. (In the East they were called lumberjacks; in the Midwest, shanty boys; and in the West, loggers.)

Franz wrote his mother that maybe he would take a year off and try his hand at writing a full-length, commercial play; he thought maybe he'd pursue a doctorate at the University of Pennsylvania; and he joked with Lillian that maybe he'd become a chicken farmer.

He continued to work on the history of the "Ballad of James Bird," which he included in part in this collection (240). It had become a long-lasting hit, telling the tragic story of one James Bird. Born in Exeter, Pennsylvania, Bird enlisted in the navy as a twenty-year-old man, eager to fight in the War of 1812. He had his chance just two months later when he fought the British on Lake Erie on the sailing ship *Lawrence*. Brave in action, Bird was severely wounded and, once recovered, deserted—or at least that's how the story went. He was captured and convicted, and President James Madison sentenced him to die. Kneeling on his own coffin, Bird was shot to death onboard a ship by fellow sailors. Charles Miner, a US congressman from Pennsylvania, wrote a song about him, turning Bird into a martyr for decades to come. Franz was intrigued by the longevity of the song's popularity and the possible backstory of the execution.

THOSE WHO WALK AMONG THE STARS

But Franz's health was deteriorating and none of these plans would come to fruition. He caught the flu and it felled him like a sawed tree in the North Country. His Claremont doctor knew little about rheumatic fever but suggested that Franz "could always go to the Seventh Day Adventists in Loma Linda."

Franz was deeply religious: He took communion, sang in choirs, and played hymns on his violin. He had taught Sunday school and run the Epworth League in Galesburg. He was supportive of the YMCA, once even donating ten dollars to it, a princely sum he could ill afford. But over time he moved further and further away from traditional churches, balking at the hierarchies and bureaucracies. He had better luck finding God on the prairies of North Dakota, the pineries of Wisconsin, and the hills of Southern California. "Another church convocation like that one, Angel," he once wrote to Lillian, "and that last little toe of mine still inside the churchyard walls will be running fast to catch up with its mates down the open road!"

Franz had never met a Seventh-Day Adventist, and the little he knew about them sounded weird: full-body baptisms, feet washing, Sabbath on Saturday, the Second Coming, prophesies. But their medical school was the only one in Southern California at that time, and it had received a Class A rating from the American Medical Association. If Franz had to go somewhere, best that he went there.

Loma Linda, only thirty miles east of Claremont, an hour on the Southern Pacific, was really a sloping hill, thirty-five acres big, and 125 feet above the barren San Bernardino valley with a breathtaking view of the mountains beyond. Like Claremont, it had been a failed dream along a railroad line. In 1887 speculators had built a three-story, wooden hotel, painted white, topped by a two-story cupola and turrets. A grand staircase led directly from a tiny rail depot up the hill to a welcoming lobby. But hotel guests rarely came, and after several attempts at redefining itself the hotel went under.

From her home in Northern California, Ellen White, one of the founders of the Seventh-Day Adventists, had a vision of a hotel for sale in Southern California. She urged church leaders to find it and buy it and use it to train medical missionaries in the holistic approach that the Adventists espoused. So in 1905 the Adventists bought the hotel on the hill as well as the tiny town, hay fields, fruit trees, vegetable gardens, cows, and barns on forty acres below for $38,000.

A driver in a brand new seven-seat Studebaker met Franz and Lillian at the railroad depot to take them up the hill; Franz could not have managed the 119 steps. Patients—as well as regular guests—lived simply and comfortably in single rooms that overlooked the mountains. Friendly doctors, all general practitioners, and nurses, both men and women, were everywhere; hot and cold water therapies were routine, and a vegetarian diet with locally grown fruit and vegetables was required. They charged twenty-nine dollars for a week, not including shampoos or telephone calls.

Lillian left after a few days and Franz wrote her regularly. "The Adventists do not believe in reading novels or plays, Angel, so the volunteers bring me none of those from the library, but they do serve up platters of poetry and trays of natural history and morsels of music books so I am nourished richly."

The community also had an orchestra and a band, comprised of doctors, nurses, blacksmiths, welders, cooks, and farmhands, that played outdoors periodically. Franz could hear them from his room. "The Chaplain comes to visit me every once in awhile. He's a short and skinny man with a large barrel chest that holds a kind heart," he wrote Lillian.

She visited three or four times week. She was becoming a reluctant convert to the idea of sanatoriums. Short of jail, they seemed like the best way to keep Frenzy quiet. He would invariably be in bed when she arrived, lying quietly, sometimes sleeping, sometimes reading. Occasionally Lillian brought Wunk with her; four-year-olds could not be expected to sit quietly in sanatoriums, but Wunk lit the spark of Franz's imagination, often expressed in postcards Franz sent home.

Dear Wunk,

I saw your Daddy today. He is feeling fine . . . they take his temperature three times a day but they always bring it back. He has to stay in bed, but they will let him get up as soon as he wears this bed out in three places . . . I saw Mrs. Goose, too. She and your daddy are loving friends. I shall write again soon.

Yours truly, Johnny O'Gray

The doctors gave Franz high doses of aspirin for his joint pain and fever, and digitalis for the shortness of breath. Thanks to the introduction of stethoscopes, doctors now knew rheumatic fever was not rheumatism but a heart condition caused most likely by untreated strep throat. Consequently, doctors believed that spraying, scraping, and removing tonsils might stave off worse infections. The Loma Linda doctors suggested removing Franz's tonsils.

"My tonsils and I are not close so feel free to take them out," Franz told his doctors.

Soon after the tonsillectomy, Franz went home, but within days he was back at Loma Linda, wracked with spasms and unable to breathe. On May 18, 1925, Franz Rickaby died. He was thirty-five years old. I do not know if Lillian was with him.

Sadly for Franz, that year marked the beginning of the end of rheumatic fever. The disease mutated into a chronic condition with the number of deaths dramatically decreasing. Eventually rheumatic fever became a rare occurrence and, with antibiotics and surgery, merely an uncomfortable inconvenience, not a death threat.

Lillian put Wunk on her lap and told him his father was dead. This remained my father's only memory of his father. Lillian then arranged to have Franz cremated. Only sixteen thousand people who died nation-wide that year—less than 2 percent—were cremated. No one, not even the knowledgeable historian at Loma Linda, knows how Lillian would have gotten his corpse to the only crematorium in Southern California. I do not know where his ashes went; no headstone exists.

The night he died Lillian sent his parents the dreaded telegram. Dora, Franz's mother, left immediately for Los Angeles, and Thomas, now hav-ing lost four of his five children, wailed in his journal, "The old Hebrew King . . . found all his wisdom futile, all his riches useless . . . when the greatest blow fell so mercilessly upon him . . . all that he could do was to moan from the depths of his broken heart, 'O my son, Absalom, my son, my son, Absalom. Would God that I had died for thee, O Absalom, my son.'"

On May 26, Pomona canceled all classes so that the entire college could attend the funeral, held in Bridges Hall. Walter Hartley, who would be-come Lillian's future brother-in-law, played the organ; colleagues read Franz's poems and favorite prayers; and the Reverend John Gardner, who had enticed him to Claremont, gave the eulogy. "I would," he said, "in the name of Franz Rickaby, challenge those who especially sat with him in the classroom and listened to him and learned something and took something from his soul, to always live well and nobly, taking the bitter with the sweet but extracting sweetness out of the bitterness and turning their sorrows into music such as he was able to sing."

Pomona then dedicated a sundial to him, a fitting memorial for some-one so keenly aware of time. It stands in Memorial Court at the col-lege; the inscription reads "*nulla linea delenda* [no lines be erased] Franz Rickaby." For years it served as the pulpit for the college's annual Memo-rial Day service.

On June 9 Knox College held a service for Franz, dedicating one of its majestic elms to him—a tree that died during the Dutch elm epidemic in the 1960s. Speakers paid tribute to Franz as a student, a family man, a fraternity brother, a musician, and a scholar. A former classmate injected levity into the sad occasion when she sang a popular song Franz had writ-ten in his senior year.

Sing the praises once again,
That have so oft been sung
And give each full and loyal heart
A glad and tuneful tongue.
When the battle's hanging and
The conflict thrills us through
When the foe is pushing hard,
Why, what are we going to do?
Oh, we'll whoop 'er up for Knox.
We'll whoop 'er up for Knox
Rickety-raff, chiff-chaff!
Whoop 'er up for Knox.

Once the services were over, Lillian wrote to Professor Kittredge, scared that Franz's book, too, would die. Kittredge responded, "I am truly grieved to learn of your husband's death. Although we had never met I had come to think of him as a friend and a colleague. I will read the proof myself. That will be the best solution to this question."

It took Vachel Lindsay almost a year, but then he wrote a long tribute to Franz for Springfield's newspaper, the *Illinois State Register*, saying in part, "This is the history of a young troubadour who might have been a statesman in the United States art, had he lived. . . . His outstanding characteristics were an untiring industry, a determined disposition, which helped him overcome all sorts of obstacles . . . a keen sense of humor, an optimism that never failed him, and a friend-making ability that was far out of the ordinary."

When Harvard released *Ballads and Songs of the Shanty-Boy* in 1926, dedicated to Lillian, "A True Comrade," Edmund Wilson and Carl Sandburg and others wrote positive reviews. Sandburg, the prodigiously creative writer, poet, biographer, folk singer, journalist, performer, and self-promoter, wrote, "He had besides attainment in scholarship, the gifts of an artist. In his *Ballads and Songs of the Shanty-Boy* there is more than fact and chronicle—there is arrangement, vision, the handling of materials by a rare human being—he knew rough men, their rough work, words, weather. . . . His book is not merely of historical and documentary value. It is also humanly appealing and entertaining. . . . It is brawny, reeking and raucous. It renders the big woods . . . with the fidelity of an unimpeachable witness."

In 1927 Sandburg published his seminal collection of almost three hundred folksongs, *The American Songbag*. Still in print today, the unique book placed the "All-American songs from the hearts and voices of thousands of American men and women" right into the mainstream and, arguably, laid one of the bricks in the foundation for the American folk revival of the 1940s, '50s, and '60s. "John Henry," "Frankie and Johnny," "The Erie Canal," "Git Along Little Dogies," and "Ain' Go'n to Study War No Mo'" would become American classics. Franz would have been thrilled that Sandburg drew heavily on *Ballads and Songs of the Shanty-Boy*. "The Shanty-man's Life," "Jack Haggerty," and "The Jam on Gerry's Rocks" are right there in what Garrison Keillor calls "a bundle of American treasures."

In 1941 Alan Lomax, then at the Archive of American Folk Song at the Library of Congress, urged his bosses to obtain Franz's papers, writing in a note now in its files: "Rickaby was to lumberjacks as my father was to cowboys."

In an ironic twist, reflective of the times, the library leaders responded to Lomax that they did not know Lillian's second husband well enough to ask him for the papers, as if directly asking Lillian—unsentimental, pragmatic, ambitious, and loving—would somehow be inappropriate. The papers were, by then, scattered among several libraries in Madison, Cambridge, Grand Forks, Galesburg, and Claremont and with Lillian herself.

The most poignant tribute came, of course, from Lillian in a letter she wrote on May 24 to William Bartlett, Franz's loyal fan in Eau Claire, Wisconsin. Starting abruptly, she wrote, "Franz died last Monday after several months of illness which became acute just a week before he died. He had severe spasms the last three days but didn't give up for a moment. . . . We're sorry, of course, that he didn't get to see his book, but what are books to those who walk among the stars."

Just a few years ago—almost eighty-five years after he died—I found a black-and-white photograph of Rickaby, taken around 1917. Standing atop a large boulder with his left leg up in a gentle sweep, his arms raised, and forefingers pointing to the western sky, he's like some midwestern Mercury, indeed the Wandering Minstrel of the Midwest. That photograph sent me off in Frenzy's footsteps. They took me to places I had never

Franz as Mercury in Galesburg, Illinois, 1917. (Gretchen Dykstra collection)

seen and introduced me to history I had never known. Now I know him a bit—maybe even more than a little—and understand, I believe, what he was like and what motivated his life's work, but, more importantly, I now love—and am proud of—the grandfather I never met and the Midwest that he adored.

<h2 style="text-align:center">Sources</h2>

I set out to meet the grandfather I never knew, and for me—as a generalist—the quest was about the time and place and people who shaped him. I am happy to report that I met my grandfather and in the doing so learned much about American history. The search was lots of fun.

Many people encouraged me, including my mother and sisters, who were patient with my obsession. Numerous friends in New York City, North Dakota, California, Cold Spring, New York, and elsewhere were supportive. In particular, Jay Barksdale at the New York Public Library gave me a key to the Wertheim Study and started me on my way; Mary and Morris Rossabi offered valuable advice about how to be a historian; Eileen Sullivan read several drafts and gave me valuable feedback; Brian Miller's knowledge about lumberjack songs, Rickaby, and his informants was a generous source; Michael Swanson at the University of North Dakota (UND) and Carley Robison at Knox College were two of the most enthusiastic and helpful archivists; James Leary provided help throughout, came up with the idea of combining my work with the reissue of Rickaby's book, and offered his scholarly depth to the endeavor; and the incomparable William Zinsser (RIP) listened patiently to my reading of the manuscript over many sessions together, offered wise and invaluable assistance in his gentle and funny way, and was the one who urged me to hit the road.

Like Rickaby, I followed some leads that took me nowhere, but many led somewhere. One of my favorites was discovering a tiny self-published pamphlet, written in 1920, that described a summer when the caddie master in Charlevoix recruited girl caddies for the first time. It charmingly substantiated what I had read in Rickaby's papers and underscored the wonders of the New York Public Library.

The following list of resources is not comprehensive, but it illustrates which avenues led me to the most valuable material. The Wisconsin

Historical Society owns Rickaby's journal from his walk from Charlevoix in 1919; the Mills Music Library at the University of Wisconsin has some of Rickaby's lecture notes and additional materials he collected; Knox College has the songs, poems, yearbook contributions, and essays he wrote while a student there; the University of North Dakota has many helpful materials, including extensive files about the Dakota Playmakers and Rickaby's involvement with the group; Pomona College's collection of college newspapers from 1923–25 was interesting for Rickaby's final years; Harvard University's Houghton Library has his original manuscript, complete with Professor Kittredge's marginal notes. I have a journal Rickaby's father kept and letters Lillian wrote to her mother and me. I own copies of Franz's poems, complete with Vachel Lindsay's comments; I have all his articles in *Golf* magazine, his published plays, photographs, notes, and letters he wrote that my grandmother kept. She included in that trunk multiple copies of "Fiddle and I: The Story of Franz Rickaby" by Daniel W. Greene (*Journal of American Folklore* 81 no. 322 [1968]), which helped me greatly.

Historical societies are rich resources, and their archivists are invariably curious and helpful. I would cite, in particular, the historical societies in Saint Paul, Bemidji, Virginia, Cloquet, and Stillwater, Minnesota; University of Wisconsin–Eau Claire and Ladysmith, Wisconsin; Grand Forks, North Dakota; Galesburg, Illinois; and, of course, the Library of Congress. The Mayo Clinic and Loma Linda Hospital have both published histories of their respective institutions, and, in the case of Loma Linda, my interview with Richard Shaefer was particularly helpful. In that same vein, Dr. Peter English, who wrote a definitive book on rheumatic fever, generously provided his time and expertise.

Much has been written about Galesburg and Springfield, Illinois. I drew heavily on Jerusha L. Farnham and Samuel Holyoke, *Log City Days: Two Narratives on the Settlement of Galesburg, Illinois* (Galesburg: Knox College Centenary Publications, 1937); Earnest Elmo Calkins, *They Broke the Prairies* (New York: Scribners, 1937); Jack Finney, *I Love Galesburg in the Springtime* (New York: Simon and Schuster, 1963); Carl Sandburg, *Always the Young Strangers* (New York: Harcourt, Brace, 1952) and *Ever the Winds of Chance* (Urbana: University of Illinois Press, 1983); Hermann R. Muelder, *Missionaries and Muckrakers: The First Hundred Years of Knox*

College (Urbana: University of Illinois Press, 1984); Eleanor Ruggles, *The West-Going Heart: A Life of Vachel Lindsay* (New York: Norton, 1959); Vachel Lindsay, *The Golden Book of Springfield* (New York: Macmillan, 1920); and Edgar Lee Masters, *Vachel Lindsay: A Poet in America* (New York: Biblo and Tannen, 1969). In all cases, the archives of the local newspapers, Chicago and New York newspapers, various student theses, and the Arcadia History series provided valuable information.

For information on Charlevoix, Michigan, I drew on Rickaby's eight articles for *Golf* magazine; Bob Miles, *Bob Miles' Charlevoix II* (Charlevoix, MI: Charlevoix Historical Society, 2002); Robert Browning, *A History of Golf* (n.p.: Classics of Golf, 1985); Edith Gilbert, *Summer Resort Life* (Charlevoix, MI: Charlevoix Historical Society, 1920); and A. K. Sandoval-Strausz, *Hotel: An American History* (New Haven, CT: Yale University Press, 2007).

The following all gave me a solid footing in the state's history: Elwyn B. Robinson, *History of North Dakota* (Lincoln: University of Nebraska Press, 1966); Hiram Drache, *The Day of the Bonanza: A History of Bonanza Farming in the Red River Valley of the North* (Fargo: North Dakota Institute for Regional Studies, 1964); Works Progress Administration, *North Dakota: A Guide to the Northern Prairie State* (Fargo: 1938); Louis Geiger, *University of the Northern Plains: A History of the University of North Dakota, 1883–1958* (Grand Forks: University of North Dakota Press, 1958); Charles Glaub et al., *The North Dakota Political Tradition* (Ames: Iowa State University Press, 1981); D. Jerome Tweton, *North Dakota: The Heritage of a People* (Fargo: North Dakota Institute for Regional Studies, 1976); and D. Jerome Tweton and Everett C. Albers, eds., *The Sod-Busters*, vol. 1 of *The Way It Was: The North Dakota Frontier Experience* (Fessenden, ND: Grass Roots Press, 2003). Frederick Jackson Turner's *The Significance of the Frontier in American History* (first published in 1893 and many times thereafter, including by Penguin Books in 2008) was essential, even if now somewhat refuted. A senior thesis prepared for UND in 1972 by Robert Mjoen on Grand Forks in 1914, *Forty Years in North Dakota in Relation to Grand Forks County*, self-published in 1921 by Henry Vernon Arnold, and *The City of Grand Forks Illustrated* by W. L. Dudley (Grand Forks, ND: Herald, 1897) were all helpful. I appreciate the *North Dakota Quarterly* 77, no. 4 (Fall 2010), for publishing "Franz

Rickaby: The Wandering Minstrel of North Dakota," a shorter version of this piece.

These books provided a glimpse into other dimensions of North Dakota: Jonathan Raban, *Bad Land: An American Romance* (New York: Pantheon, 1996); Kathleen Norris, *Dakota: A Spiritual Geography* (Boston: Houghton Mifflin, 2001); O. E. Rølvaag, *Giants in the Earth: A Saga of the Prairie* (New York: Harper and Brothers, 1927); and Willa Cather, *O Pioneers!* (first published in 1913 and reissued by Bantam Books, 1989).

Much has been written—or produced—about the Nonpartisan League, and I cite, in particular, Robert Loren Morlan, *Political Prairie Fire: The Nonpartisan League, 1915–1922* (Minneapolis: University of Minnesota Press, 1955); Charles Russell, *The Story of the Nonpartisan League: A Chapter in American Evolution* (New York: Harper and Brothers, 1920); Larry Remele, *The Lost Years of A. C. Townley* (Bismarck: North Dakota Humanities Council, 1988); Herbert Gaston, *The Nonpartisan League* (New York: Harcourt Brace, 1920); the documentary *Plowing Up a Storm* by Nebraska Educational TV Network (1985); and *Northern Lights*, an independent film produced in 1978 by John Hanson and Rob Nilsson.

For folklore and, in particular, those early days of ballad collecting, I depended on D. K. Wilgus, *Anglo-American Folksong Scholarship since 1898* (New Brunswick, NJ: Rutgers University Press, 1959); Louise Pound, *American Ballads and Songs* (New York: Scribner, 1922); Scott Spencer, ed., *The Ballad Collectors of North America: How Gathering Folksongs Transformed Academic Thought and American Identity* (Lanham, MD: Scarecrow Press, 2012); Nolan Porterfield, *Last Cavalier: The Life and Times of John A. Lomax, 1867–1948* (Urbana: University of Illinois Press, 1996); Mickey Hart with K. M. Kostyal, *Songcatchers: In Search of the World's Music* (Washington, DC: National Geographic, 2003); Benjamin Filene, *Romancing the Folk: Public Memory and American Roots Music* (Chapel Hill: University of North Carolina Press, 2000); Robert Cantwell, *When We Were Good: The Folk Revival* (Cambridge, MA: Harvard University Press, 1996); and Carl Sandburg, *American Songbag* (New York: Harcourt Brace, 1927).

For the lumber industry in the Upper Midwest I drew on Stewart Edward White, *The Blazed Trail* (New York: Grosset and Dunlap, 1902); Francis M. Carroll, *Crossroads in Time: A History of Carlton County, Minnesota* (Cloquet, MN: Carlton County Historical Society, 1987); Stewart

Hall Holbrook, *Holy Old Mackinaw: A Natural History of the American Lumberjack* (Sausalito, CA: Comstock, 1981); Eric Rutkow, *American Canopy: Trees, Forests, and the Making of a Nation* (New York: Scribner, 2012); and the archives at the University of Wisconsin–Eau Claire, including William Bartlett's files. In addition, I consulted Harold Felton, ed., *Legends of Paul Bunyan* (Minneapolis: University of Minnesota Press, 2008); Michael Edmonds, *Out of the Northwoods: The Many Lives of Paul Bunyan* (Madison: Wisconsin Historical Society Press, 2009); and various newspaper articles and letters about logging held by the Wisconsin Historical Society.

Finally, E. Wilson Lyon, *The History of Pomona College, 1887–1969* (Claremont, CA: Pomona College, 1977), and Frank Brackett, *Granite and Sagebrush: Reminiscences of the First Fifty Years of Pomona College* (Los Angeles: Ward Ritchie Press, 1944), were helpful. *California History* 88, no. 3 (2011), published a shorter piece I wrote focused on Pomona: " *'Boes in Facultate*: The Short, Creative Life of Franz Rickaby." But nothing was as useful as following Franz's footsteps, and, for that, I heartily thank Bill Zinsser, again. He was so right.

PART TWO

Ballads and Songs of the Shanty-Boy

Collected and Edited by Franz Rickaby

"O ye noble big pine tree!"

TO

A True Comrade

MY WIFE

Preface

THE BALLADS AND SONGS recorded in the following pages have been gathered by me during the past seven years from men who worked in the woods of Michigan, Wisconsin, and Minnesota, mainly during the Golden Age of American Lumbering (1870–1900).

Even a cursory acquaintance with the shanty-boy reveals him as a striking American frontier figure, with a mode of life as peculiarly his own, a personality as marked, as that of any of our other frontiersmen. He was, it must be admitted, destructive in his occupation; he cannot be credited with having been anything like the constructive factor in our national development that the cowboy was. But he was the product of a mighty industry blindly forced by the sudden growth of a mightier nation; and the person who shall study that industry and the men it required and produced may find the shanty-boy to have preserved and contributed to the American Spirit some very desirable qualities.

The definition of these qualities is not the purpose of the present volume, except as they may appear in songs and ballads. It is rather to pay tribute to the shanty-boy, and perhaps enrich the holdings of subsequent generations as well, by recording in as effective form as possible the songs and ballads he made and sang. No group ever celebrated itself in song and ballad more than did the shanty-boys of the Golden Age.

The preservation of song anywhere except in the human soul and voice is at best a process of questionable success. It may be as the little old lady of the North Countree sadly intimated to Sir Walter Scott: that to print a ballad of the people is to destroy it. But printing seems to be about the best method we have at our disposal, inasmuch as the number of those who care to learn and sing the old songs seems to be even less than negligible. The printing of the bare words of a ballad, however, without its melodic medium, seems to me to fall far short of preservation. This statement may be entirely debatable; but my feeling, based upon a considerable experience in presenting folksong to present-day audiences, is that American balladry without its "air" is ineffective, sometimes even ugly, like a boat hauled up on the shore. It is in accordance with this feeling that the melodies given me for the various pieces in this collection receive their full share of attention. It is with regret that I am obliged to record a few compositions for which no tunes were furnished me. I have done so only on the supposition that half a loaf is better than none.

The original intention of making this an anthology of only such songs and ballads as belonged body and soul to the shanty-boy, and of including all obtainable variants and fragments of all of these, gave way later to the idea of excluding for the most part variants and fragments and including instead a number of other songs and ballads which the shanty-boy sang, although they did not directly reflect life in the woods. Thus in this volume of shanty songs the sea, the Great Lakes, the battlefield (at home and abroad), the prize-ring, and the paths of common life are represented, as well as the pineries.

In the course of my work I have naturally obligated myself to many people besides those who so patiently sang and recited for me. First among these is Mr. William W. Bartlett, since 1867 a citizen of Eau Claire, Wisconsin, whose active interest in this work and whose benevolent hospitality I shall always remember gratefully. I take this opportunity to pay a sincere tribute to this far-sighted man, who has by timely action caused to be preserved literally hundreds of pounds of valuable records, both literary and pictorial, of the lumber industry in Wisconsin from the eighteen-sixties onward. The illustrations in this volume are from pictures in Mr. Bartlett's possession. His gracious permission to reproduce these is one of his many kindnesses toward me.

I am also deeply indebted to Mr. Chris M. Forbes, of Perth, Ontario, for certain texts and historical material. Similar acknowledgment is due Mr. C. L. Clark, of Greenville, Michigan, and Mr. George F. Will, of Bismarck, North Dakota.

To Professor G. L. Kittredge, under whose benevolent influence I suppose all collectors and students of balladry come sooner or later, I render grateful acknowledgment for assistance in the form of several texts, many helpful editorial suggestions, and a most generous array of bibliographical material.

To Mr. Stewart Edward White and Doubleday, Page and Company I owe the privilege of using material from Mr. White's novel *The Blazed Trail*. I acknowledge obligation also to Mr. John Lomax for material, and to him and the Macmillan Company for permission to reprint matter from his *Cowboy Songs*; to G. P. Putnam's Sons for permission to reprint a text from their *American War Ballads*, edited by George Cary Eggleston; to Mr. M. C. (Mike) Dean, of Virginia, Minnesota, old shanty-boy and sailor, "singer," and indefatigable dispenser of good fellowship, whose collection, entitled *The Flying Cloud and 150 Other Old Time Songs and Ballads*, he gave me with the remark, "Go as far as you like"; and to Professor Roland P. Gray and Harvard University Press for permission to use, from Mr. Gray's *Songs and Ballads of the Maine Lumberjacks*, a few eleventh-hour bits with which I have enriched my Notes on certain ballads.

CLAREMONT, CALIFORNIA, January 2, 1925

Introduction

I

WHEN THE ENGLISH SETTLER reached New England shores, in the early years of the seventeenth century, he found a land of forests, and he was immediately obliged to fell trees, not only that he might have material with which to build his home, but also that he might have arable land. But hardly two decades had elapsed after his landing before occasional shiploads of lumber began to find their way from the Colonies back to Old England—an exportation not based upon any conception of lumber as a source of wealth, but upon the fact that this was the first and most desirable commodity which the New Englander had to exchange for such goods as he needed from across the Atlantic.

By the time of the signing of our Declaration of Independence, while Canadian lumbering was practically just beginning, the American Colonies had been over a hundred years "in the business." For close on the heels of augmented settlement and the resultant increase in population and diversity of occupation had come the growing call for lumber within the Colonies themselves. It was no longer practicable for every man to serve himself in this respect, and thus entered industrial history those men whose calling it became to hew timber that their neighbors might have houses and their country, ships. It might be impossible to say exactly when or where, but somewhere in that century appeared the professional woodsman, the incipient shanty-boy, foot-loose and fancy-free, who was to become the courageous, physically powerful, proud, swaggering, audacious, self-extolling "white water bucko" of the next century.

By 1850 the steam-driven circular saw had supplanted the primitive water-power jig-saw mill, and the supremacy in lumber production had moved successively from New England to New York, and from New York to Pennsylvania. The Army of the Axes had advanced even into the awe-inspiring columned vastnesses of Michigan, and across the intervening lake into the illimitable pineries of Wisconsin. What had previously been a steadily growing call for lumber, by 1870 swept suddenly upward into a reverberating clamorous roar of demand, as the hundreds of thousands, following the Argonauts of '49 and '50, surged out into the New West. It was then that American lumbering literally leaped into its Golden Age. Over Michigan, Wisconsin, and Minnesota hovered for thirty years the far-seen glow of its romantic climax. Immense fortunes fell into the hands of far-sighted men, as into the spring-swollen streams rolled billions upon billions of logs, and the land was sown with stumps.

Meanwhile the shanty-boy came into his own. Up and down and across the country he roamed—here today, there tomorrow; chopping, skidding, rolling, hauling, driving great logs that the snarling saws might be fed. The free life called him, the thunder of falling majesties intoxicated him. Amid this stately presence, along these avenues of "endless upward reaches," he rudely trampled the whiteness of the earth. His axe bit deep as it shouted, and his saw-blade sang in the brittle air. The soft aroma of the woods at peace sharpened to an acrid redolence, acute, insistent—the cry of wounded pine. The great crests trembled, tottered, and thundered to the earth in a blinding swirl of needles and snow-dust, and the sun and sky at last looked in. The conqueror shouted as the proud tops came crashing down, though the places made vacant and bare meant nothing to him. Long hours of hard labor, simple fare, and primitive accommodations hardened him; the constant presence of danger rendered him resourceful, self-reliant, agile. It was as if the physical strength and bold vitality, the regal aloofness of the fallen giants, flowed in full tide into him and he thus came to know neither weariness nor fear. Neither Life nor Death was his master. He loved, hated, worked, played, earned, spent, fought, and sang—and even in his singing was a law unto himself.

The relationship between the Northern lumbering communities of the United States and the Canadian provinces across the boundary was always close, not only in respect to the commercial exchange of the product, but in social ways as well. Migration took place in both directions; and, to a much greater extent, men from each side crossed over to work temporarily on the other, for profit, for a lark, or for both. The camps on both sides were similar, as were the logging operations themselves, until the American, with his mechanical and executive genius, outstripped his Northern neighbor. In the Golden Age of lumbering this cross-boundary visiting was most marked, particularly America-ward. Canadian "boys" came across in droves to work in American camps, especially those of Michigan. They brought their songs and left them in the memories and on the lips of the Americans. They learned American shanty songs and took them back across the Lakes. In all probability the word "shanty-boy" itself came to our camps in the vocabulary of the Irishman via Canada. American jobbers logged off "limits," or grants, in Ontario; Canadian jobbers and companies boomed their cuts across the Lake to be sawed in Michigan sawmills.

So far as the contents of this volume are concerned, it is of no moment where next the lumber industry gloried in the United States; for the day of singing passed in the period of the Lake states supremacy. A few years, perhaps ten, before 1900, it was evident that some grim change was taking place, killing the song in the hearts of workers, not only in the forests, but abroad in the world as well. Instead of singing, they read or talked or plotted; or if they did sing, the song was no longer of themselves. The complexion of the shanty crews changed. Where once had been the free-moving wit, the clear ringing voice of the Irishman, the Scotchman, the French-Canadian, there appeared in greater numbers the stolid Indian, the quiet, slow-moving, more purposeful Scandinavian.

> Ten thousand Swedes
> Ran through the weeds
> Shouting the battle-cry of Copenhagen,

ran a maudlin lumberjack parody of the later day. In the place of the old unattached shanty-boy, whose sole home was the camp, came more and more the men from the farms, men who tended to save their money and whose morals were more or less safely anchored in homes to which they returned in the spring.

The insistent cry for quantity, the feverish prayer for efficiency, brought machines, massive, grim, powerful, ultra-human creatures of steel; and they, not singing, taught silence. Then one morning the romance of logging was gone. Gone were the feats of skill and prowess on the drive, for gone was the drive. The age of steel was upon lumbering—the impersonal age, the non-singing age.

The lumber industry still moves on. In the East, the North, the South, and the far West the trees still fall; for men must still have lumber, even more than ever. But it is now a cold and calculated process, with careful emphasis on selection, salvage, and by-product. The riot of wasteful harvest is no more: the unexpected vision of impending want, of imminent ugly barrenness, has quenched the thrill of destruction. The nation, having allowed the candle to be burned at both ends, tardily awakes to the necessity of conservation, a sort of cold gray "morning after." Such a morning has its good and holy uses; but whatever forms of exultation may finally come of it, it must be noted that song is not one of its immediate possessions.

II

Song did not serve in logging as it did in other gang occupations, such as that of sailors, railroad laborers, and the like, where efforts in unison were timed, or the general rhythm of the work was maintained, by the singing of the group or of an individual in it. The shanty-boy made no appreciable use of his songs while actually at work. He apparently preferred quip and jest, or wordy by-play of various sorts. He was not by nature a "gang" worker; he was predominantly an individualist, an artist with cant-hook, peavy, axe, or saw.

But back in the shanty, particularly on Saturday evenings, secure from the outer cold—his supper stowed safely within him, the old iron stove throwing out its genial heat, and the mellowing ministrations of tobacco well begun—the shanty-boy became story-teller and singer. The emotional thaw set in, and a great many of his songs were, in the words of an old shanty-boy, "as fine as any you'll hear."

One would like to assume unreservedly that this circle of deacon-seat gods required of each member a song as his turn came, as was the custom among our Anglo-Saxon forefathers. But such an assumption does not seem to be warranted. In the very early days, when singing was an integral part of common life, provided for in the human soul and mechanism just as talking and walking are, the evidence is that all woodsmen sang, just as all other people sang, individually and collectively. But in that day the singing of a song could hardly be called a requirement; it was neither duty nor privilege: it was merely an element in the composite phenomenon of living.

Only on two occasions have I been told that each man around the deacon seat was obliged to sing a song or tell a story. One of these informants added that if a fellow sang a song, he might sing an old one, but if he elected to tell a story, he had to tell a new one. These were evidently particular instances rather than general practice. They illustrate what came to be a common form of amusement at social gatherings in that day of song: each person seated around the room was required to sing a song, not being allowed to repeat one already sung on that occasion. Failure to sing made necessary the payment of a forfeit, which had later to be redeemed as in the game of Forfeits.

In all ages, however, there have been those whose natural gifts have singled them out as performers more able than their fellows. In the case of the shanty-boy, by 1860, which is about as far back as can be reached effectively by the memories of men still living, although all shanty-boys sang on occasion (even the monotones!), the group generally liked to hear certain individuals sing. These individuals were called "singers," not because of any technical training, but because of the gifts of a naturally good voice, a particularly retentive memory, and an inherent inclination to sing. Such men were extremely popular in the camps, and in the saloons and resorts where the shanty-boy off the drive reached poverty through glittering doors.

A specific instance of the popularity of such a "singer" in camp was furnished me by Mr. Will Daugherty, of Charlevoix, Michigan, some years ago. After explaining that the position of the "singer" in the camp was unique, he went on to relate how one winter, when he was in a Michigan camp, a man named George Burns, an old Scotsman, wandered into the shanties in a freezing condition. He was of course taken in, and in the natural order of events was asked if he could sing. In reply he sang "Bonnie Doon" in a fine tenor voice, and after that, as Daugherty put it, "he couldn't get away." He was given work all that winter, "although he couldn't shovel snow and do it right," and left the camp the following spring with a stake of $135, "a favorite member of the crew."

The majority of men from whom songs and ballads of the older men are now to be secured were "singers." It is only in the memories of these men, some of whom in their prime knew literally scores of songs, that the old melodies and verses rooted themselves sufficiently to stand a silence of thirty years, or even longer, and remain traceable now after a generation of rusting in disuse.

Whether the singing in the shanties was solo or ensemble would depend upon several conditions, prime among which would be the nature of the song and the spirit of the group at the particular moment. Some shanty-songs lend themselves to chorus singing; others do not. A song with a refrain would naturally bespeak a soloist for the stanza and all in chorus on the refrain. This principle is involved in the hoisting chantey, and possibly in the very origins of popular balladry. In *The Blazed Trail* Mr. White records "Bung Yer Eye" (No. 33) as sung by soloist and chorus. He also illustrates the other type of song in the fragment of "The Logger's Boast," which is reprinted in the Notes for "Bung Yer Eye." This song, boisterous and boastful in tone, and composed in the third-person plural, calls for chorus expression; whereas such a song as "Jim Whalen" (No. 3), or any of that tragic type, or as "Jack Haggerty" (No. 1), or the autobiographical type, belongs just as definitely to the individual singer.

An examination of the names of the heroes in the songs recorded in this collection, and of the names of those from whom the songs were obtained, will support the assertion that in the logging camp the hegemony in song belonged to the Irish. Although the Scotch and French-Canadian occur occasionally, the Irish were dominant, and the Irish street-song was the pattern upon which a liberal portion of the shanty-songs were made.[1] Irishmen sailed the seas of the world. In the armies of England they fought against Russia and died on the fields of Indian insurrection. In Canada and the United States, whither they migrated in hordes, they fought wherever there was fighting. And in this New World those of them who were thrifty and provident laid the foundations of homes, and those who were not, did not. But whatever they did, they made and sang songs, and wherever they went roving, they took them along. Thus it was that the shanties rang with songs of ships and piracy, of American battle charges, and of prize-fights in far-lying ports of the world; of charging the heights of Alma, of dying in India for Britannia and Britannia's Queen, and of sailing the Lakes with red iron ore—of all these, as well as of harvesting the mighty pine.

In regard to the origin of woods songs there is no problem: they were composed by individuals who set out definitely to compose. No other theory of origin is logically possible, it seems to me. So far as I know, the shanty-boy had no ballads of the type of certain amoeba-like Negro pieces; nor of the unsettled hoisting chantey type, such as "Sally Black" or "Blow the Man Down" of the sailors; nor even of the type which includes "The Old Chisholm Trail" of the cowboys. I presume "Fred Sargent's Shanty Song" (No. 21) would be the nearest approach to these. A shanty-boy of modest ingenuity might construct new stanzas for this song as the group sang the refrain. But even so, the song is under no necessity of having originated that way. Mr. Ava Smith, of Charlevoix, Michigan, gave me an account of a case of authorship which came under his observation one spring after a drive. The name of the song, the song itself, and the name of the man, had all vanished from his memory, but the occasion he recalled.

At a boarding and rooming house where a number of shanty-boys were staying, there was a waitress with very red hair. An "affair" between this lady and one of the boys became the occasion of a great deal of fun-making. Mr. Smith related that one of the men, a sort of ringleader among them, was noticeably absent from the group for several days—a fact which occasioned no little wonder on the part of the rest. For some reason known only to himself, he spent most of his time in his room, even missing some of his meals. Finally, however, he appeared at supper one evening, and after the meal was over sang for the group a song which he had "made up on" the red-haired girl and her shanty-boy. There was no evidence that the man had written in the course of composition. Mr. Smith was of the opinion that the fellow couldn't write anyway. Of the melody or its probable origin Mr. Smith could say nothing. His expression was merely that the composer of the verses had "fitted them to a tune." It is more than probable that the song was a short-lived one on account of its undramatic nature and its limited local appeal. I was told that it was highly successful at the time, however: it made the young lady "good an' hot."[2]

This incident suggests some consideration of the material and inspiration behind shanty-songs. Through the kindness of a patient friend I have been able to record in the Notes on "Jim Whalen" (No. 3) the historical data behind that classic. And it is more than likely that "Jack Haggerty" is built upon fact of some sort, although the material presented in the Notes establishes with certainty only Jack's historicity. The historical foundation of a great many ballads and songs of the generations which sang, especially of the ballads, is easily demonstrable, although the degree of visible dependence upon specific incident varies considerably in different instances. For example, "The Cumberland's Crew" is built definitely upon the sinking of the Cumberland by the Merrimac. At least one ballad and three songs rest upon the spectacular death of Colonel E. E. Ellsworth, "the first hero of the Civil War," and "James Bird" rests squarely upon the execution of the man of that name in 1814, just as "Jim Whalen" does upon the Phalen tragedy. On the other hand, in such pieces as "The Charge at Fredericksburg" (sometimes called "The Last Fierce Charge"), "The Drummer Boy of Shiloh," "The Texas Rangers," and "The Battle of Buena Vista," there is little if anything that would serve to tie the story definitely to the locality or occasion announced in the title or assigned by investigators. Such shanty-songs as "The Maine-ite in Pennsylvania" (No. 19), any of the various "shanty-man's life" songs, or "The Shanty-boy and the Farmer's Son" (No. 10) would illustrate the song of indefinite foundation.

Imitation, not only of form but of theme as well, was a prime resource in the making of shanty-songs. This is true in American folksong generally. A rich example is afforded in the old-world song called "The Unfortunate Rake," which is held responsible in a way for the well-known cowboy song "The Dying Cowboy." I have heard a version of "The Dying Hobo" which was patently an adaptation, probably of the cowboy song, and the shanty-boys sang an adaptation known as "The Dying Whore." The relation of "The Cowboy's Lament," beginning

Oh, bury me not on the lone prairee

to the earlier "Ocean Burial" (or "The Deep, Deep Sea"), which begins thus,

Oh, bury me not in the deep, deep sea,

has been pointed out.[3] It would seem also that "The Shanty-boy and the Farmer's Son" (No. 10) was patterned after "I Love My Sailor Boy." That "The Pinery Boy" (No. 18) is a direct adaptation of the older ballad "Sweet William, or The Sailor Boy," a fragment of which is included in the Notes, there can be no doubt.

But, whatever the degree of imitation and of relationship and faithfulness to specific event, the shanty-song involved individual authorship, "the mere act of composition"; and later, on the lips of the folk, falling into multitudes of variants, it came into full acquaintance with "the second act of composition."[4]

It is common knowledge that anonymity is the rule in popular balladry. Only comparatively rarely, through some chance recording of author and song together at the time of composition (as in the case of "James Bird," "The Hunters of Kentucky," and "The Fatal Oak"), is the name of the "mere composer" known. Ballad collectors soon grow accustomed to being told who wrote this song or that, but in the majority of cases the information must simply be listed as another phase of folk expression! Several years ago, however, Mr. William W. Bartlett, of Eau Claire, Wisconsin, sent me the original manuscripts of some old woods songs, which had been sent him by the author, Mr. W. N. Allen, of Wausau, Wisconsin. Among these I was surprised to find a copy of a ballad which I had picked up in Minnesota some time before: "Johnny Murphy, or On the Banks of the Little Eau Pleine" (No. 5). It was perfectly clear that this version was actually the original, and some months later I had the privilege of visiting the author, a genial octogenarian, at his home. On the occasion of this visit I found that Billy Allen was also the composer of "The Shanty-boy on the Big Eau Claire" (No. 11), a number of folk versions of which I had also found. He had composed these and most of his other pieces under the pseudonym of "Shan T. Boy." His relation to the two ballads just mentioned is not at all known, even in his own state, where they were most used. I have never had anyone tell me who wrote them, but Mr. Allen said that on several occasions he had heard men sing one or the other of them and then give a complete account of "the feller that wrote that song," name and all. In none of these cases, however, was the "feller" Mr. Allen, who considered the joke a good one, but kept it to himself, mainly because he would not have been believed, I imagine.

Inasmuch as Mr. Allen is the only folk-author I have ever known, and as he seems to be about my closest possible approach to those shadowy persons responsible for the songs the shanty-boy sang, some biographical notice of him may not be amiss.

He was born, the oldest of eight children, in St. Stephens, New Brunswick, December 20, 1843, of parents who had emigrated from Ireland to Canada. The family left Canada in 1855 and came to Cedar River, Michigan, a settlement near where Escanaba now is. After fourteen months there, they moved to Manitowoc County, Wisconsin, and a short time after, up to Wausau. There the mother of the family died. Billy left home at the age of seventeen, his first job being that of helper to a timber cruiser over in the Green Bay region of Wisconsin. It was in practical apprenticeship of this sort that he learned his trade. His formal schooling, all of which came prior to his leaving home, was very meager—not more than three years in all, he thought.

In 1868, at the age of twenty-five, Allen returned to Wausau and worked that winter on the Wisconsin River. Since that year he has called Wausau his home, although he has traveled the length and breadth of the United States, and somewhat in Mexico, as timber cruiser for various companies. He has served as County Surveyor of his home county (Marathon) for several terms, twelve years in all. He has never married, and at the time I visited him was living with a sister in quiet retirement in his home in Wausau.

About 1870 he began composing his ballads and songs (he calls them all "poems"). He told me he had written lots of poetry when he was "a kid," but "it wasn't much good." In composing his poems he had no idea of their achieving currency as songs, although he invariably composed them with tunes in mind, and, being himself a "singer," he sang them in the camps which he visited in the course of his work as cruiser. Nor did he make any attempt to preserve the pieces himself, other than in his memory—a fact he later regretted.

The following notes are from Mr. Allen to Mr. Bartlett, sent with the manuscripts already referred to:

Wausau, Wisconsin
April 10, 1923

W. W. Bartlett:

Dear Sir,

Yours of recent date at hand. Cap. Henry mentioned your name in his correspondence with me, and he wanted some of my poems. I presume it is immaterial whether I furnish them to him or to you. My business in by-gone days was cruising and surveying for the lumbermen in the Wisconsin valley. Consequently I had occasion to visit a great many logging camps in the course of each winter, and it was customary for me to sing for the lumber-jacks in lumber-jack style. But I am old and feeble now (in my 80th year) and my memory is not as fruitful as it was in former years. I was not careful enough about preserving my poems (which I should have done), and now I have to depend upon my memory for a great many of them. Several of my poems are sarcastic descriptions of characters and failings of our respectable (?) citizens, and I have been threatened with libel suits and shot-guns on several occasions. But most of my subjects are dead, so that I am now practically safe for the time being.

Yours truly, etc.

Wausau, Wisconsin
April 18, 1923

W. W. Bartlett:

Dear Sir,

Yours to hand. I scribbled off a couple of poems which I enclose. Those others you mention I have heard sang, but am not the author of any of them. Several of my poems have been published far and wide and have generally been murdered, some of them I couldn't tie together with a string.

Truly yours, etc.

As indicated here, Mr. Allen turned his poetic efforts in various directions. It happens that in two of his attempts, the two ballads mentioned earlier, he utilized such good narrative germs that the pieces caught in the popular fancy and rooted themselves there successfully, in spite of the author's conscious attempts at humor and satire. It so happens that neither of these ballads is based on actual fact—"just pure imagination," he told me, except for the mention, in each of them, of a local character. Indeed, Mr. Allen seemed always more interested in local characters and conditions than in dramatic narrative. Satire and derision were his favorite modes, and he recounted for me at great length some of his experiences as a writer of caustic verse, experiences to which he merely alludes in the last of the letters quoted above. The following stanzas from his "Ballad of a Blow-hard" are typical of his work in this vein.

> My song is not a song of love; 't is not a song of flowers.
> 'Tis not about the babbling brooks, nor of the shady bowers.
> It is not about the ocean where the briny billow rolls.
> But 'tis of a hump-backed blow-hard: his name is S. D.
>   Knowles.

> When he was a little baby in the good old State of Maine,
> His father was a homely cuss, his mother somewhat plain.
> But the sun in all its glory as this planet round it rolls,
> Ne'er gazed upon a cherub half so fair as S. D. Knowles.

> He'll tell you of the dangers, of the hardships he went
>   through;
> How he can ride a Norway log and pole a bark canoe;
> What havoc he has made among the spruces and the pines,
> And how many miles on snow-shoes he has walked on section
>   lines.

> His manifold adventures to you he will explain,
> When he was a shanty-boy in the good old State of Maine.
> And you will wonder to yourself as you meander home,
> Why so smart a man as S. D. Knowles is not more widely
>   known.

The ballad contained twelve more stanzas of this general style, and a refrain of two lines.

Many of Mr. Allen's pieces were political, and of course intensely partisan. He recounted with some pride how, during a political struggle in the city of Wausau, someone handed the editor of one of Wausau's three newspapers a copy of one of the rival papers in which was prominent one of these political poems. "Yes," said the editor, "I see it, and I wish to God that editor had even half as much sense as the man who wrote that poem."

It would of course be dangerous to generalize too freely about folksong authorship from one or two examples. Taking even the three clearly known authors represented in the present volume—Billy Allen, Mrs. Payne, author of "The Fatal Oak" (No. 29), and Samuel Woodworth, author of "The Hunters of Kentucky [Kaintucky]" (No. 40)—one might find almost any number of differing details in matters of dependence upon historical event, purpose in composing, stanza form, utilization of older songs, and so on.[5]

Certain points of apparent similarity also suggest themselves. Mr. Allen and Mr. Woodworth, for instance, might have thought and felt a great deal in common, their difference being rather in degree than in kind. The mood of "The Shanty-boy on the Big Eau Claire" is very similar to that of "The Hunters of Kentucky [Kaintucky]." In "The Old Oaken Bucket" Mr. Woodworth sounded a universal note of homely sentiment; Mr. Allen achieved nothing of this magnitude, but he was no stranger to such sentiment, for he adapted the greater song to his own community when he wrote "The Hemlock That Stood by the Brook," and recorded the traveler's yearning for his home when he composed "Wisconsin Again." Mr. Allen invariably appropriated his tunes from elsewhere; Mr. Woodworth was able to devise melodies for his verses, but did not always bind himself to do so, as witness his utilization of "Miss Bailey" for "The Hunters of Kentucky [Kaintucky]." It is easy to imagine also that the author of "Jack Haggerty" would have been a kindred spirit with him who composed "The Banks of the Little Eau Pleine." Whoever wrote "Harry Bail" would very likely have furnished congenial company for the writer of "The Fatal Oak." It is not improbable that the makers of "Gerry's Rocks" and "James Bird" would also have been entirely compatible. And finally, "The Shanty-man's Alphabet," "Fred Sargent's Shanty Song," "The Crow

Wing Drive," "Ole from Norway," and many other pieces in this collection might easily have taken form in the unlettered mind of the shanty-boy who drew aloof from his boarding-house fellows to "think up" the song on the red-haired girl and her jolly riverman.

It was in spite of his satire and his various other modes of conscious humor that Mr. Allen achieved folk-currency, certainly not because of them. It is axiomatic that the folk tends to drop from its ballads all that does not appeal to it—which is to say, it pares the story to the very core, dropping aside all artistic device which exists for its own sake or for the sake of anything except the narration. Cases in point are furnished by the ballad "Jack Haggerty" (No. 1), which, although probably not much, if any, older than Mr. Allen's compositions, has been more widely known and sung. In this ballad the paring has taken place in good style, a difference measured by four or five stanzas. The paring had begun on Mr. Allen's "The Banks of the Little Eau Pleine," and with a wider and longer usage, all of this author's genial comedy would most likely have been left drying up along the wayside with Haggerty's poetic description of his unfaithful Annie.

In regard to Mr. Allen's methods another fact is salient and significant— the fact of his recourse to imitation and adaptation. For instance, "Driving Saw-logs on the Plover" is a straight imitation of an older song about a mother's words to her son who went to the Crimean War; his "Little Log Shanty on Rib Hill" is an adaptation of the much-parodied "Little Old Log Cabin in the Lane"; in "The Lass of Dunmore" (for a text see Dean, 4–7, 4–8) he apparently found his initial suggestion for "The Banks of the Little Eau Pleine"; in "The Hemlock That Stood by the Brook" he parodied "The Old Oaken Bucket"; and in "The Ballad of a Blow-hard" he followed the pattern of "Brennan on the Moor."

Being a "singer," he had at his tongue's end many old-world songs, mainly Irish. He not only had these always at his disposal as patterns for his verses, but for melodies for his new compositions he seemed invariably to turn to them. He sang "The Banks of the Little Eau Pleine" to the tune of "Erin's Green Isle"; "Ye Noble Big Pine Tree" to that of "Will the Weaver"; "The Ballad of a Blow-hard" to that of "Brennan on the Moor"; and "The Shanty-boy on the Big Eau Claire" and "Driving Saw-logs on the Plover" to old tunes the names of which he had forgotten by the time of my acquaintance with him.[6]

Bona-fide singers of shanty-song—that is, the shanty-boys themselves—have many peculiarities in singing, as they have, or had, in doing everything else in their lives. Some of these peculiarities have been hinted at here and there in the Notes on various pieces. But the recording of the individualistic touches and mannerisms found in the different singers, interesting and amusing as most of these touches and mannerisms would be, belongs to a detailed exposition of shanty-boy character rather than to this brief introduction. Two or three outstanding traits may be mentioned here, however.

Intense application to the matter in hand was apparently a cardinal trait of those singers, if their performances today may be taken as evidence. That the concentration may be greater, I suppose, many of them sing with their eyes closed. Some prefer (nowadays at least) to sit in a rocking-chair and rock nervously as they sing; others sit bolt upright and stiff, as they might have been moulded by the harsh lines of the deacon seat itself. Stiffness and want of relaxation are present in the vocal organs themselves practically without exception, for the relaxation of proper singing comes usually only with training such as the folk never had. It would not be fair to judge, without very liberal allowance at least, what these voices were like in the Golden Age, for most of the old fellows are past man's three-score-and-ten allotment. But in the Golden Age the story and not the voice was the principal element. A good voice was appreciated, but it was in no sense a requirement.

Willingness to sing is another general trait of the old shanty-boy. I have yet to encounter one of them who hesitated to give me all he had, once common understanding and confidence had been established.

Many of the men, though not by any means all of them, have the habit of dropping from a singing to a speaking voice on the last words of a song, sometimes "talking" the entire last line. This habit is spoken of by Mr. Chris Forbes (see Notes on "Jim Whalen") as being common among shanty-boys and sailors. He explains it as being a sort of indication that the song is finished. Mr. Andrew Ross, of Charlevoix, Michigan, closed his songs with the last few words spoken, and invariably added as he opened his eyes, "That's all there is to that song."

An examination of most of the songs recorded in this collection, where the music is included, will reveal the fact that the stanzas following the first one do not seem to "fit" the melody given. In such cases anyone attempting to sing the songs simply has to make them fit. The melody given is arranged for the first stanza that is complete in the particular version. To sing the song entire, one must do as the old singers did: have the melody clearly in mind, then merely juggle the notation in each measure so that the sum total takes care of the whole stanza. For instance, the first line of stanza 1 of a certain song runs thus:

Oh, a shan - ty-man's life is a wear - i - some life.

For the first line of stanza 4, however, this becomes

But when spring it does set in, doub - le hard-ships then be - gin.

In a certain version of No. 14, for the first line of stanza 2:

We all go out with a welcome heart, with a well content-ed mind.

But for the same line in stanza 4:

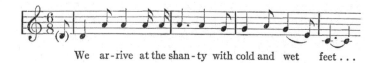

We ar - rive at the shan - ty with cold and wet feet . . .

And this passage in stanza 2 of the same piece—

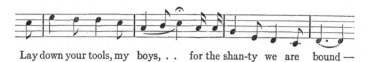

Lay down your tools, my boys, . . for the shan - ty we are bound —

becomes this for the same line of stanza 4:

It's not the style of one of our boys to lose his hash, you know.

It is with these songs and ballads just as my good friend, Mr. Otto Rindlisbacher, of Rice Lake, Wisconsin, said of the logging camp fiddler: "He gets the swing of the tune and then plays it to suit himself." Getting the swing of the melody of a song, and then bending both melody and words into a satisfactory union, is fundamental in folksong. The singing of a ballad is a free and unconfined process. The story is the clear unmortgaged possession of the personality whose lips happen to be forming it at the time; word and note must serve, but they must not get in the way. Thus it is that a singer, in three successive renditions of the same line, may sing it no twice alike. Not only may the melody vary slightly, but "they" may become "we," "though" may become "although," "Willie" may become "William," or even another person entirely. "Oh" may be omitted, or supplied, or "it's" or "then" or "now," and so on through a hundred similar or greater possibilities. This may all sound slovenly and unkempt to the conscious artist; but in the realm of popular balladry, until one does it, the ballad is not truly his.

NOTES

1. Examples of these street-songs are to be found in *A Treasury of Irish Poetry in the English Tongue*, edited by Brooke and Rolleston (Macmillan, 1900); in *Ballad Poetry of Ireland*, edited by Sir Charles Gavan Duffy; and in *Old-Time Songs and Ballads of Ireland* (*Irish Com-All-Ye's*), edited by Manus O'Conor.

2. For another such case of authorship see the Notes on "The Festive Lumberjack" (No. 23).

3. Cf. Pound, *American Ballads and Songs*, notes on "The Dying Cowboy" and "Bury Me Not on the Lone Prairie" (253), for further references.

4. These expressions are Professor Kittredge's, and are to be found in his Introduction to the Cambridge Edition of Child's *English and Scottish Popular Ballads*.

5. While speaking of ballad authors it seems entirely fitting to mention briefly Mr. Charles Miner, the author of the ballad "James Bird," which had a

place among the songs of the shanty-boy, and a melody for which is included in this collection (No. 38). Mr. Miner was a Congressman, an editor, a man of affairs, of good education and possessing considerable literary sense—all of which qualities would normally be set down as inimical to any feeling for popular balladry. Yet in "James Bird" he composed a ballad which clung in the hearts of the American folk for nearly a century, a ballad which, in my experience at least, varies less in its countless folk-versions than any other popular song. No detail in it has seemed superfluous, no stanza unnecessary, no sentiment false to the emotional realities of the thousands who heard, learned, sung, and believed it. (For further comment and reference see Notes on "James Bird.")

6. Illustrative examples of the practice of appropriating existing tunes this way are numberless. "The Little Brown Bulls" (No. 13), a genuine woods song, and "Red Iron Ore" (No. 45), a Great Lakes song, have variants of the same tune; "Ye Maidens of Ontario" (No. 16), another woods song, made in Ontario, uses the same tune, with a different measure, as does "Morrissey and the Russian Sailor" (No. 48), a sea ballad telling of a prize-fight which took place in Terra del Fuego. "The Lost Jimmie Whalen" (No. 4), still another woods song, was sung to a portion of the melody used for "The Cumberland's Crew" (No. 39), a war song, probably originating on the ships, which became general. "The Shanty-boy's Song (Jim Porter's Shanty Song)" (No. 14) uses a tune used also by "The Bigler's Crew" (No. 47), "California Joe," and "Grandfather's Story." In my collecting I have found the "Casey Jones" tune used for four different songs besides the original: a song of a deer hunt over in Minnesota; a decadent shanty-boy song, "The Crow Wing Drive" (No. 24); a forest ranger song from the Klamath country; and an Idaho version of "The Old Chisholm Trail." On the other hand, "James Bird" was sung to at least four different tunes, three besides the one recorded in this collection, which is incidentally the only one I have heard used for it by the shanty-boys: one a famous old church tune ("Nettleton"), another a fife-and-drum tune of the soldiers, and the third a favorite published song of the nineties ("The Tempest").

I

In every direction the woods—
the grandeur,
the remoteness,
the solemnity of the great pine forests.

II

The wilderness
sent forth its old-time challenge
to the hardy.

III

Each night
the men returned to the camp
in the beautiful dream-like twilight.
There, after eating,
they sat smoking their pipes.
Much of the time they sang.

IV

We regret the passing,
each after his manner;
for they are of the picturesque.

Adapted from *The Blazed Trail*
by STEWART EDWARD WHITE

I

Jack Haggerty's Flat River Girl

This ballad, usually known by its shorter name, "Jack Haggerty," is native to the Flat River in southern Michigan. It was a great shanty favorite and is still widely met with in the Lake states. Furthermore, every man who has sung or recited this ballad for me has stoutly averred that he "knew Jack Haggerty himself." B. L. Jones records the piece, with specimen stanzas (*Folk-Lore in Michigan*, 4). Shoemaker prints a version (*North Pennsylvania Minstrelsy*, 2d ed., 212–13). [References to Shoemaker are to the first edition (1919), unless the second (1923) is specified.]

I quote the following from Mr. C. L. Clark, of Greenville, Michigan, from whom I secured Version A:

"I found one old-timer who told me that this song was sung by thousands of men on the Flat River, which flows through Greenville, and on the big river [Big Muskegon], and by farm girls in this neighborhood. . . . Jack Haggerty was a lumberjack, and from a man who used to run a livery stable and rent him horses I have learned that he was not quite so rough as most of those birds, and was a little more dressy. Also wasn't very strong on fighting. In other words, he was a sort of gentleman lumberjack. It is believed he died about eight years ago [1915]. Thousands of people hereabouts knew and sang the song, and many knew the heroine."

The manuscript sent me by Mr. Clark (Version A), which was not in his own handwriting, closes with this legend: "As written and sung by Jack Haggerty." The version, though close to Jack's day, is plainly not the original. I include three versions of this ballad because of its popularity and of the interesting variations of phrase which occur. Other strange variations, in versions not recorded here, are as follows: "the strong darts of Cupid" becomes "a dartsman of cubic"; "my heart it's asunder" becomes "my heart's a broken cinder"; "Flat River" becomes "Platt River"; "to her mother, Jane Tucker," becomes "her mother, Jane, took her."

A

From Mr. C. L CLARK, Greenville, Michigan

1 I'm a heart-broken raftsman, from Greenville I came.
My virtues departed, alas! I declaim.
The strong darts of Cupid have caused me much grief.
Till my heart bursts asunder I will ne'er find relief.

2 I am by occupation a raftsman where the Flat River rolls.
My name is engraved on its rocks, sands, and shoals.
In shops, bars, and households I'm very well known.
They call me Jack Haggerty, the pride of the town.

3 I'll tell you my trouble without much delay,
How a sweet little lassie my heart stole away.
She was a blacksmith's daughter from the Flat River side,
And I always intended to make her my bride.

4 Her face was as fair as the rose on the lea.
Her eyes they resembled the calm smiling sea.
Her skin was as white as the lilies of Spain,
Or the wing of the sea-gull as he skims o'er the main.

5 Her form like the dove was so slender and neat.
Her hair hung in ringlets to her tiny white feet.
Her voice was like music or the sigh of the breeze,
As she whispered she loved me as we strolled through the trees.
I thought her my darling—what a gem for a wife.
When I think of her treachery it near takes my life.

6 I worked on the river, I earned quite a stake.
I was steadfast and steady and ne'er played the rake;
But buoyant and happy on the boiling white stream,
My thoughts were of Annie, she haunted my dreams.

7 I would have dressed her in jewels and the finest of lace,
In the choicest muslins her form would embrace.
I thought not of sorrow, of trouble or gloom,
My heart light and happy as the rays of the moon.

I gave her my wages, the same to keep safe;
I begrudged her of nothing I had on this earth.

8 One day on the river a letter I received.
She said from her promise herself she'd relieved.
My brain whirled with anguish, it near drove me mad.
My courage all left me, I wished myself dead.

9 "I have no doubt this letter will cause you surprise,
And for disappointment must apologize.
My marriage to another I've a long time delayed,
And the next time you see me I shall ne'er be a maid."

10 To her mother, Jane Tucker, I lay all the blame.
She caused her to leave me and blacken my name.
She cast off the rigging that God would soon tie,
And left me a wanderer until the day that I die.

11 I will bid farewell to virtues divine.
I'll live in debauchery, fast women, and wine.
I'll leave Flat River, there I ne'er can find rest.
I'll shoulder my peavy and start for the West.

12 Now come all you young fellows with hearts brave and true,
Don't believe in a woman: you're beat if you do.
But if ever you see one with a brown chestnut curl,
Just think of Jack Haggerty and his Flat River girl.

13 Now my song it is ended, I hope it's pleased all.
I sail in a packet that sails from White Hall.
The canvas is hoisted, and the wind blowing free,
As over the ocean sails Jack Haggerty.

B

The Flat River Girl

Sung by Mr. ARTHUR MILLOY, Omemee, North Dakota

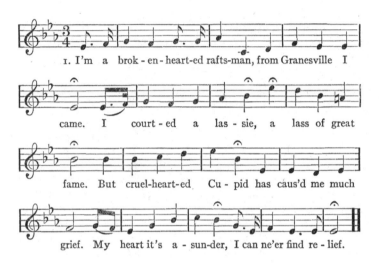

1 I'm a broken-hearted raftsman, from Granesville I came.
  I courted a lassie, a lass of great fame.
  But cruel-hearted Cupid has caused me much grief.
  My heart it's asunder, I can ne'er find relief.

2 My troubles I'll tell you without more delay.
  A comely young lassie my heart stole away.
  She was a blacksmith's only daughter from Flat River side,
  And I always intended for to make her my bride.

3 I bought her rich jewels and the finest of lace,
  And the costliest of muslins it was her I'd embrace.
  I gave her my wages for her to keep safe.
  I begrudged her of nothing that I had myself.

4 My name is Jack Haggerty where the white waters flow.
  My name it's engraved on the rocks on the shore.
  I'm a boy that stands happy on a log in the stream.
  My heart was with Hannah, for she haunted my dreams.

5 I went up the river some money to make.
   I was steadfast and steady, I ne'er played the rake.
   Through _____ and _____ ¹ I am very well known.
   They call me Jack Haggerty and the pride of the town.

6 One day on the river a letter I received,
   That it was from her promises she would be relieved.
   She'd be wed to a young man who a long time delayed,
   And the next time I'd see her she would not be a maid.

7 Then adieu to Flat River. For me there's no rest.
   I'll shoulder my peavy and I'll go out West.
   I will go to Muskegon some pleasures to find,
   And I'll leave my own darling on Flat River behind.

8 So come all ye jolly raftsmen with hearts stout and bold,
   Don't depend to the women; you're left if you do.
   For if you chance to meet one with dark chestnut curls,
   You will think of Jack Haggerty and his Flat River girl.

---

1. Mr. Milloy said these should be names of two small towns near Muskegon.

C

Jack Haggerty

Sung by Mr. W. H. UNDERWOOD, Bayport, Minnesota

2. I will tell you my sto - ry with - out much de -
lay. 'T is of a neat lit - tle las - sie my heart stole a -
way. She was a blacksmith's daughter on the Flat Riv - er
side, And I al - ways in - tend - ed to make her my bride.

1 I'm a heart-broken raftsman, from Greensville I came.
. . . .
The strong darts of Cubit have caused me much grief.
My heart's broke within me. I can ne'er get relief.

2 I will tell you my story without much delay.
'Tis of a neat little lassie my heart stole away.
She was a blacksmith's daughter on the Flat River side,
And I always intended to make her my bride.

3 My occupation is raftsman when the white waters roll.
My name is engraved on the rocks and sand shores.
Through shabbers and housetops I'm known of renown,
And they call me Jack Haggerty, the pride of the town.

4 I dressed her in jewels and the finest of lace,
The costliest muslins herself to embrace.
I gave her my wages for to keep safe.
I begrudged her of nothing I had on this earth.

5 To her mother, Jane Tucker, I owe all the blame.
She has caused her to leave me and go back on my name.
She has cast off the riggin' that God would soon tie,
And has left me to wander till the day that I die.

6 I'll bid adieu to Flat River. For me there's no rest.
I will shoulder my peavy and I will go West.
I will go to Muskegon some comfort to find,
And I'll leave my own sweetheart on Flat River behind.

7 So come all you bold raftsmen with hearts stout and true,
Don't depend on the women, you're beat if you do.
For when you meet one with a dark chestnut curl,
Oh, just remember Jack Haggerty and his Flat River girl.

D

Jack Haggerty

As sung by Mr. ED SPRINGSTAD, Bemidji, Minnesota

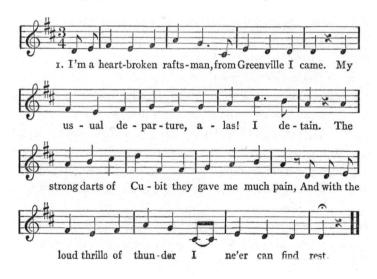

1. I'm a heart-broken rafts-man, from Greenville I came. My us - ual de - par - ture, a - las! I de - tain. The strong darts of Cu - bit they gave me much pain, And with the loud thrills of thun - der I ne'er can find rest.

2

Gerry's Rocks

This ballad, one of several celebrating death by that most spectacular of all hazards in lumbering, the log jam, was easily the most widely current of all lumber woods songs. Some of the old fellows have told me that anyone starting "Gerry's Rocks" in the shanties was summarily shut off because the song was sung to death; others vow that of all songs it was ever and always the most welcome.

The nativity of the ballad, like that of many another, is variously assigned. All the singers I have met have ascribed the song either to Canada or to Michigan, usually the latter. Professor Gray, in his recently published *Songs and Ballads of the Maine Lumberjacks*, xv–xvi, 3–9, wherein he records several versions of the ballad (cf. Cox, *Folk-Songs of the South*, 236–38), calls it a native of Maine, the accident having taken place on the West Branch of the Penobscot River. His evidence is not quite conclusive. The line that refers to Monroe's sweetheart as "a girl from Saginaw town," which occurs in every version I have seen, at least accords with the Middle West assumption that the song was composed in Michigan. The discovery of a place known as Gerry's Rocks in Michigan, or of a Saginaw town in Maine, would help considerably!

In Dean's text (25), we have "Garry's Rocks"; in a version which I have from Mr. C. M. Forbes, of Perth, Ontario, the name appears as "Garie's Rocks." A much wider variation appears in the spelling of the name of the town for which the boys are to steer after the jam is broken (stanza 2, line 4). Besides "Agonstown" and "Eagleton," we have "Egantown," "Hagenstown," "Eagontown," "Eganstown"; two versions disown the place entirely, one steering for "Saginaw town," and the other for "freedom's land." The date of the hero's burial appears as the first, fourth, fifth, sixth, seventh, tenth, or twelfth of May.

The popularity of the ballad is further attested by the fact that it was parodied. To the best of my knowledge these parodies were far from quotable. The following line was given me as coming originally from one of these, apparently an American-made satire: "The Canadians were drownded, but the oxen swum ashore."

One of the most interesting elements in the story, one which appears in all versions, and happily one reflecting a well-authenticated shanty-boy habit, is the subscription presented to the bereaved sweetheart. In actual life this contribution was sent the wife or other dependent; but the practice was common. In *The Blazed Trail* Mr. White, showing in the course of his story this practice in operation, gives the following glint from this facet of shanty-boy character: "The men were earning from twenty to thirty dollars a month. They had, most of them, never seen Hank Paul before this autumn. He had not, mainly because of his modest disposition, enjoyed any extraordinary degree of popularity. Yet these strangers, as a matter of course, gave up the proceeds of a week's hard work, and that without expecting the slightest personal credit. The money was sent 'from the boys.'"

Sung by Mr. A. C. HANNAH, Bemidji, Minnesota

1 Come all ye true born shanty-boys, whoever that ye be,
I would have you pay attention and listen unto me,
Concerning a young shanty-boy so tall, genteel, and brave.
'Twas on a jam on Gerry's Rocks he met a wat'ry grave.

2 It happened on a Sunday morn as you shall quickly hear.
Our logs were piled up mountain high, there being no one to
keep them clear.
Our boss he cried, "Turn out, brave boys. Your hearts are void
of fear.
We'll break that jam on Gerry's Rocks, and for Agonstown we'll
steer."

3 Some of them were willing enough, but others they hung back.
'Twas for to work on Sabbath they did not think 'twas right.
But six of our brave Canadian boys did volunteer to go
And break the jam on Gerry's Rocks with their foreman, young
Monroe.

4 They had not rolled off many logs when the boss to them did
say,
"I'd have you be on your guard, brave boys. That jam will soon
give way."
But scarce the warning had he spoke when the jam did break
and go,
And it carried away these six brave youths and their foreman,
young Monroe.

5 When the rest of the shanty-boys these sad tidings came to
hear,
To search for their dead comrades to the river they did steer.
One of these a headless body found, to their sad grief and woe,
Lay cut and mangled on the beach the head of young Monroe.

6 They took him from the water and smoothed down his raven
hair.
There was one fair form amongst them, her cries would rend
the air.

There was one fair form amongst them, a maid from Saginaw
town.
Her sighs and cries would rend the skies for her lover that was
drowned.

7 They buried him quite decently, being on the seventh of May.
Come all the rest of you shanty-boys, for your dead comrade
pray.
'Tis engraved on a little hemlock tree that at his head doth
grow,
The name, the date, and the drowning of this hero, young
Monroe.

8 Miss Clara was a noble girl, likewise the raftsman's friend.
Her mother was a widow woman lived at the river's bend.
The wages of her own true love the boss to her did pay,
And a liberal subscription she received from the shanty-boys
next day.

9 Miss Clara did not long survive her great misery and grief.
In less than three months afterwards death came to her relief.
In less than three months afterwards she was called to go,
And her last request was granted—to be laid by young Monroe.

10 Come all the rest of ye shanty-men who would like to go and
see,
On a little mound by the river's bank there stands a hemlock
tree.
The shanty-boys cut the woods all round. These lovers they lie
low.
Here lies Miss Clara Dennison and her shanty-boy, Monroe.

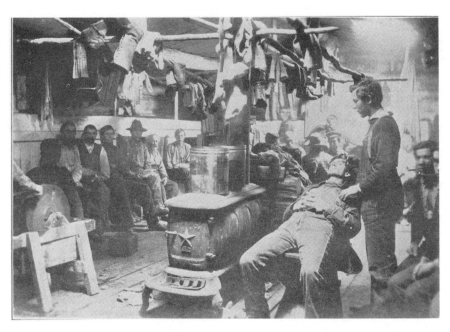

"'Twas on one Sunday morning, as you shall quickly hear." A comparatively recent picture (perhaps 1905), but as good as any that ever could have been taken for showing the interior arrangement of the bunkhouse. The location and relationship of bunks, stove, drying rack, etc., are traditional.

B
Geary's Rock

Sung by Mr. C. D. DONALDSON, Eau Claire, Wisconsin

1. Come all you jol-ly fel-lows where-ev-er you may be, I hope you'll pay at-ten-tion and list-en un-to me. It's all a-bout some shan-ty-boys, so

man - ly and so brave. 'Twas on the jam on

Gear - y's Rock where they met their wa - ter - y grave.

1 Come all you jolly fellows, wherever you may be,
I hope you'll pay attention and listen unto me.
It's all about some shanty-boys, so manly and so brave.
'Twas on the jam on Geary's Rock where they met their watery
grave.

2 'Twas on one Sunday morning as you shall quickly hear,
Our logs were piled up mountain high; we could not keep them
clear.
"Turn out, brave boys," the foreman cried, with a voice devoid
of fear,
"And we'll break the jam on Geary's Rock and for Eagletown
we'll steer."

3 Some of the boys were willing, while the others they hung
back,
For to work on Sunday morning, they thought it was not right.
But six American shanty-boys did volunteer to go
To break the jam on Geary's Rock with their foreman, young
Monroe.

4 They had not rolled off many logs before the boss to them did
say,
"I would you all to be on your guard, for the jam will soon give
way."
He had no more than spoke those words before the jam did
break and go,
And carried away those six brave youths with their foreman,
young Monroe.

5 As soon as the news got into camp and attorneys came to hear,
In search of their dead bodies down the river we did steer,
And one of their dead bodies found, to our great grief and woe,
All bruised and mangled on the beach lay the corpse of young
    Monroe.

6 We took him from the water, smoothed back his raven black
    hair.
There was one fair form amongst them whose cries did rend
    the air.
There was one fair form amongst them, a girl from Saginaw
    town,
Whose mournful cries did rend the skies for her lover that was
    drowned.

7 We buried him quite decently. 'Twas on the twelfth of May.
Come all you jolly shanty-boys and for your comrade pray.
We engraved upon a hemlock tree that near his grave did grow
The name, the age, and the drownding date of the foreman,
    young Monroe.

8 His mother was a widow living down by the river side.
Miss Clark she was a noble girl, this young man's promised
    bride.
The wages of her own true love the firm to her did pay,
And a liberal subscription she received from the shanty-boys
    that day.

9 She received their presents kindly and thanked them every one,
Though she did not survive him long, as you shall understand.
Scarcely three weeks after, and she was called to go,
And her last request was to be laid by her lover, young Monroe.

C
Shanty-boys

As sung by Miss GLENNIE TODD, Eau Claire, Wisconsin

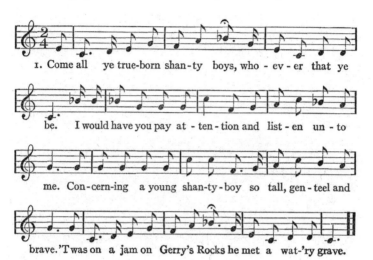

1. Come all ye true-born shan-ty boys, who-ev-er that ye be. I would have you pay at-ten-tion and list-en un-to me. Con-cern-ing a young shan-ty-boy so tall, gen-teel and brave. 'Twas on a jam on Gerry's Rocks he met a wat-'ry grave.

D

The Foreman Monroe

As sung by Mr. ART MILLOY, Omemee, North Dakota

1. Oh, come all you true-born shan-ty boys where-ev - er that you
be. I would have you pay at - ten - tion and
list - en un - to me, Con - cern - ing those bold
shan - ty - boys who did a - gree to go And to
break the jam on Garry's rocks with their foreman young Monroe.

3

Jim Whalen

The ballad of Jim Whalen, the stirring Canadian counterpart of "Gerry's Rocks," was composed in Ontario but enjoyed a wide popularity in our pine woods. The following letter from Mr. Christopher Forbes, of Perth, Ontario, gives the facts:

The Phalen family live in this district. The name is pronounced Whalen locally. James's brother, Thomas, whom I knew intimately, died a few years ago. [The letter was written in 1923.]

Regarding the James Phalen tragedy, John Smith, of Lanark Village, an old-timer and singer of the 'come all ye' type, wrote the words which I now enclose [Version B]. He sings the Jim Whalen song with much pathos, and with that peculiar dropping off of the last word from a singing tone to a speaking voice. This style of finishing a song is used by sailors and shanty-men.

I was fortunate in meeting an old shanty foreman, Peter McIlquham, well known on the Mississippi River for over half a century, who told me he was present at Jim Whalen's death.

It happened 45 years ago [1878] at King's Chute on the Mississippi River. Whalen was a riverman under 'Old Quebec,' a French-Canadian whose real name was Edward Leblanc. McIlquham was also a foreman on the River at this time. Both rafts of logs had come out of Cross Lake, known as Crotch Lake by the rivermen. McIlquham came to assist 'Old Quebec' putting over King's Chute. A dangerous and difficult jam formed in the Chute. 'Quebec,' McIlquham, and Phalen were close together when the jam shifted and precipitated Phalen into the water.

Immediately he was swept under the logs, but as the jam was close and tight he went only a short distance. Foreman 'Quebec' called for a pike-pole in an attempt to release Phalen. He, however, gave such a mighty pull that the pike-pole broke and he himself overbalanced into the water and was hurled and tossed all the way through the Chute. Others tried to get

Phalen, and in about an hour's time were successful by forming a bight on the end of a small sweeping-line and getting it over one of Phalen's boots, by which means he was recovered from the jam, McIlquham assisting in pulling him out . . .

The Peter McLaren referred to is the lumberman who operated on the Mississippi for many years. He accumulated a large fortune and became a Canadian Senator. Died a few years ago.

In response to further inquiries Mr. Forbes described King's Chute thus: "King's Chute is in the township of Palmerston, county of Frontenac. It is a small white water section of the Mississippi River, difficult and dangerous for the driving of logs. It is caused by the contraction of the stream flowing over a pegmatite dyke at this point."

According to Mr. Hannah, the singer of Version A, there were in the course of King's Chute two particularly precipitous passages known as the Falls, Upper and Lower. Mr. Hannah was born and raised in Canada, not ten miles from the scene of the Phalen tragedy. He remembered Phalen's death very well, being sixteen years old at the time. His account of the affair accords with that of Mr. Forbes, even to the names of the two men referred to in the first line of stanza 4.—A version from Michigan ("James Whalen") is published by Tolman and Eddy, *Journal of American Folklore*, xxxv, 383–84.

A

Sung by Mr. A. C. Hannah, Bemidji, Minnesota

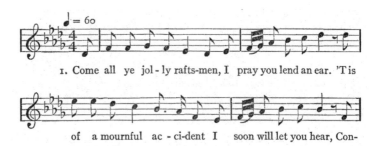

1. Come all ye jol-ly rafts-men, I pray you lend an ear. 'T is

of a mournful ac-ci-dent I soon will let you hear, Con-

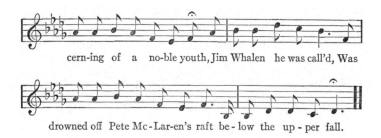

cern-ing of a no-ble youth, Jim Whalen he was call'd, Was

drowned off Pete Mc-Lar-en's raft be-low the up-per fall.

1 Come all ye jolly raftsmen, I pray you lend an ear.
'Tis of a mournful accident I soon will let you hear,
Concerning of a noble youth, Jim Whalen he was called,
Was drowned off Pete McLaren's raft below the upper fall.

2 The rapids they were raging, the waters were so high.
Says the foreman unto Whalen, "This jam we'll have to try.
You're young, you're brave and active when danger's lurking near.
You're just the man to help me now these waters to get clear."

3 Young Whalen then made answer unto his comrades bold,
Saying, "Come on, boys, though it's dangerous, we'll do as we
are told.
We'll obey our orders manfully, as young men they should
do"—
But while he spoke the jam it broke, and Whalen he went
through.

4 Three of them were in danger, but two of them were saved,
But noble-hearted Whalen met with a watery grave.
No mortal man could live in such a raging watery main,
And although he struggled hard for life, his struggles were in
vain.

5 The foaming waters roared and tossed the logs from shore to
shore.
Now here, now there his body seen tumbling o'er and o'er.
One awful cry for mercy—"O God, look down on me!"
And his soul was freed from earthly cares, gone to eternity.

6 Come all ye jolly raftsmen, think on poor Jimmy's fate.
  Be careful and take warning before it is too late,
  For death is lurking near you ever eager to destroy
  The pride of a fond father's heart, likewise a mother's joy.

B

James Phalen

From Mr. CHRIS M. FORBES, Perth, Ontario

1 Gentlemen and maidens, I pray you to draw near.
  An accident most terrible I mean to let you hear,
  All of a young and comely youth, James Phalen he was called.
  He was drowned off McLaren's raft upon the upper falls.

"That jam we'll have to try." Probably no really satisfactory picture of a log jam
has ever been secured. This one, of the famous jam at Big Eddy, above
Chippewa Falls, Wisconsin, in 1903, will give some idea of the nature and
extent of this classic spectacle of the drive.

2 The waters they were raging fierce, the rivers they ran high.
The foreman says to Phalen, "That jam we'll have to try.
You're bold, brave, and active when danger's lurking near.
You are the man to help me now those waters to get clear."

3 Young Phalen he made answer unto his comrades bold,
"Come ye all. Though it's dangerous, we'll do as we are told.
We'll obey our orders bravely, as noble men should do—"
And as he spoke, the jam it broke and let poor Jimmie through.

4 There were three of them in danger, while two of them were
saved,
While noble-hearted Jimmie he received a watery grave,
Which no mortal man could live upon that foaming watery
main.
Although he struggled hard for life, his struggles were in vain.

5 The foaming waters tossed and tore the logs from shore to
shore.
Now here, now there his body went, now tumbling o'er and
o'er.
One fearful cry for mercy, "O God, look down on me!"
And his soul was freed from earthly bonds, gone to eternity.

6 Come all you jolly raftsmen, look on poor Jimmie's fate.
Take warning and be cautious before it is too late,
For death's still lurking round you, still seeking to destroy
The pride of many a father's heart, likewise a mother's joy.

4

The Lost Jimmie Whalen

The ballad of which these stanzas are a part plainly has no relationship to the ballad just preceding, although it may have arisen from the same tragedy. The melody is similar to the first part of that given for "The Cumberland's Crew" (No. 39), which was a great favorite in the woods.

Sung by Mr. WILL DAUGHERTY, Charlevoix, Michigan

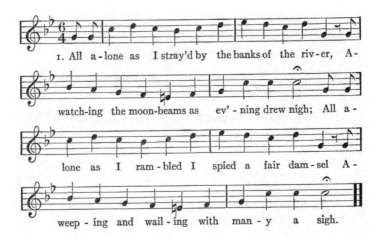

1 All alone as I stray'd by the banks of the river,
  A-watching the moon-beams as evening drew nigh;
  All alone as I rambled I spied a fair damsel,
  A-weeping and wailing with many a sigh.

2 A-weeping for one who is now lying lowly,
  A-mourning for one who no mortal can save,
  As the dark foaming waters flow sadly about him,
  As onward they speed over young Jimmie's grave.

3 "O Jimmie, can't you tarry here with me,
   Not leave me alone, distracted in pain?
   But since death is the dagger that has cut us asunder,
   And wide is the gulf, love, between you and I . . ."

5

The Banks of the Little Eau Pleine

By Shan T. Boy

This ballad, widely current in Wisconsin, Michigan, and Minnesota, is interesting as being one of those whose origin and authorship are definitely known. The author, Mr. W. N. ("Billy") Allen, having received considerable attention in the General Introduction, needs no comment here. The song is compounded wholly of imagination except for the character of Ross Gamble, who was a well-known pilot on the Wisconsin River at the time the verses were composed. Mr. Allen placed the time of composition "somewhere in the 70s." He was living at Wausau, Wisconsin, at that time.

The following old-world song, some lines of which are reprinted from Mr. Dean's *Flying Cloud* collection, 47–48, seems to have been Mr. Allen's pattern.

The Lass of Dunmore

As I went a-walking one morning,
    Bright Phœbus so early did shine,
And the meadow larks warbled melodious,
    While the roses in the valley did twine;
It was down by a grove where I wandered
    Awhile to repose in the shade,
On my destiny for to ponder,
    It was there I beheld a fair maid.

I raised up on my feet for to view her,
    And those tender words I did say,
"Who are you, my fairest of creatures?
    How far through this grove do you stray?"
. . . .

128

"Oh, once I did love a bold seaman,
  And he too my fond heart had gained;
No mortal on earth could love dearer,
  But now he is crossing the main
With Nelson, that hero of battle,
  In the English navy so brave,
Where cannons and guns loud do rattle,
  For to fight the proud French on the wave."

Version A is the original. The words are from a manuscript in Mr. Allen's handwriting sent me by Mr. William W. Bartlett, of Eau Claire, Wisconsin. The melody I secured from Mr. Allen himself upon visiting him later at his home in Wausau. The manuscript of the stanzas was headed thus:

The Banks of the Little Eau Pleine
By Shan T. Boy
Tune, "Erin's Green Shore"

For "Erin's Green Shore," see Cox, *Folk-Songs of the South*, No. 181.

The ballad is a peculiar composite of humor and pathos, a combination characteristic of Mr. Allen's work. In singing it in public, I have noted the varying reaction, a sort of ebb and flow of emotions, in the audience. Through the first five stanzas the story builds well, its genre in no wise indicated. The description in the following three stanzas seems to be a bid for smiles, if not for outright laughter. But the initial lines of stanza 9 prepare the hearers for the answer, which falls with brutal realism and invariably precipitates a tense and sympathetic hush. The episode of the hatful of water again is rather more humorous than not. The protracted curse in stanzas 11 and 12 is remarkable for its completeness and its extremity, and is in no way comical for those audiences familiar with the lumbering industry. The final stanza is saved by its last two lines.

The Little Eau Pleine is a small tributary of the Wisconsin River, lying entirely within Marathon County, Wisconsin.

"Fifty-foot oar": a reference to the long oars or sweeps, operated by several men, used in propelling, or more especially for guiding, rafts of logs or lumber on the large rivers. Note how, in Folk-Version B, the dimension shrinks. I have never found it "fifty" in any variant.

The ballad is often known as "Johnny Murphy." An interesting variant of "a field of ripe grain" (stanza 11), a remarkably effective simile, is "a fever-wracked brain," which sounds terrible, but in this connection means nothing. "Ross Gamble" appears usually as "Ross Campbell."

A

Sung by Mr. WM. N. ALLEN ("Shan T. Boy"), Wausau, Wisconsin

1. One eve-ning last June as I ram-bled .. The green woods and val-leys a - mong. The mos-qui-to's notes were me-lod-ious, .. And so was the whip-poor-will's song. .. The frogs in the marsh-es were croak-ing, . . . The tree-toads were whist-ling for rain, . . . The par-tridg-es round me were drum-ming . . . On the banks of the Lit-tle Eau Pleine.

1 One evening last June as I rambled,
    The green woods and valleys among,
The mosquito's notes were melodious,
    And so was the whip-poor-will's song.
The frogs in the marshes were croaking,
    The tree-toads were whistling for rain,
And partridges round me were drumming,
    On the banks of the Little Eau Pleine.

2 The sun in the west was declining
    And tinging the tree-tops with red.
My wandering feet bore me onward,
    Not caring whither they led.
I happened to see a young school-ma'am.
    She mourned in a sorrowful strain,
She mourned for a jolly young raftsman
    On the banks of the Little Eau Pleine.

3 Saying, "Alas, my dear Johnny has left me.
    I'm afraid I shall see him no more.
He's down on the lower Wisconsin,
    He's pulling a fifty-foot oar.
He went off on a fleet with Ross Gamble
    And has left me in sorrow and pain;
And 'tis over two months since he started
    From the banks of the Little Eau Pleine."

4 I stepped up beside this young school-ma'am,
    And thus unto her I did say,
"Why is it you're mourning so sadly
    While all nature is smiling and gay?"
She said, "It is for a young raftsman
    For whom I so sadly complain.
He has left me alone here to wander
    On the banks of the Little Eau Pleine."

5 "Will you please tell me what kind of clothing
    Your jolly young raftsman did wear?

For I also belong to the river,
    And perhaps I have seen him somewhere.
If to me you will plainly describe him,
    And tell me your young raftsman's name,
Perhaps I can tell you the reason
    He's not back to the Little Eau Pleine."

6 "His pants were made out of two meal-sacks,
        With a patch a foot square on each knee.
    His shirt and his jacket were dyed with
        The bark of a butternut tree.
    He wore a large open-faced ticker
        With almost a yard of steel chain,
    When he went away with Ross Gamble
        From the banks of the Little Eau Pleine.

7 "He wore a red sash round his middle,
        With an end hanging down at each side.
    His shoes number ten were, of cowhide,
        With heels about four inches wide.
    His name it was Honest John Murphy,
        And on it there ne'er was a stain,
    And he was as jolly a raftsman
        As was e'er on the Little Eau Pleine.

8 "He was stout and broad-shouldered and manly.
        His height was about six feet one.
    His hair was inclined to be sandy,
        And his whiskers as red as the sun.
    His age was somewhere about thirty,
        He neither was foolish nor vain.
    He loved the bold Wisconsin River
        Was the reason he left the Eau Pleine."

9 "If John Murphy's the name of your raftsman,
        I used to know him very well.
    But sad is the tale I must tell you:
        Your Johnny was drowned in the Dells.

They buried him 'neath a scrub Norway,
　　You will never behold him again.
No stone marks the spot where your raftsman
　　Sleeps far from the Little Eau Pleine."

10　When the school-ma'am heard this information,
　　　She fainted and fell as if dead.
　　I scooped up a hat full of water
　　　And poured it on top of her head.
　　She opened her eyes and looked wildly,
　　　As if she was nearly insane,
　　And I was afraid she would perish
　　　On the banks of the Little Eau Pleine.

11　"My curses attend you, Wisconsin!
　　　May your rapids and falls cease to roar.
　　May every tow-head and sand-bar
　　　Be as dry as a log schoolhouse floor.
　　May the willows upon all your islands
　　　Lie down like a field of ripe grain,
　　For taking my jolly young raftsman
　　　Away from the Little Eau Pleine.

12　"My curses light on you, Ross Gamble,
　　　For taking my Johnny away.
　　I hope that the ague will seize you,
　　　And shake you down into the clay.
　　May your lumber go down to the bottom,
　　　And never rise to the surface again.
　　You had no business taking John Murphy
　　　Away from the Little Eau Pleine.

13　"Now I will desert my vocation,
　　　I won't teach district school any more.
　　I will go to some place where I'll never
　　　Hear the squeak of a fifty-foot oar.
　　I will go to some far foreign country,
　　　To England, to France, or to Spain;

But I'll never forget Johnny Murphy
Nor the banks of the Little Eau Pleine."

B

The Little Auplaine

Sung by Mr. M. C. DEAN, Virginia, Minnesota (Text from Dean, 11–12)

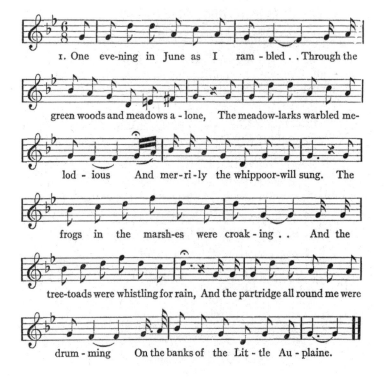

1 One evening in June as I rambled
    Through the green woods and meadows alone,
The meadow larks warbled melodious,
    And merrily the whip-poor-will sung;
The frogs in the marshes were croaking,
    And the tree-toads were whistling for rain,
And the partridge all round me were drumming
    On the banks of the Little Auplaine.

2 The sun to the west a-declining
    Had shaded the tree-tops with red,
My wandering feet led me onward,
    Not caring wherever I strayed.
Till by chance I beheld a fair school-ma'am
    Who most bitterly did complain.
It was all for the loss of her lover
    From the banks of the Little Auplaine.

3 I boldly stepped up to this fair one,
    And this unto her I did say,
"Why are you so sad and so mournful
    When all nature is smiling and gay?"
"It's all for a jolly young raftsman,
    But I fear I will see him no more,
For he is down on the Wisconsin River
    A-pulling a fifteen-foot oar."

4 "If it's all for a jolly young raftsman
    You are here in such awful despair,
Pray tell me the name of your true love,
    And what kind of clothes did he wear?"
"His pants were made of two meal-sacks,
    With a patch a foot wide on each knee,
And his jacket and shirt they were dyed
    With the bark of the butternut tree.

5 "His hair was inclined to be curly,
    His whiskers as red as the sun;
He was tall, square-shouldered, and handsome,
    His height was six feet and one.
His name was young Johnnie Murphy,
    And his equal I ne'er saw before;
But he is down on the Wisconsin River
    A-pulling a fifteen-foot oar."

6 "If Johnnie Murphy was the name of your true love,
    He was a man I knew very well.

But sad is the tale I must tell you:
    Your Johnnie was drowned in the Dalles.
We buried him 'neath a scrub Norway,
    And his face you will ne'er see again;
No stone marks the grave of your lover,
    And he is far from the Little Auplaine."

7 When she heard me say this she fainted,
    And fell at my feet like one dead;
I scooped up a hat full of water
    And threw it all over her head.
She opened her eyes and looked wildly;
    She acted like one that's insane.
I thought to myself she had gone crazy
    On the banks of the Little Auplaine.

8 "My curse be upon you, Ross Campbell,
    For taking my Johnnie away;
May the eagles take hold of your body
    And sink it way down in the clay.
May your lumber all go to the bottom,
    Never rise to the surface no more;
May all of your creeks and your sandbars
    Go as dry as the log schoolhouse floor.

9 "And now I will leave this location,
    I'll teach district school no more;
I will go where never, no never,
    I will hear the screech of a fifteen-foot oar.
I will go to some far distant country,
    To England, to France, or to Spain,
But I will never forget Johnnie Murphy
    Or the banks of the Little Auplaine."

C

Johnny Murphy

As sung by Mr. Ed Springstad, Bemidji, Minnesota

1. One eve-ning last June as   I   rambled The green woods and

val - leys   a - mong.   The mo-squi - to's notes were mel-

o - di-ous, And   so   was   the whippoorwill's song. . .   The

frogs in   the marsh-es were croak-ing, The tree-toads were

whist-ling for   rain,   And par-tridg - es round me were

drum-ming On the banks of   the   Lit - tle Eau Pleine.

6

The Shanty-man's Alphabet

A far cry from true balladry, but a genuinely interesting bit of shanty-boy composition for the light it throws, not only on certain phases and facts of camp life and atmosphere, but also on the character of the group which found entertainment in such song. It is an example of that singing of self which so characterized the old-time shanty-boy.

For Maine and Michigan versions of this song see Gray's *Songs and Ballads of the Maine Lumberjacks*, 10–14.

The "iron" mentioned in stanza 3 is the tool with which logs were marked to denote ownership. The mark usually consisted of a letter, a figure, or some specific design. It was put in the end of the log and called the "end mark." The "bark mark," which was also used, was notched in the side of the log with an axe. Paul Bunyan, the greatest logger who ever lived (ask any shanty-boy if he wasn't!) never troubled himself to use an axe for this, but simply pinched a piece out of the log with his thumb and forefinger.

To "stag" a camp with moss (stanza 4) was to stuff the cracks of the log shanties with it. It made a very warm camp.

The varying injunction in the refrain is noteworthy. Some of the old-timers have explained to me that the appeal for liquor must have been an addition of later years; that, although the shanty-boy off duty was and had always been devoted to whiskey, the early camps had no whiskey in them, and no shanty-boy of that day expected to have it there. On the other hand, the men did like to have reasonably comfortable quarters and good food, especially plenty of the latter.

A

Sung by Mr. JOE BAINTER, Gordon, Wisconsin

1. A is for axe as you all ve - ry well know, And
B is for boys that can use them just so.
C is for chop - ping, and now I'll be - gin; And
D is for dan - ger we oft - times run in. And so

CHORUS

mer - ry and so mer - ry are we. No
mor - tals on earth are so hap - py as we.
Hi der - ry hi, and a hi der - ry down. Give the
shan - ty - boys grub and there's noth - ing goes wrong.

1 *A* is for axe as you all very well know,
   And *B* is for boys that can use them just so.
   C is for chopping, and now I'll begin;
   And *D* is for danger we ofttimes run in.

   Chorus
   And so merry and so merry are we.
   No mortals on earth are so happy as we.
   Hi derry hi, and a hi derry down.
   Give the shanty-boys grub and there's nothing goes wrong.

2 *E* is for echo that through the woods ring,
   And *F* is for foreman, the head of our gang.
   G is for grindstone, so swift it doth move,
   And *H* is for handle so slick and so smooth.

3 *I* is for iron we mark our pine with,
   And *J* is for jobber that's always behind.
   K is for keen edge our axes do keep,
   And *L* is for lice that around us do creep.

4 *M* is for moss we stag our camp with,
   And *N* is for needle we patch our pants with.
   O is for owl that hoots in the night,
   And *P* is for pine that always falls right.

5 *Q* is for quarrels we never allow,
   And *R* is for river our logs they do plow.
   S is for sleigh, so stout and so strong,
   And *T* is for teams that will haul them along.

6 *U* is for use we put our teams to,
   And *V* is for valley we haul our logs through.
   W's for woods we leave in the spring . . .

7 There's three more letters I ain't put in rhyme,
   And if any of you know them, please tell me in time.
   The train has arrived at the station below,
   So fare you well, true love, it's I must be gone.

"*T* is for teams that will haul them along." A load of white pine logs. This was the method of hauling from the skidway to the landing. The load pictured here, though a good one, is not extraordinary.

B

Shanty-man's Alphabet

Sung by Mr. ARTHUR MILLOY, Omemee, North Dakota

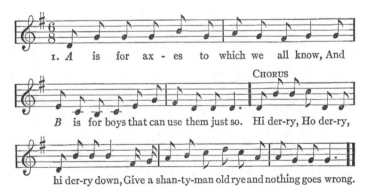

1. *A* is for ax-es to which we all know, And
B is for boys that can use them just so. Hi der-ry, Ho der-ry, hi der-ry down, Give a shan-ty-man old rye and nothing goes wrong.

1 *A* is for axes to which we all know,
And *B* is for boys that can use them just so.

 Chorus
Hi derry, ho derry, hi derry down,
Give a shanty-man old rye and nothing goes wrong.
C is for choppers . . .
L is for loaders that roll the logs on . . .
T is for teamsters that pull them along . . .

7

Save Your Money When You're Young

Through the words and notes of this song move the dim spirit-beings of thousands of shanty-boys, the story of whose improvident lives is dramatically implied in the reiterated admonition born of sad experience, one which needs no glossing, either in our generation or in any to come. As many an old fellow sang this, or heard it sung, there must have welled up and overflowed within him a poignant but unavailing regret that life for him should have come to this: all the glory and strength of his young manhood gone, his thousands of hard-earned dollars poured periodically into the fathomless tides of dissolute hours; his earning capacity far waned and more swiftly waning, but life lingering on, demanding support; all his magnificent heritage of warmth and recuperative power and the length of days miserably bartered for a mess of pottage.

If a ballad can be defined as "a song which tells a story," then I might still feel prompted to call this song a ballad!

Sung by Mr. ARTHUR MILLOY, Omemee, North Dakota

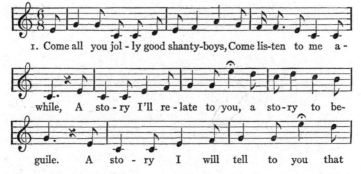

1. Come all you jol - ly good shanty-boys, Come lis-ten to me a -
while, A sto - ry I'll re - late to you, a sto - ry to beguile. A sto - ry I will tell to you that

man-y's a man has told. It's save your mon-ey

when you're young, you'll need it when you're old. . . .

1 Come all you jolly good shanty-boys, come listen to me awhile,
   A story I'll relate to you, a story to beguile.
   A story I will tell to you that many's a man has told.
   It's save your money when you're young, you'll need it when
       you're old

2 Oh, if you are a single man, I'll tell you what to do,
   Just court some pretty fair maid that always will prove true.
   Just court some pretty fair maid that is not over-bold,
   That will stick to you when you are young, find comforts when
       you're old.

3 And if you are a married man, I'll tell you what to do,
   Support your wife and family, you're sworn that to do.
   Keep away from all those grog-shops where liquor's kept and sold,
   For all they want is your money, boys. You'll need it when you're
       old.

4 Oh, once I was a shanty-boy, and wasn't I the lad?
   I spent my money foolish, I swear it was too bad.
   And now I'm old and feeble, and wet out in the cold.
   Oh, save your money when you're young, you'll need it when
       you're old.

5 . . . .
   . . . .
   But yet you'll see the day, my boys, when wet out in the cold,
   Oh, save your money when you're young, you'll need it when
       you're old.

8

Michigan-I-O

The general sentiment found in this ballad seems to have developed into quite a "family" of songs commemorating the hardship involved in going to one place or another. It seemed to be applicable to any locality or occupation against which a singer wished to inveigh.

Gray records two adaptations of it, one from Maine (called "Canaday-I-O"), the other from Pennsylvania ("The Jolly Lumbermen"), the latter with the refrain line, "On Colley's Run, i-oh!" He mentions also a railroad adaptation of it, retailing the hardship of a man who agreed to go and work on the Oregon Short Line "way out in Idaho." Lomax, in his *Cowboy Songs*, 158–63, records another adaptation known as "The Buffalo Skinners," or "The Range of the Buffalo." Still another ("Boggus Creek") refers to cowboys and "the hills of Mexico" (Webb, *Publications of the Texas Folk-Lore Society*, No. 2, 45).

The melody recorded here for "Michigan-I-O" is substantially that given by Mr. Lomax for "The Range of the Buffalo" (162–63).

"The preacher of the gospel": according to Mr. Milloy, this was a fancy name for the agent recruiting men to go across into the Michigan woods.

Sung by Mr. ARTHUR MILLOY, Omemee, North Dakota

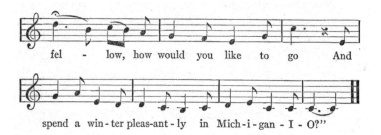

fel - low, how would you like to go And

spend a win-ter pleas-ant-ly in Mich-i-gan - I - O?"

1 It being on Sunday morning, as you shall plainly see,
   The preacher of the gospel at morning came to me.
   He says, "My jolly good fellow, how would you like to go
   And spend a winter pleasantly in Michigan-I-O?

2 "Oh, we will pay good wages; we will pay your passage out,
   Providing you'll sign papers that you will stand the route,
   For fear that you'll get homesick and swear out home you'll go.
   I'll never pay your passage out of Michigan-I-O."

3 He had a kind of flattering. With him we did agree.
   Some thirty-five or forty stout able men were we.
   We had a pleasant journey on the road we had to go.
   We landed safe in Saginaw, called Michigan-I-O.

4 . . . .
   . . . .
   The grub the dogs would laugh at. Our beds were on the snow.
   God send there is no worse than hell or Michigan-I-O.

5 . . . .
   Along yon glissering river no more shall we be found.
   We'll see our wives and sweethearts, and tell them not to go
   To that God-forsaken country called Michigan-I-O.

9

The Shanty-man's Life

The life of the shanty-man was undoubtedly a rigorous one, as all kinds of pioneer life were. And if one judges from the number of songs in which the shanty-man spoke of the fact, he was fond of telling himself and others that it was a rigorous life. But all this was in no spirit of complaint or whining. At the bottom of his heart he was proud of the fact that he was "both stout and hardy and fit to stand the squall." It was part of his intense belief in himself.

Gray includes a New Brunswick version of this song in his *Songs and Ballads*, 53–55. A broadside version (also given by Gray, 55–57), printed by Andrews, New York (List 5, No. 98), purports to have been "composed and written by Geo. W. Stace, La Crosse Valley, Wis." See Dean, 87–88. Cf. "The Cowboy's Life," in Lomax's *Cowboy Songs*, 20–21.

A

Sung by Mr. A. C. HANNAH, Bemidji, Minnesota

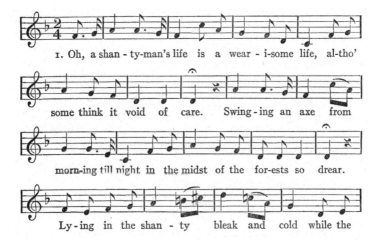

1. Oh, a shan-ty-man's life is a wear-i-some life, al-tho' some think it void of care. Swing-ing an axe from morn-ing till night in the midst of the for-ests so drear. Ly-ing in the shan-ty bleak and cold while the

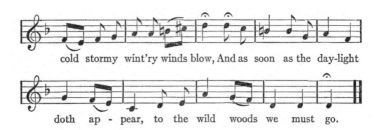

cold stormy wint'ry winds blow, And as soon as the day-light

doth ap - pear, to the wild woods we must go.

1   Oh, a shanty-man's life is a wearisome life, altho' some think it
     void of care,
     Swinging an axe from morning till night in the midst of the
     forests so drear.
     Lying in the shanty bleak and cold while the cold stormy wintry
     winds blow,
     And as soon as the daylight doth appear, to the wild woods we
     must go.

2   Oh, the cook rises up in the middle of the night saying,
     "Hurrah, brave boys, it's day."
     Broken slumbers ofttimes are passed as the cold winter night
     whiles away.
     Had we rum, wine, or beer our spirits for to cheer as the days so
     lonely do dwine,
     Or a glass of any shone while in the woods alone for to cheer up
     our troubled minds.

3   But transported from our lass and our sparkling glass, these
     comforts which we leave behind,
     Not a friend to us so near as to wipe the falling tear when
     sorrow fills our troubled mind.

4   But when spring it does set in, double hardships then begin,
     when the waters are piercing cold,
     And our clothes are dripping wet and fingers benumbed, and
     our pike-poles we scarcely hold.
     Betwixt rocks, shoals, and sands gives employment to all hands
     our well-handed raft for to steer.

And the rapids that we run, oh, they seem to us but fun, for we're void of all slavish fear.

5 Oh, a shanty-lad is the only lad I love, and I never will deny the same.
My heart doth scorn these conceited farmer boys who think it a disgraceful name.
They may boast about their farms, but my shanty-boy has charms so far, far surpassing all.
Until death it doth us part he shall enjoy my heart, let his riches be great or small.

"Oh, the rapids that we run, they seem to us but fun." A striking picture of the wanigan, or wangan, negotiating an interesting piece of white water. The wanigan was the cook's headquarters on the drive.

B

Sung by Mr. M. C. DEAN, Virginia, Minnesota

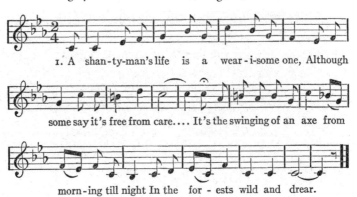

1. A shan-ty-man's life is a wear-i-some one, Although some say it's free from care.... It's the swinging of an axe from morn-ing till night In the for-ests wild and drear.

1 A shanty-man's life is a wearisome one,
     Although some say it's free from care.
   It's the swinging of an axe from morning till night
     In the forests wild and drear.

2 Or sleeping in the shanties dreary
     When the winter winds do blow.
   But as soon as the morning star does appear,
     To the wild woods we must go.

3 At four in the morning our greasy old cook calls out,[1]
     "Hurrah, boys, for it's day."
   And from broken slumber we are aroused
     For to pass away the long winter's day.

4 Transported as we are from the maiden so fair
     To the banks of some lonely stream,
   Where the wolf, bear, and owl with their terrifying howl
     Disturb our nightly dreams.

5 Transported from the glass and the smiling little lass,
     Our life is long and drear;

---

1. This is the line as Mr. Dean sang it. In his *Flying Cloud* collection (87–88) it is given, "At four o'clock in the morning our old greasy cook calls out."

No friend in sorrow nigh for to check the rising sigh
    Or to wipe away the briny tear.

6 Had we ale, wine, or beer our spirits for to cheer
    While we're in those woods so wild,
  Or a glass of whiskey shone while we are in the woods alone,
    For to pass away our long exile.

7 When spring it does come in, double hardship then begins,
    For the water is piercing cold;
  Dripping wet will be our clothes and our limbs they are half froze,
    And our pike-poles we scarce can hold.

8 O'er rocks, shoals, and sands give employment to old hands,
    And our well-bended raft we do steer.
  Oh, the rapids that we run, they seem to us but fun.
    We're the boys of all slavish care.

9 Shantying I'll give o'er when I'm landed safe on shore,
    And I'll lead a different life.
  No longer will I roam, but contented stay at home
    With a pretty little smiling wife.

C

As sung by Mr. I. B. KEELER, Bemidji, Minnesota

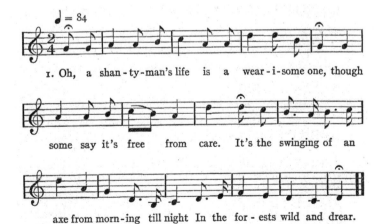

1. Oh, a shan-ty-man's life is a wear-i-some one, though
some say it's free from care. It's the swinging of an
axe from morn-ing till night In the for-ests wild and drear.

10

The Shanty-boy and the Farmer's Son

This song (Dean, 51–52, "Shanty-Boy"), in form reminiscent of the medi-
aeval *debat*, owed its popularity to the fundamental fact of a social distinc-
tion. Although the farms came to furnish the camps with many an efficient
woodsman in the winter seasons, it could hardly be otherwise than that
the dyed-in-the-wool shanty-boy, the courageous, daring, pent-up animal who, after the spring drive, roared into the cities and towns for his
riotous and spendthrift holiday, should hold in some degree of contempt
the quieter, more provident farmer fellow with his less hazardous occupation, who, if he did winter in the camps, pocketed his stake and retired to
his friendly acres, or his father's. But the shanty-boy's contempt, for all his
singing about it, was more apparent than real; for in his innermost being
the shanty-boy, unattached and utterly without home except the camps,
knew that, although his experience was the larger, it was the more costly.
He knew that the "mossback," with all his diffidence and handicapping
greenness, was the better off. There were probably very few shanty-boys
who did not form and nourish annually the intention of acquiring farms
of their own. This hypothesis finds support in the final stanzas of many
shanty songs and ballads. It was thus over a substance of tragedy that the
shanty-boy laid his veneer of fun and had his flings at the "mossback."

The rivalry, barring the action of liquor, was not deep or vital, and did
not reach the fatal intensity of that between the cowboy and the sheepherder, or the ranchman and the fence-farmer, in our western country. For
there the dominant motif was self-preservation—always potentially terrible. There was no such rivalry between shanty-boy and farmer, for where
one plied his trade the other, by the very nature of things, could not.

Over the padded lists of this jousting quite frequently hovered the
spirit of Woman. On the one side it was righteous and lovely.

[Big Junko, one of Thorpe's men, has announced his intention of
securing a wife and a farm with that year's stake.] "Thorpe looked at his
companion fixedly. Somehow the bestial countenance had taken on an
attraction of its own. . . . 'You've changed, Junko,' said he.

"'I know,' said the big man. 'I been a scalawag all right. I quit it. I don't know much, but Carrie she's smart, and I'm goin' to do what she says. When you get stuck on a good woman like Carrie, Mr. Thorpe, you don't give much of a damn for anything else. Sure! That's right. It's the biggest thing top o' earth.'"

But on the other it was destructive and hideous.

"The towns of Bay City and Saginaw alone in 1878 supported over fourteen hundred tough characters. Block after block was devoted entirely to saloons. In a radius of three hundred feet from the famous old Catacombs could be numbered forty saloons where drinks were sold by from three to ten 'pretty waiter girls.' When the boys struck town, the proprietors and waitresses stood in their doorways to welcome them. . . .

"Or if Jack resisted temptation and walked resolutely on, one of the girls would remark audibly to another, 'He ain't no lumber-jack! You can see that easy 'nuff. He's just off the hay-trail.'

"Ten to one that brought him." [Both of these quotations are from Mr. White's *The Blazed Trail*.]

For a version from Michigan (with further references) see *Journal of American Folklore*, xxxv, 399–401. Cf. Shoemaker, 2d ed., 215–17.

There is an old-world song, called "I Love My Sailor Boy," or at least recorded under that name in Mr. Dean's *Flying Cloud* collection, which expresses an earlier and similar comparison between the farmer's son and the sailor. It may have been the pattern for the later song. I reprint the following lines to show points of similarity.

I Love My Sailor Boy

Abroad as I rambled one morning in May,
So carelessly I rambled down Liverpool's streets so gay.
I overheard a fair maid, and this was all her cry,
"And let my friends say what they will, I love my sailor boy.

"For he is constant and true-hearted; he's proper, tall, and trim.
No country clown or squire's son could ever equal him.
He is crossing the wide ocean now where the tempests loud do
    roar,
My blessings do attend him, he's the lad I do adore."

Then up spoke her mother, those words to her did say:
"You are but a young and foolish girl, take counsel now, I pray.
Forsake your tarry sailor; he'll rove from shore to shore,
Leave his sweetheart broken-hearted, have wives on every shore.

"Then wed a steady farmer's son that whistles at the plow,
And then you will have time enough to tend both sheep and
    cows.
But your sailor he'll carouse and drink whenever he comes on
    shore,
And when his money is spent and gone, he'll sail the seas for
    more."

"A fig for all your farmer's sons! Such lovers I disdain.
There is not one among them dare face the raging main.
And when the winds are howling and the billows are white as
    snow,
I'll venture my life with the lad that dare go where stormy winds
    do blow."

A

Sung by Mr. ED D. SPRINGSTAD, Bemidji, Minnesota

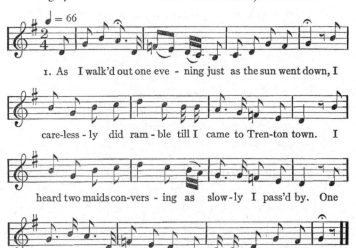

1. As I walk'd out one eve - ning just as the sun went down, I

care-less - ly did ram - ble till I came to Tren-ton town. I

heard two maids con-vers - ing as slow-ly I pass'd by. One

say'd she lov'd a farm-er's son, the oth-er a shan-ty-boy.

1 As I walk'd out one evening just as the sun went down,
I carelessly did ramble till I came to Trenton town.
I heard two maids conversing as slowly I passed by.
One say'd she loved a farmer's son, the other a shanty-boy.

2 The one that loved her farmer's son those words I heard her say:
"The reason that I love him, at home with me he'll stay.
He'll stay at home all winter; to the shanties he will not go,
And when the spring it doth come in, his land he'll plow and
     sow."

3 "All for to plow and sow your land," the other girl did say,
"If crops should prove a failure and the grain market be low,
The sheriff he would sell you out to pay the debts you owe."

4 "All for the sheriff selling us out, it doth not me alarm.
You have no need to be in debt when you're on a good farm.
You raise your bread all on your farm; you don't work through
     storms of rain,
While your shanty-boy he must work each day his family to
     maintain.

5 "Oh, how you praise your shanty-boy, who off to the woods
     must go.
He's ordered out before daylight to work through storms and
     snow,
Whilst happy and contented my farmer's son doth lie,
And he tells to me sweet tales of love until the storm goes by."

6 "That's the reason I praise my shanty-boy. He goes up early in
     the fall.
He is both stout and hearty, and he's fit to stand the squall.
It's with pleasure I'll receive him in the spring when he comes
     down,
And his money quite free he'll share with me when your
     farmer's sons have none.

7 "I could not stand those silly words your farmer's son would say.
They are so green the cows ofttimes have taken them for hay.

How easy it is to know them when they come into town.
Small boys will run up to them sayin', 'Mossback, are ye
  down?'"

8 "What I say'd about your shanty-boy, I hope you'll excuse me,
And of my ignorant farmer's son I hope I do get free.
Then if ever I do get a chance, with a shanty-boy I'll go,
And I'll leave poor mossback stay at home his buckwheat for
  to sow."

B

Sung by Mr. M. C. DEAN, Virginia, Minnesota (Text from Dean, 51–52)

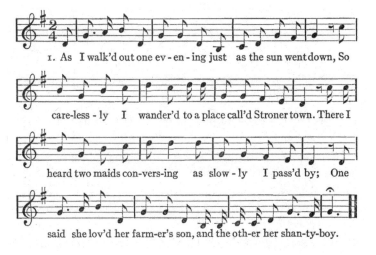

1 As I walk'd out one evening just as the sun went down,
So carelessly I wander'd to a place called Stroner town.
There I heard two maids conversing as slowly I passed by;
One said she loved her farmer's son, and the other her shanty-boy.

2 The one that loved her farmer's son, those words I heard her say,
The reason why she loved him, at home with her he'd stay;
He would stay at home all winter, to the woods he would not go,
And when the spring it did come in, his grounds he'd plow and
  sow.

3 "All for to plow and sow your land," the other girl did say,
   "If the crops should prove a failure, your debts you couldn't pay.
   If the crops should prove a failure, or the grain market be low,
   The sheriff often sells you out to pay the debts you owe."

4 "As for the sheriff selling the lot, it does not me alarm,
   For there's no need of going in debt if you are on a good farm;
   You make your bread from off the land, need not work through
      storms and rain,
   While your shanty-boy works hard each day his family to
      maintain."

5 "I only love my shanty-boy, who goes out in the fall.
   He is both stout and hardy, well fit for every squall.
   With pleasure I'll receive him in the spring when he comes
      home,
   And his money free he will share with me when your farmer's
      son has none."

6 "Oh, why do you love a shanty-boy? To the wild woods he must
      go.
   He is ordered out before daylight to work through rain and
      snow;
   While happy and contented my farmer's son can lie
   And tell to me some tales of love as the cold winds whistle by."

7 "I don't see why you love a farmer," the other girl did say;
   "The most of them they are so green the cows would eat for
      hay.
   It is easy you may know them whenever they're in town,
   The small boys run up to them saying, 'Rube, how are you
      down?'"

8 "For what I have said of your shanty-boy, I hope you will
      pardon me,
   And from that ignorant mossback I hope to soon get free.
   And if ever I get rid of him, for a shanty-boy I will go—
   I will leave him broken-hearted his grounds to plow and sow."

II

The Shanty-boy on the Big Eau Claire

By Shan T. Boy

This is another of old Billy Allen's creations, written, he told me, in 1875 or 1876. It is in his characteristic style, which leaves one wondering a good deal of the time if he was not composing with his tongue in his cheek. This ballad achieved almost as wide a popularity as his "The Banks of the Little Eau Pleine." Versions of it exist among the cowboys and on the home-steads of the Middle West. Mr. George F. Will, of Bismarck, North Dakota, comments on the ballad thus (*Journal of American Folklore*, xxii, 259):

"This song, which has been transplanted from the Wisconsin camps of the seventies, . . . hardly belongs with the cowboy songs, but it seems permissible to insert it as it has become quite widely known in this region [central and western North Dakota]. It came from Wisconsin with some of the first settlers in this region and is more properly a shanty than a cowboy song."

Shoemaker prints a text (2d ed., 178–79) and credits the piece to Charles Evans.

This ballad, like "The Banks of the Little Eau Pleine," is entirely with-out historical basis except that Sailor Jack (Jack O'Brien) was a real char-acter just as Ross Gamble was, and, like him, was a widely known pilot on the Wisconsin River in the later eighteen-seventies. The inclusion of these characters of course gave the songs significance and flavor locally, but variants show in what esteem the folk hold proper names. The "fleet of Sailor Jack's" usually becomes "a fleet of lumberjacks." Similarly, "a suburban pest-house" becomes "Asa Baldwin's pest-house," "a rapids piece" becomes "a precipice," and "grim death" becomes "old Grimdad." The three cities mentioned are all well-known cities in Wisconsin, and the names have remained unaltered in the singing, so far as I have seen. But alterations would have taken place had the ballad lived longer as a folk-possession, and travelled farther afield.

Mr. Allen said that he himself introduced this ballad to the camps a great deal, in his travels from community to community as timber cruiser. But unfortunately he was unable to recall for me the melody he had used for it. The tune, whatever it was, was that of another old song. This was his usual method of obtaining melodies for "new" songs, he explained to me.

A

From the Author (Mr. W. N. ALLEN), Wausau, Wisconsin

1 Every girl she has her troubles; each man likewise has his.
   But few can match the agony of the following story, viz.
   It relates about the affection of a damsel young and fair
   Who dearly loved a shanty-boy up on the Big Eau Claire.

2 This young and artless maiden was of noble pedigree.
   Her mother kept a milliner shop in the town of Mosinee.
   She sold waterfalls and ribbons and bonnets trimmed with lace
   To all the gay young ladies that lived around that place.

3 Her shanty-boy was handsome, a husky lad was he.
   In summer time he tail-sawed in a mill at Mosinee.
   And when the early winter blew its cold and biting breeze,
   He worked upon the Big Eau Claire a-chopping down pine trees.

4 The milliner swore the shanty-boy her daughter ne'er should wed.
   But Sally did not seem to care for what her mother said.
   So the milliner packed her ribbons and bonnets by the stack
   And started another milliner shop 'way down in Fond du Lac.

5 Now Sal was broken-hearted and weary of her life.
   She dearly loved the shanty-boy and wished to be his wife.
   And when brown autumn came along and ripened all the crops,
   She went 'way out to Baraboo and went to picking hops.

6 But in that occupation she found but little joy,
   For her thoughts were still reverting to her dear shanty-boy.
   She caught the scarlet fever and lay a week or two
   In a suburban pest-house in the town of Baraboo.

7 And often in her ravings she would tear her raven hair
And talk about her shanty-boy upon the Big Eau Claire.
The doctors tried, but all in vain, her hapless life to save;
And millions of young hop-lice are dancing over her grave.

8 When the shanty-boy heard these sad news, his business he did
leave.
His emotional insanity was fearful to perceive.
He hid his saw in a hollow log and traded off his axe,
And hired out for a sucker on a fleet of Sailor Jack's.

9 But still no peace or comfort he anywhere could find,
That milliner's daughter's funeral came so frequent to his mind.
He often wished that death would come and end his woe and
grief,
And grim death took him at his word and came to his relief.

10 For he fell off a rapids piece on the falls at Mosinee,
And ended thus his faithful love and all his misery.
The bold Wisconsin River is now roaring o'er his bones.
His companions are the catfish, and his grave a pile of stones.

11 The milliner is a bankrupt now; her shop's all gone to wrack,
And she talks of moving some fine day away from Fond du Lac.
Her pillow is often haunted by her daughter's auburn hair
And the ghost of that young shanty-boy from up the Big Eau
Claire.

12 And often in her slumbers she sees a dreadful sight
Which puts the worthy milliner into an awful fright.
She sees horrid ghosts and phantoms, which makes her blood
run cool.
By her bedside in his glory stands the ghost of Little Bull.

13 Now let this be a warning to other maidens fair,
To take no stock in shanty-boys up on the Big Eau Claire;
For shanty-boys are rowdies, as everybody knows.
They dwell in the dense forest where the mighty pine tree
grows.

14 And stealing logs and shingle-bolts, and telling awful lies,
And playing cards and swearing, is all their exercise.
But seek the solid comfort and bliss without alloy,
And play their cards according for some one-horse farmer's boy.

B

The Shanty-boy on the Big Eau Claire

Sung by Mrs. MATHILDE MYER, Eau Claire, Wisconsin

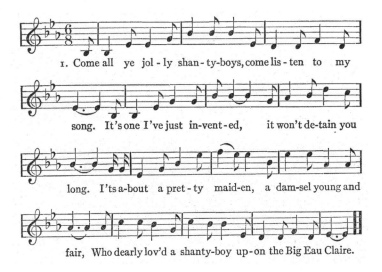

1. Come all ye jol-ly shan-ty-boys, come lis-ten to my song. It's one I've just in-vent-ed, it won't de-tain you long. I'ts a-bout a pret-ty maid-en, a dam-sel young and fair, Who dearly lov'd a shanty-boy up-on the Big Eau Claire.

1 Come all ye jolly shanty-boys, come listen to my song.
It's one I've just invented, it won't detain you long.
It's about a pretty maiden, a damsel young and fair,
Who dearly loved a shanty-boy upon the Big Eau Claire.

2 This young and artful maiden with a noble pedigree,
Her mother she kept a milliner shop 'way down in Mosinee.
She sold waterfalls and ribbons and bonnets trimmed with lace
To all the high-toned people in this gay and festive place.

3 This shanty-boy was handsome, there was none so gay as he.
In the summer time he labored at the mills of Mosinee,

Till stern keen winter came along with cool and blistering
    breeze,
He went upon the Big Eau Claire to fall the big pine trees.

4 He had a handsome black mustache and a curly head of hair.
    A finer lad than he was not upon the Big Eau Claire.
    He loved this milliner's daughter, he loved her long and well,
    Till circumstances happened, and this is what I tell.

5 The milliner swore her daughter the shanty-boy never to wed.
    But Sally, seeming not to care for what her mother said,
    So she packed down her waterfalls and bonnets by the stack,
    And started another milliner shop 'way down by Fond du Lac.

6 It was in her occupation she found but little joy.
    Thoughts came rushing through her mind about the shanty-boy.
    Till one fine autumn came along to ripen all the crops,
    She then went down to Baraboo and went to picking hops.

7 Sal is broken-hearted and tired of her life.
    She's thinking of the shanty-boy, and wished to be his wife.
    She caught the scarlet fever, was sick a week or two
    Down in the shabby pest-house 'way down in Baraboo.

8 It was ofttimes in her raving she tore her auburn hair.
    . . . .
    The doctors tried, but all in vain; her life they could not save,
    And now this weeping willow stands drooping o'er her grave.

9 When the shanty-boy heard these sad news, he became a
    lunatic.
    He acted just as others do when they become lovesick.
    He hid his saw in a hollow log and traded off his axe,
    And hired out to pull an oar [in] a fleet for Sailor Jack.

10 He fell off from a rapids place at the falls of Mosinee,
    Which put an end to his career and all his misery.
    The bold Wisconsin River is waving o'er his bones;
    His friends and his companions are weeping for him at home.

11 The milliner now is bankrupt; her shop is gone to wrack.
She's thinking now of some fine day to move from Fond du Lac.
Her pillow sobbed every night in spite of her daughter fair,
And by the ghost of the shanty-boy upon the Big Eau Claire.

12 Come all ye young and pretty fair maids, come take an advice
   of me,
Not to be too fast to fall in love with everyone you see;
For the shanty-boys are rowdish, which everybody knows.
They dwell in the mighty pine woods where the mighty pine
   tree grows.

13 Stealing logs or shingle booms, telling other lies,
Playing cards, or swearing, is all their exercise.
But if you want to marry for comfort or for joy,
I advise you to get married to an honest farmer's boy.

C

The Shanty-boy on the Big Eau Claire

As sung by Mrs. A. J. Fox, Eau Claire, Wisconsin

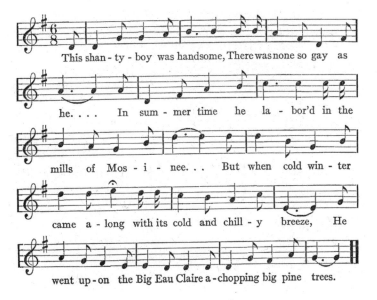

This shan-ty-boy was handsome, There was none so gay as
he. . . . In sum-mer time he la-bor'd in the
mills of Mos-i-nee. . . But when cold win-ter
came a-long with its cold and chill-y breeze, He
went up-on the Big Eau Claire a-chopping big pine trees.

12

Ye Noble Big Pine Tree

By Shan T. Boy

There may be some question as to the eligibility of this composition of Mr. Allen's for a place in these pages, as I do not know that it ever had any folk-currency. The composer sang it a great deal, however, on his rounds, and it is exactly the sort of detailed account of familiar processes that one finds elsewhere appealing to the shanty-boy.

At the head of the manuscript from which I copied this text, a manuscript in Mr. Allen's handwriting, appeared the words, "Air—Will the Weaver"; later, when I visited him, he sang "Ye Noble Big Pine Tree" as here recorded, and told me that the following were the opening words of the old song whose melody he had appropriated for his verses:

> Gentlemen of every station,
> 'Tend unto this kind relation.
>   As to you the truth I bring,
>   Never was so strange a thing.
>
> A lady left by her good grand-ma'am
> Full five thousand pounds per annum,
>   This she held 'neath her control.
>   Thus she did in riches roll.

It seems, however, that these words do not belong to "Will the Weaver," although "Will the Weaver" may have been sung to the recorded tune. "Will the Weaver" begins—

> Mother, mother (O, dear mother) I am married,
> I wish that I had longer tarried;
> For the womankind, I do declare,
> They often will the breeches wear.

See broadsides printed by H. P. Such (London, No. 843) and W. Armstrong (Liverpool); Ford, *Massachusetts Broadsides*, Nos. 3045, 3046, p. 449; Ford, *Proceedings of the American Antiquarian Society*, New Series, xxxiii, 101; Shoemaker, *North Pennsylvania Minstrelsy*, 115–16; A. Williams, *Folk-Songs from the Upper Thames*, 106–8; Ebsworth, *Roxburghe Ballads*, viii, 187.

Sung by Mr. W. N. ALLEN ("Shan T. Boy"), Wausau, Wisconsin

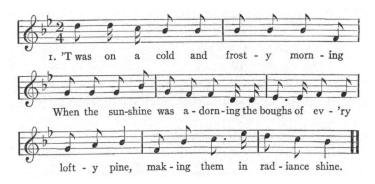

1   'Twas on a cold and frosty morning
    When the sunshine was adorning
    The boughs of ev'ry lofty pine,
    Making them in radiance shine.

2   Through the forest lone I wandered
    Where a little brook meandered,
    Gurgling o'er the rocks below,
    Wading deep through ice and snow.

3   On its banks and right before me
    Stood a pine in stately glory.
    The forest king he seemed to be.
    He was a noble Big Pine Tree.

4   I gazed upon his form gigantic.
    Thoughts ran through my head romantic.
    These were my musings as I stood
    And viewed that monarch of the wood.

5 "For ages you have towered proudly.
The birds have praised you long and loudly.
The squirrels have chattered praise to thee,
O ye noble Big Pine Tree.

6 "When the lumberjacks first spy you,
They'll step up to you and eye you.
With saw and axe they'll lay you down
On the cold snow-covered ground.

7 "Your fall will sound like distant thunder
And fill the birds and squirrels with wonder.
The snow thy winding-sheet will be,
O ye noble Big Pine Tree.

8 "Were you punky, were you hollow,
You had been a lucky fellow;
Then they would have let you be,
O ye noble Big Pine Tree.

9 "But seeing you're so sound and healthy,
You'll make some lumberman more wealthy.
There's scads of wealth concealed in thee,
O ye noble Big Pine Tree.

10 "They will measure, top, and butt you.
Into saw-logs they will cut you.
The woodsman's chains will fetter thee,
O ye noble Big Pine Tree.

11 "When your branches cease to quiver,
They will haul you to the river,
And down the roll-ways roll you in
Where you'll have to sink or swim.

12 "In spring the agile river-driver
Will pick and punch you down the river.
There'll be little rest for thee,
O ye noble Big Pine Tree.

13 "Up the mill-slide they will draw you.
   Into lumber they will saw you.
   Then they'll put you in a pile,
   Where they'll let you rest awhile.

14 "In spring, when gentle showers are falling,
   And the toads and birds are squalling,
   They will take and raft you in
   Where once more you'll have to swim.

15 "Over dams and falls they'll take you,
   Where the rocks will tear and break you,
   You'll reach the Mississippi's breast
   Before they'll let you have a rest.

16 "Then they'll sell you to some farmer
   To keep his wife and children warmer.
   With his team he'll haul you home
   To the prairie drear and lone.

17 "Into a prairie house he'll make you,
   Where the prairie winds will shake you.
   There'll be little rest for thee,
   O ye noble Big Pine Tree.

18 "The prairie winds will sing around you.
   The hail and sleet and snow will pound you,
   And shake and wear and bleach your bones,
   On the prairie drear and lone.

19 "Then the prairie fires will burn you.
   Into ashes they will turn you.
   That will be the end of thee,
   O ye noble Big Pine Tree."

13

The Little Brown Bulls

This is an old Wisconsin classic, dating from the days when oxen were used in the woods almost entirely. It resounds with that valorous spirit of the days when supremacy among men and animals was measured in terms of ability to do work, to stand physical exertion. Competition between camps, teams, and even individual men, was a tremendous driving force. A direct reflection of this is found in stanza 3 of "The Merry Shanty Boys" (No. 31). One cannot help regretting the ballad "leap" between stanzas 9 and 10; for, although one gets from the ballad as it is a considerable reflection of the spirit in which the contest was waged, there is no word of the battle itself, which must have had its Homeric aspects.

According to Mr. Fred Bainter, the singer of Version A, the ballad was composed in Mart Douglas's camp in northwestern Wisconsin in 1872 or 1873. It was in this camp and at this date, he said, that the contest between the big spotted steers and the little brown bulls was waged.

"When he drew the stick": that is, the goad.

"Our skidding was full": "thought he was O.K. at it" (Fred Bainter).

"Said Gordon to Stebbin": Stebbin was the chainer, Gordon's teammate, whose full name was evidently "Kennebec" John Stebbin, very likely a "State of Maine" man. In the previous stanza McCluskey addresses his chainer, not named.

"With the belt ready made": the championship belt, a symbolism taken over from the prize ring, of which every shanty-boy was a devout follower. The idea of defeat was evidently entirely foreign to the big Scotchman. He of course did not know Gordon's score, as the two had probably not worked in sight of each other. The scaler was the only person, with the possible exception of the foreman, in actual possession of the tally.

The refrain used in Version A is common among woods and lake ballads. Mr. Underwood sang no refrain to his version, but upon being asked, he said he had heard this one used with this ballad: "Down, down rye derry down."

A

Verses from Mr. JOE BAINTER, Gordon, Wisconsin
Sung by Mr. FRED BAINTER, Ladysmith, Wisconsin

1. Not a thing on the riv-er Mc-Clus-key did fear When he drew the stick o'er the big spot-ted steers. They were young, quick and sound, girt-ing eight foot and three. Says Mc-Clus-key the Scotchman, "They're the lad-dies for me." Der-ry down, down, down der-ry down.

1 Not a thing on the river McCluskey did fear
When he drew the stick o'er the big spotted steers.
They were young, quick, and sound, girting eight foot and
three.
Says McCluskey the Scotchman, "They're the laddies for me."
Derry down, down, down derry down.

2 Bull Gordon, the Yankee, on skidding was full,
As he cried "Whoa-hush" to the little brown bulls.
Short-legged and soggy, girt six foot and nine.
Says McCluskey the Scotchman, "Too light for our pine."

3 It's three to the thousand our contract did call.
Our hauling was good and the timber was tall.
McCluskey he swore he'd make the day full
And skid two to one of the little brown bulls.

4 "Oh no," says Bull Gordon; "that you cannot do,
Though it's well do we know you've the pets of the crew.
And mark you, my boy, you would have your hands full,
If you skid one more log than the little brown bulls."

5 The day was appointed and soon it drew nigh,
For twenty-five dollars their fortunes to try.
Both eager and anxious that morning were found,
And scalers and judges appeared on the ground.

6 With a whoop and a yell came McCluskey in view,
With the big spotted steers, the pets of the crew,
Both chewing their cuds—"O boys, keep your jaws full,
For you easily can beat them, the little brown bulls."

7 Then out came Bull Gordon with a pipe in his jaw,
The little brown bulls with their cuds in their mouths;
And little we think, when we seen them come down,
That a hundred and forty could they jerk around.

8 Then up spoke McCluskey: "Come stripped to the skin.
We'll dig them a hole and tumble them in.
We'll learn the damned Yankee to face the bold Scot.
We'll mix them a dose and feed it red hot."

9 Said Gordon to Stebbin, with blood in his eye,
"Today we must conquer McCluskey or die."
Then up spoke bold Kennebec, "Boy, never fear,
For you ne'er shall be beat by the big spotted steers."

10 The sun had gone down when the foreman did say,
"Turn out, boys, turn out; you've enough for the day.
We have scaled them and counted, each man to his team,
And it's well do we know now which one kicks the beam."

11 After supper was over McCluskey appeared
With the belt readymade for the big spotted steers.
To form it he'd torn up his best mackinaw.
He was bound he'd conduct it according to law.

12 Then up spoke the scaler, "Hold on, you, awhile.
    The big spotted steers are behind just one mile.
    For you have a hundred and ten and no more,
    And Gordon has beat you by ten and a score."

13 The shanty did ring and McCluskey did swear.
    He tore out by handfuls his long yellow hair.
    Says he to Bull Gordon, "My colors I'll pull.
    So here, take the belt for the little brown bulls."

14 Here's health to Bull Gordon and Kennebec John;
    The biggest day's work on the river they done.
    So fill up your glasses and fill them up full;
    We'll drink to the health of the little brown bulls.
    Derry down, down, down derry down.

"It's three to the thousand our contract did call." Skidding logs with oxen.
Under the forward end of the big log to the left is a go-devil, to which the two
yoke of oxen in the foreground are hitched.

B

The Brown Bulls

As sung by Mr. W. H. UNDERWOOD, Bayport, Minnesota

1. Not a thing on the riv-er Mc-Clus-ky did fear When

he drew the stick o'er the big spot-ted steers. They were

quick, young and sound, girt-ing eight foot and three. Says Mc-

Clus-ky, the Scotchman, "They're the laddies for me."

14

Jim Porter's Shanty Song

Here is a general song, one of the "Shanty-man's Life" type, apparently appropriated to celebrate a special crew by the addition of a particularized final stanza. The tendency to celebrate special crews is further illustrated by "Fred Sargent's Shanty Song" (No. 21); adaptation by the method used in "Jim Porter's Shanty Song" was probably the easiest solution of the problem.

Gray, *Songs and Ballads*, xvii, mentions a song "called 'The Shanty Boy,' which originated about 1847 near Muskegon, Michigan," and prints the initial and final stanza thus:

> Come boys, if you will listen, I'll sing to you a song.
> It's all about the pinery boys and how they get along;
> A set of jovial fellows, so merry and so fine,
> They spend a jovial winter in cutting down the pine.

> So now my song is ended, you'll find those words are true,
> But if you doubt one word of this, just ask Jim Lockwell's
>   crew.
> 'Twas in Jim Lockwell's shanty this song was sung with glee,
> And that's the end of "The Shanty Boy," and it was composed
>   by three.

Comparison with homologous stanzas in "Jim Porter's Shanty Song" is basis for two suggestions: (1) the song was probably thus appropriated rather frequently by various crews and sung to celebrate themselves; (2) such information as to authorship as is directly offered in folksong is not necessarily authentic. I am reminded of the following line from the ballad of "Jesse James": "This song was made by Billy Gashade." Billy's argument would have been more convincing, as would that in the present instance, if it had been offered somewhere free of the requirement of rhyme!

The melody used for Version B is the same as that given for "The Bigler's Crew" (No. 47). I have it also for "California Joe" and another interminable ballad known as "Grandfather's Story." If the truth be known, I think that this was the tune originally heard for this song by Mrs. Murphy, the singer of Version A; she sang fairly definitely, but was unable to recognize a tune when it was "sung back" to her. Shoemaker prints a version in his *North Pennsylvania Minstrelsy*, 2d ed., 90–93.

A

Sung by Mrs. J. S. MURPHY, Minto, North Dakota

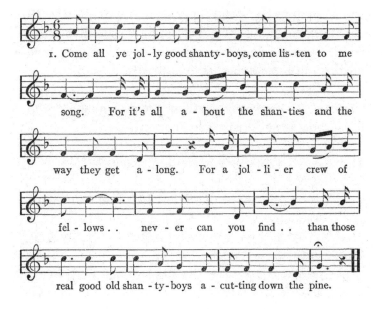

1 Come all ye jolly good shanty-boys, come listen to me song,
　For it's all about the shanties and the way they get along.
　For a jollier crew of fellows never can you find
　Than those real good old shanty-boys a-cutting down the pine.

2 The choppers and the sawers they lay the timbers low,
　The skidders and the swampers they holler to and fro.
　Next comes the sassy loaders before the break of day.
　"Come, load up your teams, me boys!" And to the woods they sway.

3 For the broken ice is floating, and our business is to try.
Three hundred able-bodied men are wanted on the drive.
With cant-hooks and with jam-pikes these noble men do go
And risk their sweet lives on some running stream, you know.

4 On a cold and frosty morning they shiver with the cold.
The ice upon their jam-pikes, which they can scarcely hold.
The axe and saw does loudly sing unto the sun goes down.
Hurrah, my boys! For the day is spent. For the shanty we are
bound.

5 Arriving at the shanty with cold and with wet feet,
Pull off your boots, me boys, for supper you must eat.
Then supper being ready, to supper we must go,
For it's not the style of one of us to lose our hash, you know.

6 Then supper being over, to the apartments we must go.
We'll all load up our pipes and smoke till all is blue,
To nine o'clock or thereabout. Our bunks we then do climb.
. . . .

7 At four o'clock in the morning our foreman he will say,
"Come, roll out, ye teamsters! It's just the break of day."
The teamsters they get up, and their things they cannot find.
They'll blame it on the swampers, and they'll curse them till
they're blind.

8 But as springtime rolls on, how happy we will be,
Some of us arriving home, and others far away.
It takes farmers and sailors, likewise merchants too—
It takes all sorts of tradesmen to make up a shanty crew.

9 So now my song is ended. Those words they say are true.
But if you doubt a word of it, go ask Jim Porter's crew.
For it was in Jim Porter's shanty this song was sung with glee.
So that's the end of me shanty song. It was composed by me.

"Arriving at the shanty with cold and with wet feet, pull off your boots, me boys, for supper you must eat." An interior view of the bunk shanty, showing the upper and lower bunks, and the deacon seat—in use. The men sitting in the middle are wearing calked rivermen's boots. All wear their trousers "stagged," or cut off just below the knee.

B

Shanty-boy and the Pine

As sung by Mr. FRED BAINTER, Ladysmith, Wisconsin

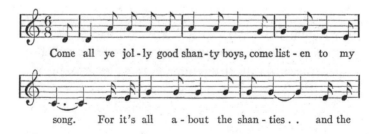

Come all ye jol-ly good shan-ty boys, come list-en to my song. For it's all a-bout the shan-ties . . and the

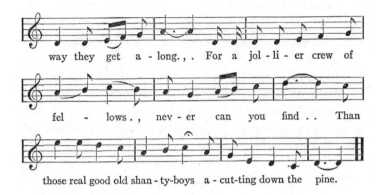

way they get a - long. , . For a jol - li - er crew of

fel - lows ., nev - er can you find . . Than

those real good old shan - ty-boys a - cut-ting down the pine.

C

The Shanty-boy's Song

Reprinted from *Delaney's Song Book No. 13*, 23 (1896)

1 Now, boys, if you will listen, I will sing to you a song,
It's all about the shanty-boys and how they get along;
They are a jovial set of boys, so merry and so fine,
They spend a pleasant winter in cutting down the pine.

2 Some will leave their homes, and friends whom they love dear,
And for the lonesome pine woods their pathway they will
steer;
They are going to the pine woods, all winter to remain
Awaiting for the springtime ere they return again.

3 There are farmers, and sailors, likewise mechanics, too,
And all sorts of tradesmen found with a lumber crew;
The choppers and the sawyers, they lay the timber low,
While the swampers and the skidders, they haul it to and fro.

4 Noon time rolls around, the foreman loudly screams,
"Lay down your saws and axes, boys, and haste to pork and
beans!"
Arrived at the shanty, the splashing does begin;
There's the rattle of the waterpail, and the banging of the tin.

5 It is, "Hurry in, my boys! you, Tom, Dick, or Joe,
For you must take the pail and for some water go!"
The cook he halloos, "Dinner!" they all get up and go;
It's not the style of a shanty boy to miss his pie, you know.

6 Dinner being over, to their shanty they all go;
They all load up their pipes, and smoke till all is blue.
"It's time you were out, boys," the foreman soon will say;
They all take up their hats and mitts, to the woods they haste
away.

7 Oh, each goes out with cheerful heart, and with contented
mind,
For wintry winds do not blow cold among the waving pine;
Loudly their axes ring, until the sun goes down.
"Hurrah! my boys, the day is done, for the shanty we are
bound."

8 Arrived at the shanty, with wet and cold feet,
They off with their boots and packs, for supper they must eat;
The cook he halloos, "Supper!" they all get up and go,
It's not the style of a shanty boy to miss his hash, you know.

9 The boots, the packs, the rubbers, are all thrown to one side,
The mitts, the socks, the rags, are all hung up and dried;
At nine o'clock or thereabouts into their bunks they crawl,
To sleep away the few short hours until the morning call.

10 At four o'clock next morning, the foreman loudly shouts:
"Hurrah, there! you teamsters, 'tis time that you were out!"
The teamsters then get up, all in a fretful way;
Says one, "I've lost my boot-packs, and my socks have gone
astray."

11 The choppers they get up, and their socks they cannot find,
They lay it to the teamsters, and curse them in their mind;
One says, "I've lost my socks—I don't know what to do."
Another has lost his boot-packs, and he is ruined too.

12 Springtime rolls around; the foreman he will say:
    "Lay down your saws and axes, boys, and haste to break away";
    And when the floating ice goes out, in business we'll thrive;
    Hundreds of able-bodied men are wanted on the drive.

15

The Three McFarlands

Mr. Gallagher insisted on calling this ballad, in a deprecatory way, "just a home-made song," although he knew nothing of what camp it was made in and knew no such people as the McFarlands, or any of the rest; nor could he locate any of the three towns mentioned in stanza.[1] He sang a version of "Gerry's Rocks" to the same melody that he gave for this. It was apparently his general utility tune.

"A fine concern team": a team belonging to the company, or "concern."

Sung by Mr. James Gallagher, Minto, North Dakota

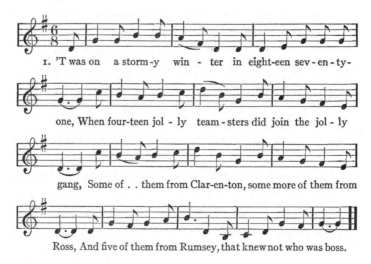

1. 'Twas on a storm-y win - ter in eight-een sev - en - ty-
one, When four-teen jol - ly team - sters did join the jol - ly
gang, Some of . . them from Clar-en-ton, some more of them from
Ross, And five of them from Rumsey, that knew not who was boss.

1 'Twas on a stormy winter in eighteen seventy-one,
  When fourteen jolly teamsters did join the jolly gang,
  Some of them from Clarenton, some more of them from Ross,
  And five of them from Rumsey that knew not who was boss.

2 There were the three McFarlands: there was Tom and Jim and
  Bob;

And Alec Tois, their rollway man, to load the timber on.
They loaded our hosses heavy with three sticks every time,
And we did think it early if we were home at nine.

3 As for our leadin' teamster, he is a very nice man.
I do intend to tell his name; it's Louie Culberson.
He drives a fine concern team, he starts us up at three,
Sayin', "Go and harness your horses, for you must follow me."

4 Bein' in the month of January, a very cold time indeed,
When seven of our jolly teamsters left our gang with speed.
Bein' in the month of February, it would make your poor heart
    ache
To see such loads and drifted roads our horses had to take.

5 Here's a word to the three McFarlands: They are a most
    damnable crew.
They all stood at their stations, they mean to put us through.
They never did show mercy to man nor beast was there,
But when they had to leave a stick, they all began to swear.

6 Come all ye jolly teamsters, wherever you are from,
Oh, do not blame poor Culberson, for he's not in the wrong.
We never did blame Louie to drive through frost and snow;
He bein' our leadin' teamster, he always had to go.

7 So now the cold winter's o'er, an' spring is comin' on,
And with the help of God, brave boys, we'll all get home again.
We'll kiss the girls and court them, and play with them for fun.
This lovin' maid will ask us when we'll come back again.

16

Ye Maidens of Ontario

"The Long Soo": a rapid in the St. Lawrence River.

"Lake St. Peter": a lake in the course of the St. Lawrence; the "Lac San Pierre" mentioned in No. 22.

"Red pine oars": long sweeps used in controlling rafts on the rivers. Seven or eight men were used at each oar. (See "The Banks of the Little Eau Pleine.") (The foregoing glosses are by Mr. Hannah.)

The same melody, with a change in rhythm, is used for this and "Morrissey and the Russian Sailor" (No. 48).

Sung by Mr. A. C. Hannah, Bemidji, Minnesota

1. O ye maid-ens of On-tar-i-o, give ear to what I write, In driv-ing down these ra-pid streams where rafts-men take de-light, In driv-ing down these ra-pid streams as rafts-men they must do, While these low and loaf-ing farm-er boys they stay at home with you.

1 O ye maidens of Ontario, give ear to what I write,
In driving down these rapid streams where raftsmen I take delight,
In driving down these rapid streams as raftsmen they must do,
While these low and loafing farmer boys they stay at home with
you.

2 Oh, these low and loafing farmer boys they tell the girls great tales.
They'll tell them of great dangers in crossing o'er the fields,
While the cutting of the grass and weeds is all that they can do,
While we poor jolly raftsmen are running the Long Soo.

3 And when the sun is going down, their plows they'll cast aside.
They'll jump upon their horse's back and homeward they will ride.
And when the clock strikes eight or nine, then into bed they'll
crawl,
While down on Lake St. Peter we stand many a bitter squall.

4 Oh, the wind blew from the south and east; it blew our cribs
along.
It blew so very hard it shook our timbers up and down.
It put us in confusion for fear we should be drowned.
Our pilot cried, "Cheer up, brave boys! Your red pine oars bring
on."

5 Oh, when we get down to Quebec town, the girls they dance
for joy.
Says one unto another one, "Here comes a shanty-boy!"
One will treat us to a bottle, and another to a dram,
While the toast goes round the table for the jolly shanty-man.

6 I had not been in Quebec for weeks 'twas scarcely three,
When the landlord's lovely daughter fell in love with me.
She told me that she loved me and she took me by the hand,
And shyly told her mamma that she loved a shanty-man.

7 "O daughter, dearest daughter, you grieve my heart full sore,
To fall in love with a shanty-man you never saw before."
"Well, mother, I don't care for that, so do the best you can,
For I'm bound to go to Ottawa with my roving shanty-man."

17

The Falling of the Pine

According to Mr. Dean (who prints the piece, 73–74), this song comes from the Georgian Bay region and belongs to the day of "square timber logging," a process once used in Canada. The following explanatory note is from *A Historical Sketch of Canada's Lumber Industry*, by James Lawler, issued by the Department of the Interior, Canada:

"For many years the export trade consisted largely of square timber, that is, timber squared by the axe in the woods. This trade, which employed many hundred sailing ships, had its centre at the port of Quebec, where sometimes as many as three hundred ships were to be seen loading at one time. It reached its highest point about 1870 and since that, owing to the wastefulness of the trade and the dangerous condition in which it left the woods, owing to the chips and debris, it has . . . dwindled away to almost nothing."

A version of this song in Shoemaker, 2d ed., 197–99, shows amusing corruptions. The "Bright Phœbus" of stanza 4 appears in strange guise:

> Feeble Phœbie there doth sit,
> And we never shall forget,
> And our work we will not quit
>   Till the sun it doth not shine.

Sung by Mr. M. C. Dean, Virginia, Minnesota

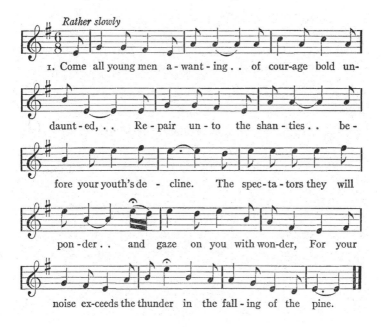

1. Come all young men a-want-ing.. of cour-age bold un-daunt-ed,.. Re-pair un-to the shan-ties.. be-fore your youth's de-cline. The spec-ta-tors they will pon-der.. and gaze on you with won-der, For your noise ex-ceeds the thunder in the fall-ing of the pine.

1 Come all young men a-wanting of courage bold undaunted,
   Repair unto the shanties before your youth's decline.
   The spectators they will ponder and gaze on you with wonder,
   For your noise exceeds the thunder in the falling of the pine.

2 The shanty is our station and lumbering our occupation,
   Where each man has his station, some for to score and line.
   It is nine foot of a block we will bust at every knock,
   And the wolves and bears we'll shock at the falling of the pine.

3 When the day it is a-breaking, from our slumbers we're
      awakened.
   Breakfast being over, our axes we will grind.
   Into the woods we do advance, where our axes sharp do glance,
   And like brothers we commence for to fall the stately pine.

4 For it's to our work we go through the cold and stormy snow,
    And it's there we labor gayly till bright Phœbus does not
        shine;
    Then to the shanties we'll go in and songs of love we'll sing,
    And we'll make the valleys ring at the falling of the pine.

5 When the weather it grows colder, like lions we're more bolder,
    And while this forms grief for others, it's but the least of mine;
    For the frost and snow so keen it can never keep us in,
    It can never keep us in from the falling of the pine.

6 When the snow is all diminished and our shanty work all
        finished,
    Banished we are all for a little time,
    And then far apart we're scattered until the booms are gathered,
    Until the booms are gathered into handsome rafts of pine.

7 When we get to Quebec, O me boys, we'll not forget,
    And our whistles we will wet with some brandy and good wine.
    With fair maidens we will boast till our money is all used,
    And, my boys, we'll ne'er refuse to go back and fall the pine.

18

The Pinery Boy

Mrs. Olin said she learned this quaint little ballad, which is redolent of the fragrance not only of the pine woods, but of classic balladry as well, shortly after she came to Wisconsin, which she did in 1867. She learned it from a neighbor boy, one Thomas Ward, "a great singer."

The following fragment, given me, without title, by Mrs. M. W. Deputy, of Bemidji, Minnesota, is a part of an older ballad which was apparently the pattern for "The Pinery Boy":

> O father, father, build me a boat
> That I may over the ocean float,
> And every ship that I sail by,
> 'Twill be that I'll inquire for my sweet
>   William, the sailor boy.
>
> O captain, captain, tell me true,
> Does my sweet William sail with you?
> Oh no, my dear, he is not here,
> He's drownded in the gulf below.
>
> She wrung her hands and tore her hair,
> Just like a lady in dying despair . . .
>
> O father, father, dig me a grave,
> And dig it wide and deep.
> Put a marble stone at my head and feet,
> And a turtle dove upon my breast.

This is the well-known English song "Sweet William," or "The Sailor Boy," often met with in this country; for references see Cox, *Folk-Songs of the South*, 353.

Sung by Mrs. M . A. OLIN, Eau Claire, Wisconsin

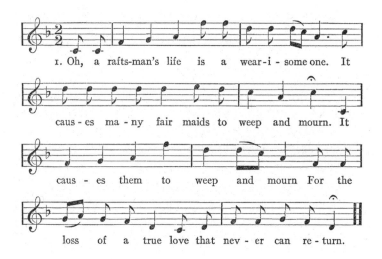

1. Oh, a rafts-man's life is a wear-i - some one. It
caus - es ma - ny fair maids to weep and mourn. It
caus - es them to weep and mourn For the
loss of a true love that nev - er can re - turn.

1 Oh, a raftsman's life is a wearisome one.
It causes many fair maids to weep and mourn.
It causes them to weep and mourn
For the loss of a true love that never can return.

2 "O father, O father, build me a boat,
That down the Wisconsin I may float,
And every raft that I pass by
There I will inquire for my sweet Pinery Boy."

3 As she was rowing down the stream,
She saw three rafts all in a string.
She hailed the pilot as they drew nigh,
And there she did inquire for her sweet Pinery Boy.

4 "O pilot, O pilot, tell me true,
Is my sweet Willie among your crew?
Oh, tell me quick and give me joy,
For none other will I have but my sweet Pinery Boy.

5 "Oh, auburn was the color of his hair,
　His eyes were blue and his cheeks were fair.
　His lips were of a ruby fine;
　Ten thousand times they've met with mine."

6 "O honored lady, he is not here.
　He's drownded in the dells, I fear.
　'Twas at Lone Rock as we passed by,
　Oh, there is where we left your sweet Pinery Boy."

7 She wrung her hands and tore her hair,
　Just like a lady in great despair.
　She rowed her boat against Lone Rock.
　You'd a-thought this fair lady's heart was broke.

8 "Dig me a grave both long and deep,
　Place a marble slab at my head and feet;
　And on my breast a turtle dove
　To let the world know that I died for love;
　And at my feet a spreading oak
　To let the world know that my heart was broke."

19

The Maine-ite in Pennsylvania

The genuine shanty-boy was a rover. Not only Pennsylvania, but Michigan and Wisconsin, had their full quotas of "State of Maine" men, many of them excellent foremen and bosses.

Mr. Underwood learned this song in 1879.

"No artificial German text": shanty-boy's tribute to Pennsylvania's heavy German settlement.

Sung by Mr. W. H. UNDERWOOD, Bayport, Minnesota

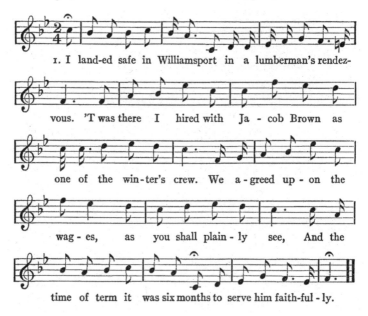

1. I land-ed safe in Williamsport in a lumberman's rendez-

vous. 'T was there I hired with Ja - cob Brown as

one of the win-ter's crew. We a-greed up - on the

wag - es, as you shall plain - ly see, And the

time of term it was six months to serve him faith-ful - ly.

1 I landed safe in Williamsport in a lumberman's rendezvous.
'Twas there I hired with Jacob Brown as one of the winter's
crew.
We agreed upon the wages, as you shall plainly see,
And the time of term it was six months to serve him faithfully.

2 It would melt your heart with pity, it would make your blood
    run cold,
   To see the work that Nature did all in her rudest mould,
   And to see those overhanging rocks along the ice-bound shore,
   Where the rippling waters fierce do rage and the cataracts do
    roar.

3 There's the tomtit and the moose-bird and the roving caribou;
   The lucifee and pa'tridge that through the forests flew;
   And the wild ferocious rabbit from the colder regions came;
   And several other animals too numerous to name.

4 So to conclude and finish, I have one thing more to say:
   When I am dead and in my grave, lying mould'ring in the clay,
   No artificial German text you can for me sustain,
   But simply say I'm a roving wreck right from Bangor, Maine.

20

Driving Saw-logs on the Plover

A Doleful Ditty, by Shan T. Boy

Another creation of Billy Allen's (composed in 1873), which he sang greatly in the days of singing and which had some currency in Wisconsin. Again the story has no historical basis, except that the Plover was an actual stream, a small tributary of the Wisconsin, joining it just below Stevens Point, Wisconsin.

The tune used, according to Mr. Allen, is that of an old song about a mother's words to her son who went away to the Crimean War. "The Persian's Crew" (No. 46) uses the same tune.

Sung by Mr. W. N. ALLEN ("Shan T. Boy"), Wausau, Wisconsin

1. There walk'd on Plo - ver's shad - y banks One eve - ning last July, . . . A moth - er of a shan - ty - boy, And
dole - ful was her cry, . . Saying, "God be with you,
John - nie, Al - though you're far a - way . . Driv-ing
saw-logs on the Plo - ver, And you'll nev-er get your pay."

1   There walked on Plover's shady banks one evening last July
    A mother of a shanty-boy, and doleful was her cry,
    Saying, "God be with you, Johnnie, although you're far away
    Driving saw-logs on the Plover, and you'll never get your pay.

2   "O Johnnie, I gave you schooling, I gave you a trade likewise.
    You need not been a shanty-boy had you taken my advice.
    You need not gone from your dear home to the forest far away,
    Driving saw-logs on the Plover, and you'll never get your pay.

3   "O Johnnie, you were your father's hope, your mother's only joy.
    Why is it that you ramble so, my own, my darling boy?
    What could induce you, Johnnie, from your own dear home to
      stray,
    Driving saw-logs on the Plover? And you'll never get your pay.

4   "Why didn't you stay upon the farm and feed the ducks and
      hens,
    And drive the pigs and sheep each night and put them in their
      pens?
    Far better for you to help your dad to cut his corn and hay
    Than to drive saw-logs on the Plover, and you'll never get your
      pay."

5   A log canoe came floating adown the quiet stream.
    As peacefully it glided as some young lover's dream.
    A youth crept out upon the bank and thus to her did say,
    "Dear mother, I have jumped the game, and I haven't got my pay.

6   "The boys called me a sucker and a son-of-a-gun to boot.
    I said to myself, 'O Johnnie, it is time for you to scoot.'
    I stole a canoe and started upon my weary way,
    And now I have got home again, but nary a cent of pay."

7   Now all young men take this advice: If e'er you wish to roam,
    Be sure and kiss your mothers before you leave your home.
    You had better work upon a farm for a half a dollar a day
    Than to drive saw-logs on the Plover, and you'll never get your
      pay.

21

Fred Sargent's Shanty Song

Mr. Horen had no name for these stanzas. Noting certain points of similarity between this and "Jim Porter's Shanty Song," I suggested the title here given, which was accepted.

Sung by Mr. EMMET HOREN, Eau Claire, Wisconsin

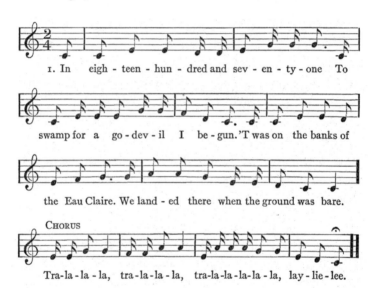

1. In eigh-teen-hun-dred and sev-en-ty-one To

swamp for a go-dev-il I be-gun.'Twas on the banks of

the Eau Claire. We land-ed there when the ground was bare.

CHORUS

Tra-la-la-la, tra-la-la-la, tra-la-la-la-la-la, lay-lie-lee.

1 In eighteen hundred and seventy-one
To swamp for a go-devil I begun.
'Twas on the banks of the Eau Claire.
We landed there when the ground was bare.

Chorus
Tra-la-la-la, tra-la-la-la,
Tra-la-la-la-la-la, lay-lie-lee.

2 Early in the morning we arose
  And manfully put on our clothes.
  'Twas not day till the horn did blow,
  And in to breakfast we did go.

3 Now to conclude and end my song,
  My shanty ditty won't be long.
  Here's a health to whiskey strong,
  And to Fred Sargent and all his gang.

22

On the Lac San Pierre

A fragment of some folk-version of "The Wreck of the Julie Plant," by the Canadian poet Drummond. Described by Mr. Hannah as a "Canuck" song, very popular among the French-Canadian shanty-boys both at home and abroad.

Sung by Mr. A. C. HANNAH, Bemidji, Minnesota

2. Come all you jol-ly raf's-men, I tell you von good plan. You mar-ry von good French voman an' leev on von good farm. For the vind she may blow from the nor', sout', eas', Bime by she be blow some more; But you ne-ver git drown' in the Lac San Pierre So long's you stay on the shore.

1 Von night on the Lac San Pierre
  The vind she blow, blow, blow;
  The vind she blow from the nor', sout', eas',
  She blow our crib from the shore. . . .
  . . . .
  . . . .

Our raf' she struck on a great beeg rock
In the beeg Lachine canawl.

2 Come all ye jolly raf'smen,
   I tell you von good plan.
   You marry von good French voman
   An' leev on von good farm.
   For the vind she may blow from the nor', sout', eas',
   Bime by she be blow some more;
   But you never git drown' in the Lac San Pierre
   So long's you stay on the shore.

23

The Festive Lumberjack

This song, a sort of cross-section of lumberjack temperament, may be said to illustrate folksong-making in its decadence. [Ed "Arkansaw"] Springstad said that he and a Negro called Bill made the song, about 1900, one day during harvest near Crystal, North Dakota. A group of lumberjacks had gone out there from the camps of Minnesota to work in the fields. Springstad reported that he furnished most of the terms and expressions belonging to the lumberjack vernacular, along with certain facts concerning the lumberjack's inner nature. The Negro, who was "quite a poet," moulded all this material into verses.

My informant said also that the tune had the same source as the stanzas, and examination of the result seems to leave no reason for doubting him. The song was very well known, in Minnesota at least, and lumberjacks have often told me of its having been made famous by "a big nigger" who used to work in the camps. It may have been Bill. According to many who must be regarded as authorities on the matter, the song presents an amazingly faithful picture of its subject.

"Porky": porcupine.

"Moose-cat": a slang expression, hard of translation, but applied to anyone possessing great ability, strength, or what not.

"The long white-aproned man": the bar-keep.

"Within a year of time," etc.: further evidence that the shanty-boy was not unaware of the difference between the steadiness of farm life and his own improvident existence.

"Peakers": top logs on sled-loads. Jack here poses as a crack loader.

"Every jack's a cant-hook man": men skilled in the use of the cant-hook were valuable and highly paid.

"That birls the crooked steel": the "crooked steel" was a fancy name for the cant-hook. To "birl" the cant-hook was to twirl it in the hands before taking hold of the log with it—an added mark of skill. The whole expression sometimes had a general meaning of handling the cant-hook skillfully.

Sung by Mr. ED SPRINGSTAD, Bemidji, Minnesota

1. I've been a-round the world a bit, an' seen beasts great an' small. The one I mean to tell a-bout for dar-in' beats 'em all. He leaves the woods with his brist-les raised the full length of his back. He's known by men of sci-ence as the fes-tive lum-ber-jack. He's a wild, rip-snort-in' dev-il ev-er' time he comes to town. *(Spoken)* He's a pork-y, he's a moose cat, too bus-y to set down. But when his sil-ver's reg-is-ter'd, an' his drinks is com-in' few, He's then as tame as oth-er jacks that's met their Wat-er-loo.

1 I've been around the world a bit, an' seen beasts both great an'
   small.
The one I mean to tell about for darin' beats 'em all.
He leaves the woods with his bristles raised the full length of his
   back.
He's known by men of science as the festive lumberjack.

Chorus
He's a wild rip-snortin' devil ever' time he comes to town.
He's a porky, he's a moose-cat, too busy to set down.
But when his silver's registered and his drinks is comin' few,
He's then as tame as other jacks that's met their Waterloo.

2 While out in camp he's very wise, he'll tell you of his plans.
He's figgered out an' knows he'll beat the long white-aproned man.
He means to cut out drinkin' booze an' climb right up in fame,
And within a year of time will own a handsome little claim.

3 He'll go down to the city with his time-check in his hand.
He's as busy as a bed bug, for an instant couldn't stand
Until he gets his pile o' silver, which will vanish soon from sight,
For he intends to log a bit, an' he will do it right.

4 One dozen drinks o' whiskey straight an' the jack feels pretty fair.
The heavy loggin' then begins, but he's loggin' with hot air.
His peakers rise above the clouds; the cross-haul man below
Works by a code, for they couldn't hear his "Whoa!"

5 Every jack's a cant-hook man; no others can be found.
They do some heavy loggin', but they do it best in town.
They're loved by all the pretty girls, who at their feet would
   kneel
If they could win that darlin' chap that birls the crooked steel.

6 But here's a proposition, boys: when next we meet in town,
We'll form a combination and we'll mow the forest down.
We then will cash our handsome checks, we'll neither eat nor
   sleep,
Nor will we buy a stitch o' clothes while whiskey is so cheap.

"His peakers rise above the clouds." A good illustration of the process of loading (see glossary, under *cross-haul*). The cross-haul line and oxen, the cant-hook men, and the top-loader are all present in the picture.

24

The Crow Wing Drive

Another example from the raveled ends of song-making, composed by the "White Pine Tom" mentioned in it, who made it and "sung it on" Springstad ("Arkansaw") when they all returned to Bemidji after the Crow Wing drive here commemorated. The year of composition was not stated, but must have been comparatively recent, as the utilization of the "Casey Jones" tune indicates.

"Crow Wing River": a small stream in central Minnesota, joining the Mississippi near Brainerd.

"The old Pine Tree": the Pine Tree Lumber Company.

"Pushing": a later term for logging, or, perhaps more specifically, driving.

"Long Jim Quinn": a foreman.

"M. & I.": the Minnesota and International, a short line of railroad from Bemidji south to Brainerd, county seat of Crow County; familiarly known as the "Mike and I."

"Humpy Russell": the oldest engineer in the service of the M. & I. at the time. In fact, Springstad accounted for all the characters in this song—all "real," and good cronies of his in times past. The tendency to include one's friends and locality, a tendency which merely tints the lines of Billy Allen, here usurps the entire song and impoverishes it.

Sung by Mr. ED SPRINGSTAD, Bemidji, Minnesota

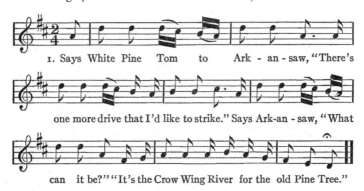

1. Says White Pine Tom to Ark - an - saw, "There's one more drive that I'd like to strike." Says Ark-an - saw, "What can it be?" "It's the Crow Wing River for the old Pine Tree."

1 Says White Pine Tom to Arkansaw,
   "There's one more drive that I'd like to strike."
   Says Arkansaw, "What can it be?"
   "It's the Crow Wing River for the old Pine Tree."

2 Says Arkansaw, "Now if that's the case,
   I can put you in the race.
   Come with me in the mornin' an' we'll begin,
   For I've a job a-pushin' for Long Jim Quinn."

3 In the mornin' we boarded the M. & I.
   Our friends in Bemidji we bid good-bye.
   Humpy Russell took us down the line
   And landed us in Brainerd right on time.

4 There was White Pine Tom and young Lazzard,
   And Mikey Stewart and his two big pards;
   Billy Domine and the Weston boys,
   And there was others from Bemidji that could make some noise.

25

The M. and I. Goo-goo Eyes

By Ed ("Arkansaw") Springstad

And here lies the Song of the White Pine Woods, *sans* originality, *sans* meaning, *sans* everything. The song that was once the embodiment of virile pioneer virtues, a faithful reflection of the ideals of a picturesque and hardy group, and the record of its deeds of valor; the song that rose, filled with the strong and simple qualities of those who made and sang it, drifting up out of the shanty clearings to melt away among the silent pines and the bright white stars, lies here in the ditch of maudlin parody.

This is Arkansaw Springstad's own work, composed at the time when "Just Because She Made Those Goo-goo Eyes" was popular. He could sing only the chorus for me, and could not recall quite all of the final stanza. Perhaps it is just as well.

Sung by Mr. ED SPRINGSTAD, Bemidji, Minnesota

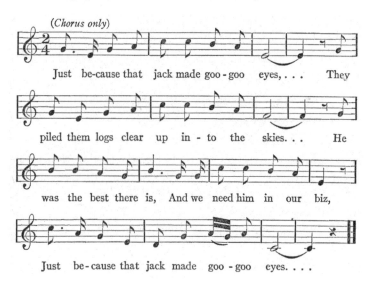

(Chorus only)

Just be-cause that jack made goo-goo eyes, . . . They piled them logs clear up in-to the skies. . . He was the best there is, And we need him in our biz, Just be-cause that jack made goo-goo eyes. . . .

1   There was an old switch-hog with a train o' logs
    All standin' on their end.
    The engineer was shovin' back,
    He had heaps o' coal to spend.
    When a lumber-jack from the timber came,
    He lowered his head and rolled his eyes,
    An' then laid back one ear,
    As much as to say, "You old switch-hog,
    I'll put you in the clear."
    The engineer gave a dynamite sign.

    Chorus
    Just because that jack made goo-goo eyes,
    They piled them logs clear up into the skies.

        He was the best there is,
        And we need him in our biz,
    Just because that jack made goo-goo eyes.

2   Then along came Russell with number seven;
    He was rubberin' straight up at his stack.
    He says, "I guess my air's all right." But just then he left the
        track
    At Hackensack, at Hackensack.
    There was Nolan's logs, there was Dolan's logs,
    And there was logs that never went through.
    But says Nolan's logs to Dolan's logs,
    "Good mornin' an' how-dy-you-do?
    I'm on to you, I'm on to you."

3   There is a spur upon this line,
    They call it seventy-five.
    If you wanta hold your job,
    You've gotta be alive
    When the pay car comes, when the pay car comes . . .

26

The Hanging Limb

The story of this ballad belongs to Michigan, but the verses may have been composed either there or back in the native country of the hero, who was clearly one of the many hundreds of men who came across into the Michigan woods to work, and who carried to those woods, and later to the camps of Wisconsin and even Minnesota, the large number of "American" woods songs born in Canada.

The falling limb was one of the three or four outstanding dangers which haunted shanty-boy life. The author of *The Blazed Trail* describes it thus.

"When the tree had fallen it had crashed through the top of another, leaving suspended in the branches of the latter a long heavy limb. A slight breeze dislodged it. . . .

"This is the chief of the many perils of the woods. Like crouching pumas the instruments of a man's destruction poise on the spring, sometimes for days. Then swiftly, silently, the leap is made. It is a danger unavoidable, terrible, ever present."

The text of Version B was copied from a scrap-book of Mrs. Hopkins's, wherein it was written in a miserable handwriting. The blanks in stanzas 8 and 12 indicate undecipherable manuscript. The owner of the book herself could not read it at these places. B. L. Jones records this song (*Folk-Lore from Michigan*, 4).

A

Printed by F. W. Waugh, in the *Journal of American Folklore*, xxxi, 75–76: "informant, ROY HUTCHISON, Manitoulin Island, Ontario."

1 Come, all ye sons of Canada, wherever you may be,
   And listen to my tale of woe, and mark it in Fort Knell;
   And do not leave your own dear homes, but by your parents
      stand:

And if ever you're forced to look for work, steer clear of
    Michigan.

2 Right well I knew that handsome lad whose name was Harry
    Done.
  His father was a farmer, the township of Aldone.
  He had everything he wished for, and a farm of good land;
  But he thought he would spend a winter in the woods of
    Michigan.

3 The morning that he left his home, his mother to him did say,
  "Now, Harry boy, take my advice and on your farm stay;
  For if you leave your mother, likewise your sister dear,
  There's something tells me that on earth your face I'll ne'er
    more see."

4 But Harry gaily laughed at her: "Say, mother, don't you fear!
  For when the spring is opened, I am coming straight back
    here."
  Then he went to Bay City, where he hired in a lumber king;
  And straight from that he took his course to the woods of
    Michigan.

5 He worked three months quite merrily, and ofttimes would
    write home,
  "The winter will soon be over, and [in] spring I am going
    home."
  As he rose one morning from his bunk, his face it wore no
    smile,
  As he called his chum outside the door, whose name was
    Charlie Loyal.

6 "O Charlie Loyal, I had a dream which fills my heart with woe.
  I fear there's something wrong at home, and home I ought to
    go."
  But his comrade only laughed at him, which cheered him for a
    while,
  Saying, "Harry boy, it's time for work; let's go and fell the pine."

7 He worked away till ten o'clock, while on that fatal day,
When a hanging limb fell down on him and crushed him where
   he lay.
His comrades gathered round him to pull the limb away,
When he opened his eyes and faintly smiled, and this to them
   did say:

8 "Now, comrades, I am dying; may the end come right soon,
And may the Lord in his mercy look on my friends at home."
In two or three days after, his body was sent home,
Containing all remained on earth of poor young Harry Done.

9 And when his mother saw him, she fell down like a stone.
They picked her up, but her heart was broke when Harry he
   came home.
His poor old aged father he lingered for a while,
But never till the day he died was known to wear a smile.

10 In less than three months after, they buried the poor old man.
Now, who can say no deadly curse hangs over Michigan?

B

Harry Dunn

From Mrs. RILEY HOPKINS, Moran, Michigan

1 Come all you sons of Canada, wherever you may dwell,
And likewise pay attention and mark its imports well.
Oh, do not leave your old homestead, but by your parents
   stand,
And if you ever get short of work, steer clear of Michigan.

2 For it's many a bold Canadian boy left home and friends so
   dear,
And longing for excitement, for Michigan would steer.
But ere many months would pass away a telegram would come,
Saying, "Your son was killed in the lumber-woods. His body
   will send home."

3 I once did know a handsome youth whose name was Harry
   Dunn.
   His father was a farmer in the county of Aldun.
   He had everything he wished for, like houses and good land,
   But he thought he would like one winter in the woods of
   Michigan.

4 The day before he went away his mother to him did say,
   "It's breaking of my heart, dear boy, to have you go away.
   Oh, do not leave your parents, likewise your sisters three,
   For something tells me that your form no more on earth
   we'll see."

5 But Harry only laughed at them, saying, "Mother, don't you
   fear.
   The winter will soon pass away, then I'll come right back here,
   With plenty of money for to spend; and don't you understand?
   I only want to have a time in the woods of Michigan."

6 He then went to Bay City and hired out to a lumber king,
   And steered his course then straightway to the woods near.
   He worked along right merrily and often did write home,
   Saying, "Winter will soon pass away, then right back home
   I'll come."

7 One morning Harry rose from bunk, his face it wore no smile.
   He called his comrade to one side, whose name was Charlie
   Lisle,
   Saying, "Charlie, my boy, I've had a dream that fills my heart
   with woe.
   I fear there's something wrong at home, and there I'd better go."

8 His comrade only laughed at him, which cheered him for a
   time,
   Saying, "Harry, dear boy . . ."
   He worked along till ten o'clock all on that fatal day,
   When a hanging limb fell from above and crushed him where
   he lay.

9 His comrades gathered around him and tore the limb away.
   He opened wide his bright blue eyes and unto them did say,
   "O comrades, I'm a-dying. The end will come right soon.
   May God in his great mercy pity my poor friend[s] at home.

10 "And Charlie Lisle, I'd have you go and take my body home
   Unto my aged mother dear. Oh, why did I leave her side?"
   And then he closed his bright eyes, he gasped, fell back and
       died.

11 And just two days after, a coffin was brought home
   Containing all that was left of poor, poor Harry Dunn.
   And when his mother saw him, she fell down like a stone.
   They picked her up, but her heart was broke when Harry was
       brought home.

12 Then that old man through sickness and woe, and from that
       day until he died,
   He was never known to smile . . .
   And just three months afterward they buried that old man.
   And who can say but what there a deadly lure hangs over
       Michigan?

27

Harry Bail

The tragedy of this ballad, which the first line of stanza 2 would seem to locate in Michigan, is not strictly one of shanty life; but it still belongs to the pine woods. These mills, of varying size and capacity, on the lakes and rivers of the logging country, gave employment to many woodsmen at one time or another, especially in the summer. The hero of "The Shanty-boy on the Big Eau Claire" in the summer time "tail sawed in a mill at Mosinee."

The maker of this song, however, shows a decided leaning toward moralizing. The narrative of the piece and the manly qualities of the hero seem to be present only that the moralizing may go forward.

Lapeer County is in the southeastern part of lower Michigan.

Mrs. Hopkins's scrap-book is again replete with undecipherable words. Some of these the context made clear; others were even beyond surmise.

This ballad has already been printed by Lomax, *Cowboy Songs*, 172–73 ("Harry Bale"); Shoemaker, *North Pennsylvania Minstrelsy*, 79–80 ("Harry Bell"); Tolman and Eddy, *Journal of American Folklore*, xxxv, 375 ("Harry Bale"). Lomax's version gives the date of the accident as April 29, 1879; Shoemaker's as April 10, 1879; Tolman and Eddy's, which is fragmentary, omits the date. Stanza 4, line 3, which is unintelligible in the present text, runs, in Lomax, "In lowering of the feed bar throwing the carriage into gear"; in Shoemaker, "He took hold of the lever, threw the carriage into gear."

From Mrs. RILEY HOPKINS, Moran, Michigan

1 Come all kind friends and parents, brother[s] one and all,
   A story I will tell to you. It will make your blood run cold.
   'Tis of a poor unfortunate boy; 'tis known both far and near.
   His parents raised him tenderly not many miles from here.

2 In the township of Arcade, in the county of Lapeer,
   There stands a little shingle mill that has run about one year.
   'Tis where the dreadful deed was done caused many to weep
      and wail.
   'Tis where this poor boy lost his life, and his name was Harry
      Bail.

3 It appears his occupation was head sawyer in the mill.
   He followed it successfully two years four months, until
   The time was come for him to leave this earth of care.
   No one knows how soon 'twill be these recorded deeds to
      share.

4 On the twenty-ninth of April in the year of sixty-nine,
   He went into the mill as usual; no fear did he discern,
   Till the roaring of the feed-box threw the carriage into gear.
   It threw him upon the saw and cut him so severe.

5 It cut clear through his shoulder-blade and halfway down.
   It threw him upon the floor as the carriage it came back.
   He started for the shanty, his strength was failing fast.
   He said, "My boys, I'm wounded. I fear it is my last."

6 His brothers they were sent for; likewise his sisters two.
   The doctor he was summoned, but alas! it was true.
   For when his cruel wound was dressed, he unto them did say,
   "I know there is no help for me. I soon will pass away."

7 No father has poor Harry to weep beside his bed,
   No kind and loving mother to soothe his aching head.
   He lingered for one night and day till death did ease his pain.
   Hushed his voice forever. He never spoke again.

8 They dressed him for his coffin and fitted him for his grave,
   While brothers and sisters mourned the loss of their brother so
      young and brave.
   They took him to the churchyard and laid him there to rest.
   His body is a-mouldering, but his spirit is with the blest.

9 This life is such a short time, which often causes many to
   frown.
   We know it is men's portion to come forth and be slain down.
   As jolly a fellow was Harry as ever you wish to know,
   But he withered like a flower; it was his time to go.

10 The springtime is returning to wait this mournful lay.
   The little birds in the leafy trees sing sweetly all the day.
   While brother[s] and sister[s] they . . . the love he fondly gave,
   By planting . . . of flowers around young Harry's grave.

28

Shanty Teamster's Marseillaise

This text is from a manuscript sent me by Mr. George F. Will, of Bismarck, North Dakota, who secured the stanzas from the recitation of Mr. E. R. Steinbrueck, of Mandan. The following comment, from Mr. Steinbrueck, accompanied the manuscript:

"When that song was sounded nights in the lumber shanty there was a break-up of the teamsters in the morning that you could bet your last pair of moccasin strings on. At no other occasion the thought of that song, among many others, entered the head of anybody. . . . That was during the years 1871–76."

The ballad has been printed by Mr. Will in the *Journal of American Folklore*, xxvi, 187.

From Mr. GEORGE F. WILL, Bismarck, North Dakota

1 Come all ye gay teamsters, attention I pray.
I'll sing you a ditty composed, by the way,
Of a few jovial fellows who thought the hours long,
Would pass off the time with a short comic song.

Chorus
Come, cheer up, brave boys, it is upward we go
Through this wretched country, the Opeongo.

2 As it happened one morning of a fine summer day,
I met Robert Conroy, who to me did say,
"Will you go to my shanty and draw my white pine?
I'll give you good wages and the best of good time."

3 "For to go to your shanty we do feel inclined,
To earn our good wages and be up in good time.
To our wives and our sweethearts we'll bid all adieu,
And go up to York Branch and draw timber for you."

4   There assembled together a fine jovial crew,
     With horses well harnessed, both hardy and true.
     All things being ready, we started away
     From fair Elmer town about noon of the day.

5   The road led o'er mountains, through valleys and plains,
     In a country where hardship and poverty reigns,
     Where the poor suff'ring settlers, hard fate to bewail,
     Are bound down with mortgage, debt dues and claims.

6   At a place called York Branch, where Conroy holds his rules,
     There assembled together his hacknaves and fools,
     And old Jimmy Edwards, that cut-throat and spy,
     Would try to deceive you by advices and lies.

7   Not long at the farm we're allowed to stay,
     But escorted by Jimmy we're hurried away,
     Where Frenchmen and Indian, their living to gain,
     Were abused by a brute—Jerry Welch was his name.

8   We read of the devil: from heaven he fell,
     For rebellion and treason was cast down to hell.
     But his son, Jerry Welch, remains here below
     To work deeds of darkness, cause sorrow and woe.

9   With the eye of a demon, the tongue of a knave,
     Those two villainous traitors should be yoked in a sleigh,
     And Jerry's old squaw for a teamster and guide
     To tip up the brutes of the Branch for to drive.

10   At length we commenced the white pine to draw.
     It was Jerry's intention to put us square through,
     To break down our horses and show no fair play,
     And he ordered brave Jimmy to drive night and day.

11   But the teamsters consulted and made up a plan,
     Since fair work won't do, to go home every man.
     So we left Conroy's shanty and Jerry the knave,
     For true loyal teamsters ain't born to be slaves.

12 So we are at home and surrounded by friends.
    We are thankful for favors that providence sends.
    We'll sing our adventures and our shantying is o'er,
    And we'll never go up the York Branch any more.

    Chorus
    Come, cheer up, brave boys! We plough and we sow,
    And adieu evermore to the Opeongo.

29

The Fatal Oak

The text of this song was sent me by Mr. Lee Todd, of Cornell, Wisconsin, with this comment: "The following verse was written by Mrs. Abbie Payne, a past resident of North Bear Lake, Wisconsin. I cannot say definitely where the accident took place, but it was on the Kickapoo River somewhere between Steuben and Wauzeka. It happened about fifty years ago [1873]. Anson DeKeans, the captain of the party, was somewhere between twenty and twenty-five years of age."

The cause of the tragedy is more easily comprehended when one remembers that the risen streams in the spring often undermine the roots of trees along the banks and cause them to fall.

Mr. Todd told me that these verses were sung in the early days, and named two old pioneers who could still sing them. Mrs. Payne was well known as a local song-maker who used as the basis of her songs happenings (usually tragic) which took place in her locality. She is credited with another song, known as "The Shattuck Song" or "The Song of Mrs. Shattuck," which records an accident much the same as that of "The Fatal Oak," and which was well known in southern Wisconsin in the seventies and eighties.

From Mr. LEE TODD, Cornell, Wisconsin

1 'Tis a mournful story I relate
Of three young men who met their fate.
While folded in the arms of sleep
They sank beneath the billows deep.

2 In blooming health they left the shore,
Ne'er thought they'd see their friends no more.
Down the Kickapoo on a raft
With DeJean the captain of the craft.

3 Down they floated down the Kickapoo,
Laughing and joking as raftmen do;
Ne'er thought their fate would come so soon
When death would rob them of their bloom.

4 When night came on, they made for shore,
Where they had often stayed before;
'Neath the same oak tree which had been their stake
They went to sleep, no more to wake.

5 The Captain viewed the tree once more
And spoke as he had oftentimes before,
Saying, "I fear, my boys, when it is too late,
This very oak will seal our fate."

6 Early next morning the Captain arose
And left his men in sweet repose.
For some wood he stepped out on the shore
For to [p]repare their breakfast o'er.

7 Scarcely had he stepped on shore
When, looking at the tree once more,
He saw it start and then did cry,
"Awake, my boys, or you must die."

8 There was none but Wilson that awoke,
When, with a crash, down came the oak.
The Captain stood out on the shore
And saw them sink to rise no more.

9 For three long hours they searched in vain,
Till at last two bodies they obtained.
'Twas Hatfield and Totten, two boys so brave,
But Robert still slept beneath the grave.

10 By land the Captain started home,
Both night and day he journeyed on,
Taking those brave boys home to their friends,
That they might see their last remains.

11   When the sun was setting in the west,
Those two brave boys were laid to rest.
Their friends stood weeping round their tomb,
No more to see them in their bloom.

12   'Twas but a glance and all was o'er,
Their friends could see their faces no more.
Poor Juliet, the Captain's wife,
It seemed 't would almost take her life.

13   The Captain strove to hide his grief,
But now he wrung his hands and cried,
Saying, "Oh, this is a bitter cup!
Aaron, how can I give up?"

14   Young Hatfield was the Captain's pride,
Long in his family did reside.
To him he seemed more like a son
Than like a child that was not their own.

15   Poor Robert's friends in deep despair,
They longed some tidings for to hear.
They searched the river for miles along
Till at Wyalusing his body was found.

16   And near the place where it was found
There may be seen a little mound.
'Twas strangers' hands that laid him there,
No friends to shed a farewell tear.

17   But since that time he was brought home.
Friends laid him in his earthly tomb.
Come, weeping mourners, dry your eyes,
Prepare to meet them in the skies.

18   Now think of those young and blooming youths
And travel no more on but what is truth.
For like a raft tied to a tree,
Every day there is a snare for thee.

30

The River in the Pines

Mr. William Bartlett, of Eau Claire, Wisconsin, sent me this piece, which he secured "from Ruth F. G." Beneath the title in the manuscript of the melody was the gloss, "The Chippewa River, Wisconsin."

From Mr. WILLIAM BARTLETT, Eau Claire, Wisconsin

1. Oh, Ma-ry was a maid-en when the birds be-gan to sing. She was fair-er than the bloom-ing rose so ear-ly in the spring. Her thoughts were gay and hap-py in the morn-ing gay and fine, For her lov-er was a riv-er-boy from the Riv-er in the Pines.

1 Oh, Mary was a maiden when the birds began to sing.
   She was fairer than the blooming rose so early in the sprmg.
   Her thoughts were gay and happy in the morning gay and fine,
   For her lover was a river-boy from the River in the Pines.

2 Now Charlie got married to this Mary in the spring,
   When the trees were budding early and the birds began to sing.

"Now, darling, I must leave you in the happiness of love,
And make some V's and X's for you, my darling dove.
And early in the autumn when the fruit is in the wine,
I'll return to you, my darling, from the River in the Pines."

3 'Twas early in the morning in Wisconsin's dreary clime
When he rode the fatal rapids for that last and fatal time.
They found his body lying on the rocky shores below,
Where the silent water ripples and the whispering cedars blow.

4 The woodsmen gathered round him on the bright and cloudless
   morn,
And with sad and tearful eyes they viewed his cold and lifeless
   form.
"I would send a message to her, but I fear she would repine,"
Spoke a friend of Charlie Williams from the River in the Pines.

5 When Mary heard these tidings from that river far away,
It was in the early springtime, in the early month of May.
At first she seemed uncertain and no more her eyes did shine,
But her saddened thoughts still wandered to that River in the
   Pines.

6 Not long ago I visited there, not many years ago;
It was a Southern city where strange faces come and go.
I spied a gray-haired maiden, both very old and gray,
And my thoughts turned back again once more to that river far
   away.

7 She smiled though when she saw me, though she looked old
   and gray.
"I am waiting for my Charlie boy," these words to me did say.
"And early in the autumn, when the fruit is in the wine,
I'll return to meet my Charlie from the River in the Pines."

8 Now every raft of lumber that comes down the Chippewa,
There's a lonely grave that's visited by drivers on their way.
They plant wild flowers upon it in the morning fair and fine;
'Tis the grave of Charlie Williams from the River in the Pines.

31

The Merry Shanty Boys

I am indebted to Professor Kittredge for this text, which pictures in vivid detail and in the most jovial of moods shanty life of the earlier day.

From a broadside published by H. J. WEHMAN, New York (No. 990)

1 We are a band of shanty boys, as merry as can be;
No matter where we go, my boys, we're always gay and free;
Blow high or low, no fear we know, to the woods we're bound
    to go,
Our axes swing, the woods do ring with shanty men, heighho!

Chorus
Blow high or low, no fear we know, to the woods we're bound
    to go,
Our axes swing, the woods do ring with shanty men, heighho!

2 At break of day the boss doth say: Hurrah, to the woods, away!
Those teams hitch up—get to the dump, the rollers are away!
The choppers are all gone, hurrah! Come, boys, do not delay—
Then whips do crack on every track, the teamsters are away.

3 And when our day's work we have done, home to the shanty
    come—
Each gang will boast who's done the most, the clerk our work
    doth sum;
Then clean and neat we take our seats, and for our suppers
    go—
Beef, pork and beans, eat all we please, bread, pie, molasses, oh!

4 When lined within, we then begin our axes to grind thin;
Come, fiddler gay, do not delay to tune up every string;
'Tis our delight!—yes, every night, to wrestle, dance, and sing,
Our songs all sung and dancing done, we roll in one by one.

5 When spring doth come we've jolly fun on the river drive away;
   Pull, ahoy! Heave away! Together, *Oh—yeh—oh!*
   The drive, when through, our lasses true, we'll meet them all so
      gay,
   And kiss for kiss will be our bliss, while we with them do stay.

6 Since shanty life is our delight, let's all together sing,
   Scorehackers, hewers, choppers, sawyers, road-cutters join in,
   Boss, cook, and clerk, for all your worth, now let your voices
      ring,
   Teamsters and all, on you we call, in chorus now dive in.

"We are a band of shanty boys." A Wisconsin crew of the 1870s or early 1880s. Note the special display of cant hook, saw, mascot, fiddle, and dinner horn. The last is held by the cook's helper, who, with the cook, is distinguishable by his apron. The exhibition of the manly art in the background is notoriously deficient in similarity to real shanty-boy fashion in fighting!

32

Silver Jack

The following comment is from Mr. Lomax, from whose *Cowboy Songs*, 331 ff., the present version of "Silver Jack" is reprinted: "I have always especially enjoyed another lumberjack ballad which you do not mention, entitled 'Silver Jack.' Silver Jack was a well-known character in the Michigan yards." As Mr. Lomax indicates, this ballad was adopted by the cowboys of the southeast. He printed the same text in the *Journal of American Folklore*, xxviii, 9–10 (1915), with the following note: "'Silver Jack' . . . was sent to me by Professor Edwin F. Gay. . . . He says that he got it from a lumber-camp in northern Michigan, and that it is probably not an original lumber-jack ballad. It is, however, very popular among the lumbermen. And Silver Jack, the hero of the poem, was a real person who lived near Saginaw, Michigan, and was well known among the camp and lumbermen as a hard case. About the same time that Professor Gay sent me this song, I received practically the identical song from Bay City, Tex. Thus one copy has come to me from lumbermen near Canada, and another from the canal-diggers close to the line of Old Mexico. . . . This particular ballad has a suspicious resemblance to newspaper verse." See also Pound, *Poetic Origins and the Ballad*, 229, where there are conjectures as to the authorship.

Reprinted from Lomax, *Cowboy Songs* (by permission)

1 I was on the drive in eighty
  Working under Silver Jack,
 Which the same is now in Jackson
  And ain't soon expected back,
 And there was a fellow 'mongst us
  By the name of Robert Waite;
 Kind of cute and smart and tonguey,
  Guess he was a graduate.

2 He could talk on any subject
    From the Bible down to Hoyle,
And his words flowed out so easy,
    Just as smooth and slick as oil.
He was what they call a skeptic,
    And he loved to sit and weave
Hifalutin' words together
    Tellin' what he didn't believe.

3 One day we all were sittin' round
    Smokin' nigger-head tobacco
And hearing Bob expound;
    Hell, he said, was all a humbug,
And he made it plain as day
    That the Bible was a fable,
And we 'lowed it looked that way.
    Miracles and such like
Were too rank for him to stand,
    And as for him they called the Savior
He was just a common man.

4 "You're a liar," some one shouted,
    "And you've got to take it back."
Then everybody started—
    'Twas the words of Silver Jack.
And he cracked his fists together
    And he stacked his duds and cried,
"'Twas in that thar religion
    That my mother lived and died;
And though I haven't always
    Used the Lord exactly right,
Yet when I hear a chump abuse him
    He's got to eat his words or fight."

5 Now this Bob he weren't no coward
    And he answered bold and free:

"Stack your duds and cut your capers,
    For there ain't no flies on me."
And they fit for forty minutes
    And the crowd would whoop and cheer
When Jack spit up a tooth or two
    Or when Bobby lost an ear.

6 But at last Jack got him under
    And he slugged him onct or twict,
And straightway Bob admitted
    The divinity of Christ.
But Jack kept reasoning with him
    Till the poor cuss gave a yell
And 'lowed he'd been mistaken
    In his views concerning hell.

7 Then the fierce encounter ended
    And they riz up from the ground,
And some one brought a bottle out
    And kindly passed it round.
And we drank to Bob's religion
    In a cheerful sort o' way,
But the spread of infidelity
    Was checked in camp that day.

33

Bung Yer Eye

This text is reprinted from *The Blazed Trail*. No title is given the song there; but on the strength of the fact that there was a well-known song called "Bung Yer Eye," and by reason of several encouraging hints, which I reproduce below, I presume to the extent of naming the song. This version of three stanzas, although it forms a sort of unity, is perhaps not the whole of the piece. Lomax, 252–53, prints a text ("The Shanty Boy") which is almost word for word identical with this.

The following comments have bearing on this song one way or another. The first is from *Paul Bunyan and His Big Blue Ox*, written and illustrated by W. B. Laughead, for the Red River Lumber Company, of Minneapolis: "After supper they [Paul's Seven Axemen] would sit on the deacon seat in the bunk shanty and sing 'Shanty Boy' and 'Bung Yer Eye' till the folks in the settlements down on the Atlantic would think another nor'wester was blowing up." Mr. Lomax ascribes the authorship of some song having the same refrain as this one to the aforementioned Silver Jack: "And I have another song by him which has the refrain 'Bung your eye, bung your eye!'" And in reply to an inquiry of mine concerning this song and a fragment (printed below), Mr. Stewart Edward White wrote: "The two songs you mention I can say very little more for than that in the eighties they were favorites with the shanty-boys. The Danny Randall song was probably 'Bung Yer Eye,' as you suggest. All these songs—like genuine cowboy songs—had many verses that varied with the locality. As to the other, I don't know its official name. Both songs are genuine, however."

In *The Blazed Trail* Mr. White describes the singing of "Bung Yer Eye" thus: "A single voice, clear and high, struck into a quick measure [here is given the stanza] . . . and then with a rattle and a crash the whole Fighting Forty shrieked out the chorus." The melody of the stanza he describes as "a mere minor chant."

The fragment (from *The Blazed Trail*), which belongs to "The Logger's Boast" (Gray, 18–21), is worth printing because it shows local adaptation:

Come all ye sons of freedom throughout old Michigan,
Come all ye gallant lumbermen, list to a shanty-man.
On the banks of the Muskegon, where the rapid waters flow,
Oh!—we'll range the wild woods o'er and a-lumbering we go.

The music of our burnished axe shall make the woods resound,
And many a lofty ancient pine shall tumble to the ground.
At night around our shanty fire we'll sing while rude winds blow.
Oh!—we'll range the wild woods o'er while a-lumbering we go.

Gray's text has "throughout the State of Maine" and "on the banks of the Penobscot."

Another fragment of this same "Logger's Boast" corresponding to Gray's sixth stanza was recited for me by Mr. Emmet Horen, of Eau Claire, Wisconsin:

When spring it does come and our ice-bound streams are free,
We will drive our logs to market our southern friends to see.
Our sweethearts they will welcome us, their eyes with rapture
    glow;
We'll spend the summer with them and again a-lumbering go.

From STEWART EDWARD WHITE, *The Blazed Trail* (by permission)

1 I am a jolly shanty-boy,
       As you will soon discover;
   To all the dodges I am fly,
       A hustling pine-woods rover.
   A peavy-hook it is my pride,
       An axe I well can handle.
   To fell a tree or punch a bull
       Get rattling Danny Randle.
           Bung yer eye! bung yer eye!

2 I love a girl in Saginaw,
       She lives with her mother.
   I defy all Michigan
       To find such another.

She's tall and slim, her hair is red,
   Her face is plump and pretty.
She's my daisy Sunday best-day girl,
   And her front name stands for Kitty.
     Bung yer eye! bung yer eye!

3 I took her to a dance one night,
   A mossback gave the bidding—
Silver Jack bossed the shebang,
   And Big Dan played the fiddle.
We danced and drank the livelong night
   With fights between the dancing,
Till Silver Jack cleaned out the ranch
   And sent the mossbacks prancing.
     Bung yer eye! bung yer eye!

34

Fragments of Shanty Songs

I. An unnamed fragment given me by Mrs. Douglas McKay, then of Park River, North Dakota. Her father, an old woodsman in Canada and Minnesota, recited the lines for her.

II. A ragged fragment of a Michigan woodsman's bacchanal, recited for me by Mr. Ava Smith, of Charlevoix, Michigan. I cannot vouch for the spelling of the proper names. The reciter could give me no help in the matter beyond reproducing the sound he remembered hearing.

III. A fragment of a ballad called "Kenneth Cameron," Mr. Springstad told me. The story of the song runs thus. Two drivers, Reading and McCrae, were out breaking a center jam which had formed on a rock in a rapids. Their boat was washed away from them, leaving them stranded on the jam, which was beginning to loosen. (In here occur the lines given.) Springstad was not sure whether Cameron succeeded in reaching the two men, but the bateau was poled for nearly an hour, he said, either by Cameron or the three of them, when finally he, or they, let the boat get too far crosswise and the swift current swamped it and the men were lost. Gilboyd was the foreman. James was a driver, and a married man. Cameron was an experienced boatman, and single.

I

'Twas on the Grand River near the falls of Chaudiere,
And these four men got into a boat and for them did steer.
There was Benjamin Moore and William Wright, and likewise
    A. C. Young.
These three men were drowned and from their boats were flung.

But James McCullum was preserved and safely swam ashore
Down by those rocks and islands where the mighty waters pour.
Let us not say in Nature God made one thing in vain,
For beneath those foaming waters does hideous rocks remain.

A little boy standing on the shore this dreadful sight did see,
And unto Benjamin's parents with the news did quickly flee.
There were fathers and mothers, kind brothers and sisters too,
They all came running to the shore to see if it were true.

And when they found their sons were lost and buried in the deep,
Their mournful cries did rend the skies, and they bitterly did
    weep,
Saying, "O you cruel waters, that brought our sons to rest,
What is your troubled motion to what lies on my breast?"

Look in the works of Nature, by water and by land,
And see the many ways God brings us to an end.
And yet, though blooming as you are, and death seems far away,
How soon it may overtake us for its easy prey.

II

Way down near Alpena in a far-distant land,
There's a hard-hearted, hard-spoken band,
Called paython, gorilla. They don't use much care,
And they're hard to keep track of when they get on a tear.

Chorus
Hurray, hurrah! For the fruit you can bet.
Less taken of the drink, boys, for their credit's good yet.

The other night they got on a tear.
Sam Gluffin he vowed he could whip any man there.
Charlie Kittson he climbed him as he laid on the sod.
Sam Gluffin fears nothing on the footstool of God.

The other night in Jim Woodrickson's saloon
Jim Todrick whipped Donnell, who thought himself some.
Sam Gluffin brought home a gallon to wind up the spree,
Saying, "That is the kind of a hairpin I be."

Whiskey, dear whiskey, from the hour of my birth,
Is dearer to me than what else on earth.

For days have I labored and days have I toiled,
And many a dollar for you I have spoiled.

III

Gilboyd gave orders to James to their assistance go,
To steer the boat through Miller's Falls that lurks the hidden
  foe.
Kenneth Cameron, he being standing by, those words to James
  did say,
"You stay on shore, and I will go, for it's dangerous to delay."

Three times the foreman warned him not, but it was of no use.
He sprang into the waitin' boat an' cut her loose . . .

35

The Backwoodsman

Mr. Bale secured this song from his grandmother, Mrs. M. A. Bearfield, of Ollie, Montana. Mrs. Bearfield was born in Wisconsin in 1851, and had learned "The Backwoodsman" from her grandparents, who came, Bale thought, from Connecticut.

From Mr. DWIGHT BALE, Grand Forks, North Dakota

1 As I got up one morning in eighteen hundred and five.
  I found myself quite happy to find myself alive.
  I geared up my horses my business to pursue,
  And went to hauling wood as I used for to do.

2 The still-house being open, the liquor being free,
  As one glass was empty there was another filled for me.
  Instead of hauling five loads, never hauled but three,
  For I got so drunk at Darby town I could hardly see.

3 On my way home I met an old acquaintance,
  He told me that night where there was to be a ball.
  Hard to persuade, but at length I did agree
  To meet him that night where the fiddle was to play.

4 I took the saddle on my back and went into the barn.
  . . . .
  I saddled up old Grey and rode away so still,
  And scarcely drew a long breath until I got to Toureneville.

5 My father followed after me, as I have heard them say.
  He must have had a pilot or he couldn't have found the way.
  He peeped through every keyhole where he could spy a light,
  Till his locks were all wet with the dews of the night.

6 Then four of us got upon the floor for to dance.
. . . .
The fiddler being willing, his arm it being strong,
Played "The Crowns of Old Ireland" full four hours long.

7 The morning star has dawned, my boys, and we have dance
enough.
We will spend one half an hour a-gathering cash for Cuff.
We'll go home to our plows and we'll whistle and we'll sing,
And never be caught in such a scrape again.

8 Come all you old people who carry the news about,
Come all you old people who make such a fuss,
. . . .
You are guilty of the same, or perhaps a damn sight worse.

36

Ole from Norway

Mrs. Hastings told me that "Ole from Norway" was a song from the "tie drive" in the Medicine Bow Mountains in southeastern Wyoming, where it has been used for the past thirty years. She knew no melody for it. The words were probably poured into the mould of some music-hall tune.

"*Som lever*," etc.: that is, *Som lever paa Lodsfisk og Sil*—"who lives on pilot-fish and launce."

From Mrs. FLO HASTINGS,
Laramie, Wyoming

1 I just come down from Minnesota,
  I've been in this country three years.
  When I got off at the depot,
  Oh, how the people they cheer!
  They say, "Here comes Ole from Norway!
  He's been on a visit up there,
  His sister she lives in Dakota,
  And his father has got light hair."

  Chorus
  And they call me Ole and Ole,
  But Ole is not my name.
  Ole, Ole, Ole, Ole just the same.
  They say I'm a Norsk from Norway,
  Som lever po Lutfisk ock Sil.
  They say I'm a rat and I better go back to Norway.

2 I got one fine job in the river
  A-chasing the ties down the stream.

235

With a big pole in hand, oh, wasn't it grand?
It seemed just like a dream.
When the ties make a bend down the river,
I give a big whoop and a yell,
My feet went co-splash in the water,
And I think I bane gone to—well—

37

Fair Charlotte

A widely prevalent song, supposed to be a native of Vermont and to be based upon an actual event. Barry (*Journal of American Folklore*, xxii, 367, 442; xxv, 156) ascribes it to William Lorenzo Carter, of Benson or Bensontown, Vermont, before 1833. For further references see Cox, *Folk-Songs of the South*, 286. Dean prints a version, 57–58, and sang the ballad for me, using a variant of the melody here recorded, which he said he learned in the shanties over in New York State in the eighteen-seventies.

Sung by Mr. ANDREW ROSS, Charlevoix, Michigan

1. Fair Char-lotte liv'd by the moun-tain side in a cold and dis-mal spot. No dwellings there for ten miles 'round ex-cept her fa-ther's cot. But oft-times on a win-ter's night young swains would gath-er there, Her fa-ther kept a so-cial board and she was ver-y fair.

1 Fair Charlotte liv'd by the mountain side in a cold and dismal
    spot.
  No dwellings there for ten miles round except her father's cot.
  But ofttimes on a winter's night young swains would gather
    there,
  Her father kept a social board and she was very fair.

2 Her father loved to see her dressed prim as a city belle.
  She was the only child he had and he loved his daughter well.
  In a village some fifteen miles off there's a merry ball to-night.
  Though the driving wind is cold as death, their hearts are free
    and light.

3 And yet how beams those sparkling eyes as the well-known
    sound she hears,
  And dashing up to her father's door young Charles and his
    sleigh appears.
  "O daughter dear," her mother said, "those blankets round you
    fold,
  For it is a dreadful night to ride and you'll catch your death of
    cold."

4 "Oh nay, oh nay," fair Charlotte said, and she laughed like a
    gipsy queen;
  "To ride with blankets muffled up one never would be seen."
  Her gloves and bonnet being on, she stepped into the sleigh,
  And away they ride by the mountain side, and it's o'er the hills
    and away.

5 There's music in those merry bells as o'er the hills we go.
  What a creaking noise those runners make as they strike the
    frozen snow!
  And muffled faces silent are as the first five miles are passed,
  When Charles with few and shivering words the silence broke at
    last.

6 "What a dreadful night it is to ride! My lines I scarce can hold."
  When she replied in a feeble voice, "I am extremely cold."

Charles cracked his whip and urged his team far faster than
  before,
Until at length five other miles in silence were passed o'er.

7 "Charlotte, how fast the freezing ice is gathering on my brow!"
When she replied in a feeble voice, "I'm getting warmer now."
And away they ride by the mountain side beneath the cold
  starlight,
Until at length the village inn and the ball-room are in sight.

8 When they drove up, Charles he got out and offered her his
  hand.
"Why sit you there like a monument that hath no power to
  stand?"
He asked her once, he asked her twice, but she answered not a
  word.
He offered her his hand again, but still she never stirred.

9 He took her hand into his own. 'Twas cold as any stone.
He tore the veil from off her face and the cold stars on her
  shone,
And quick into the lighted hall her lifeless form he bore.
Fair Charlotte was a frozen corpse, and a word she ne'er spoke
  more.

10 He took her back into the sleigh and quickly hurried home;
And when he came to her father's door, oh, how her parents
  moaned.
They mourned the loss of their daughter dear, while Charles
  wept o'er their gloom,
Until at length Charles died of grief and they both lay in one
  tomb.

38

James Bird[1]

This ballad, written by Mr. Charles Miner, of Wilkes-Barre, Pennsylvania, was first printed in Mr. Miner's paper, *The Gleaner*, sometime in April, 1814. Though Mr. Miner was not a singer, and wrote the poem with no thought of its being used as a song, it was appropriated almost overnight by the folk, and for nearly a century it held a dominant position among the songs of the American people. The stanzas have been printed so often, and with such uniformity of text, that their inclusion here is deemed unnecessary. For a text of the ballad see Pound, *American Ballads and Songs*, 93–97. For the original text, and an interesting account of the composition of the ballad and of the facts out of which the ballad grew, see Charles Francis Richardson and Elizabeth Miner (Thomas) Richardson, *Charles Miner, a Pennsylvania Pioneer*, 67–76.

Mr. Hankins learned this shanty-boy version of the ballad while working in the Minnesota woods about 1874. He had a typical folk-impression of Bird's "murder."

As sung by Mr. GEORGE M. HANKINS, Gordon, Wisconsin

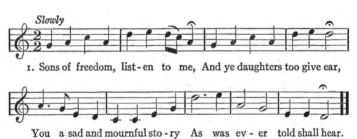

1. Sons of freedom, list-en to me, And ye daughters too give ear,
You a sad and mournful sto-ry As was ev-er told shall hear.

---

1. The full text of "James Bird" is omitted here because it is not appreciably different from those already printed many times and therefore generally accessible.

Sons of freedom, listen to me,
　And ye daughters too give ear,
You a sad and mournful story
　As was ever told shall hear.

. . . .

Farewell, Bird, farewell forever,
　Friends and home he'll see no more;
But his mangled corpse lies buried
　On Lake Erie's distant shore.

39

The Cumberland's Crew[1]

This ballad, celebrating the dramatic sinking of the Cumberland by the Confederate iron-clad, Merrimac, off Newport News in 1862, was described to me by Mr. Milloy as "a great favorite among the boys." He said further that many a time after he had sung it in the shanties one of the gang would speak up to say that if he could sing that song like Milloy could, he'd quit workin'! This was a common form of strong approval.

For a text of this ballad, with references and variant lines, see Gray, *Songs and Ballads*, 162–65. Dean, 36–37, also prints a version; also Shoemaker, 2d ed., 211–12.

As sung by Mr. M. C. DEAN, Virginia, Minnesota

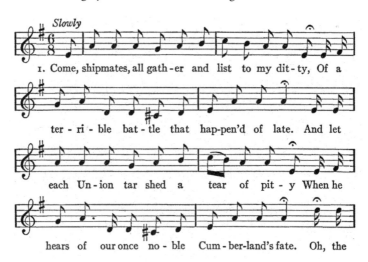

1. Come, shipmates, all gath-er and list to my dit-ty, Of a ter-ri-ble bat-tle that hap-pen'd of late. And let each Un-ion tar shed a tear of pit-y When he hears of our once no-ble Cum-ber-land's fate. Oh, the

---

1. The full text of "The Cumberland's Crew" is omitted here because it is not appreciably different from those already printed many times and therefore generally accessible.

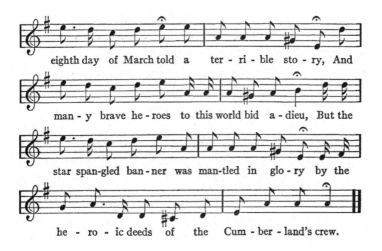

eighth day of March told a ter - ri - ble sto - ry, And

man - y brave he - roes to this world bid a - dieu, But the

star span-gled ban - ner was man-tled in glo - ry by the

he - ro - ic deeds of the Cum - ber - land's crew.

40

The Hunters of Kaintucky

"The Hunters of Kentucky"—often printed anonymously in song-books and broadsides, and included as by an "unknown" author in B. E. Stevenson's *Poems of American History*, 326–27—was written in 1822 by Samuel Woodworth, the poet of "The Old Oaken Bucket." It may be found in his *Melodies, Duets, Trios, Songs, and Ballads* (New York, 1826), 221–23, where it is said (252) to have been written for "Keene" (that is, Arthur Keene, a native of Ireland, who appeared first on the American stage in 1817, and soon became famous as a tenor singer) and the tune is designated as "Miss Baily"—that is, of course, Coleman's famous song beginning "A captain bold of Halifax." A copy in *The American Naval and Patriotic Songster* (Baltimore, 1836), 56–58, is marked "As sung by Mr. Ludlow in the New Orleans and Western Country Theatres." See N. M. Ludlow, *Dramatic Life as I Found It*, 237–38, 241, 250–51. I give the tune that was sung for me by Mr. Hankins, but as his text of the poem is slightly defective, I print instead, as Version B, the text from Woodworth's volume. Note that Mr. Hankins's refrain differs slightly from that of the original.

For this tune and an account of it, see W. Chappell, *Popular Music of the Olden Time*, ii, 713–14, under the title "The Golden Days of Good Queen Bess." I quote the following from the comment there: "The earliest form in which I have found this tune is as 'No more, fair virgins, boast your power,' introduced in *Love in a Riddle*, in 1729. It has three other names, "The Golden Days of Good Queen Bess," "Ally Croaker," and "The Unfortunate Miss Bailey." The hunters of Kentucky were the Kentucky riflemen, about two thousand in number, who figured so dominantly in General Andrew Jackson's repulse of the forces of the British General, Packenham, at New Orleans, January 8, 1815.

For most of this note I am indebted to Professor Kittredge and Mr. R. G. Shaw.

A

As sung by Mr. GEORGE M. HANKINS, Gordon, Wisconsin

1. Ye gen - tle - men and lad - ies fair, Who grace this fa - mous

cit - y, Just list - en, if you've time to spare, While

I re - hearse a dit - ty; And for the op - por -

tu - ni - ty, Con - ceive your-selves quite luck - y, For it's

hard - ly ev - er that you see a hunt - er from Kain-

CHORUS

tuck - y. Oh, Kain - tuck - y, The hunt - ers of Kain-

tuck - y; Oh, Kaintuck - y, The hunt - ers of Kain - tuck - y.

B

The Hunters of Kentucky (Air: "Miss Baily")

From *Melodies, Duets, Trios, Songs, and Ballads*, by SAMUEL WOODWORTH, New York, JAMES M. CAMPBELL, 1826, 221–23.

1   Ye gentlemen and ladies fair,
    Who grace this famous city,
Just listen, if ye've time to spare,
    While I rehearse a ditty;
And for the opportunity,
    Conceive yourselves quite lucky,
For 'tis not often that you see
    A hunter from Kentucky.
Oh! Kentucky, the hunters of Kentucky,
    The hunters of Kentucky.

2   We are a hardy free-born race,
    Each man to fear a stranger,
Whate'er the game, we join in chase,
    Despising toil and danger;
And if a daring foe annoys,
    Whate'er his strength and forces,
We'll show him that Kentucky boys
    Are "alligator horses."
Oh! Kentucky, the hunters of Kentucky,
    The hunters of Kentucky.

3   I s'pose you've read it in the prints,
    How Packenham attempted
To make Old Hickory Jackson wince,
    But soon his scheme repented;
For we with rifles ready cock'd
    Thought each occasion lucky,
And soon around the General flock'd
    The hunters of Kentucky.
        Oh! Kentucky, etc.

4 You've heard, I s'pose, how New Orleans
    Is famed for wealth and beauty—
There's girls of every hue, it seems,
    From snowy white to sooty;
So Packenham he made his brags,
    If he in fight was lucky,
He'd have their girls and cotton bags,
    In spite of Old Kentucky.
        Oh! Kentucky, etc.

5 But Jackson, he was wide awake,
    And wasn't scared at trifles;
For well he knew what aim we take,
    With our Kentucky rifles;
So he led us down to a cypress swamp,
    The ground was low and mucky;
There stood John Bull, in martial pomp,
    And here was Old Kentucky.
        Oh! Kentucky, etc.

6 A bank was raised to hide our breast,
    Not that we thought of dying,
But then we always like to rest
    Unless the game is flying;
Behind it stood our little force—
    None wished it to be greater,
For every man was half a horse,
    And half an alligator.
        Oh! Kentucky, etc.

7 They did not let our patience tire,
    Before they showed their faces—
We did not choose to waste our fire,
    So snugly kept our places;
But when so near we saw them wink,
    We thought it time to stop them;
And 'twould have done you good, I think,

To see Kentucky pop them.
 Oh! Kentucky, etc.

8 They found at last 'twas vain to fight
  Where lead was all their booty,
And so they wisely took to flight,
  And left us all the beauty.
And now, if danger e'er annoys,
  Remember what our trade is,
Just send for us Kentucky boys,
  And we'll protect you, Ladies.
   Oh! Kentucky, etc.

41

The Flying Cloud

This is the ballad of which it was said that, in order to get a job in the Michigan camps, one had to be able to sing it through from end to end!

Gray, *Songs and Ballads of the Maine Lumberjacks*, 116–23, prints two versions, one from Maine and the other from Michigan, and refers to still others from Nova Scotia (Mackenzie, *The Quest of the Ballad*, 151–53) and Scotland (Greig, *Folk-Songs of the North-East*, cxviii). Colcord, *Roll and Go*, 72–75, also prints a version with a melody and several paragraphs of comment on the song and its background. The name of the speaker varies: "Edward Hollohan" (Maine), "Edward Hallahan" (Michigan), "Robert Anderson" (Nova Scotia), "William Hollander" (Scotland), "Willie Hollander" (Dean, 1–2), "Edward Hollander" (Colcord). The melody recorded by Colcord is a variant of the one given here.

Sung by Mr. ARTHUR C. MILLOY, Omemee, North Dakota

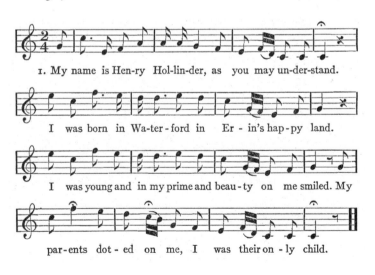

1. My name is Hen-ry Hol-lin-der, as you may un-der-stand.
   I was born in Wa-ter-ford in Er - in's hap-py land.
   I was young and in my prime and beau-ty on me smiled. My
   par-ents dot - ed on me, I was their on - ly child.

1 My name is Henry Hollinder, as you may understand.
   I was born in Waterford in Erin's happy land.
   I was young and in my prime and beauty on me smiled.
   My parents doted on me, I was their only child.

2 My father bound me to a trade in Waterford's fair town.
   He bound me to a cooper there by the name of William
      Brown.
   I served my master faithfully for eighteen months or more,
   And I stepped aboard the Ocean Queen bound for Belfraser's
      shore.

3 When I landed at Belfraser, I fell in with Captain More,
   Commander of the Flyin' Cloud goin' out from Baltimore.
   He asked me if I'd hire on a slavin' voyage to go
   To the burning shores of Africa, where the sugar cane does
      grow.

4 The Flyin' Cloud was as fine a ship as ever sailed from shore.
   She could easily sail round any craft going out from Baltimore.
   Her sheets was as white as the driven snow and on them not
      one speck,
   And forty-nine brass powder guns she carried on her deck.

5 In about three weeks sailing we reached the African shore.
   We took five hundred negro men to be slaves for evermore.
   We made them march out on our plank and stowed them down
      below.
   Scarcely eighteen inches to a man was all they had to go.

6 Next day we set sail again with our cargo of slaves.
   It would have been better for those poor souls if they were in
      their graves.
   The plague and fever came on board, swept half of them away.
   We dragged their bodies across our decks and hove them in the
      sea.

7 In about six weeks after, we reached the Cuban shores,
   And sold them to the planters there to be slaves for evermore,

To sow the rice and coffee seed and toil out in the sun,
And lead a hard and wretched life till their creear [career] was
done.

8 When our money was all spent, brave boys, we put to sea again,
And Captain More he came on board and sayed unto his men,
"There's gold and silver to be had if with me you'll remain.
We'll hist aloft a pirate's flag and scour the Spanish main."

9 We all agreed but five brave lads. We told those boys to land.
Two of them were Boston boys, two more from Newfoundland
The other was an Irish lad from the town of sweet Trymore.
I wish to God I'd joined those lads and gone with them on
shore.

10 We robbed and plundered many's the ship down on the Spanish
main.
We left many's the widow and orphan in sorrow to remain.
Their crews we made them walk our planks, gave them a watery
grave.
The saying of our captain was that dead men tells no tales.

11 Pursued we were by many a ship, by liners and frigates too,
. . . .[1]
But 'twas always in our stern-ways their cannons roared aloud.
It was all in vain for them to try to catch the Flyin' Cloud.

12 At length the Spanish man-o'-war with vengeance hove in view.
They fired a shot across our decks, a signal to lay to.
We paid to them no answer, but flew before the wind,
When a chain-shot broke our mizzen-mast and then we fell
behind.

13 We cleared our decks for action as they hove up 'longside,
And across our quarter decks, brave boys, they fired a crimson
tide.

---

1. The missing line reads: "But for to catch the Flying Cloud was a thing they
ne'er could do." [Dean.]

We fired till Captain More was shot and eighty of his men,
And a bomb-shell set our ship afire; we were forced to surrender
then.

14 Fare ye well to the shady groves and the girl that I adore.
Her dark brown eyes and curly hair I'll never see no more.
I'll never kiss her ruby lips nor press her soft white hand,
For I must die a scornful death out in some foreign land.

15 It's next to ———² I was brought, bound down in iron chains,
For the robbing and plundering of ships we saw down on the
Spanish main.
It was whiskey and bad company that made a rake of me.
So, youth, beware of my sad fate and shun bad company.

---

2. New Gate [Dean]; Newgate [Colcord].

42

The Clipper Ship Dreadnaught

Properly a sea ballad. But the "woods were full" of Irishmen who had literally sailed the Seven Seas. The high seas, mixed with piracy or not, had a largeness about them which appealed to shanty-boy nature. For other texts see Colcord, *Roll and Go*, 89–91; Whall, *Sea Songs and Shanties*, 4th edition (Glasgow, 1920), 12–13; S. B. Luce, *Naval Songs*, 2nd edition, 63; *Partridge's New National Songster*, ii, 131; Wehman broadside, No. 742.

The text here printed is from Dean, 58–59. Colcord records a melody whose relationship to the present one is slightly traceable.

Sung by Mr. M. C. DEAN, Virginia, Minnesota

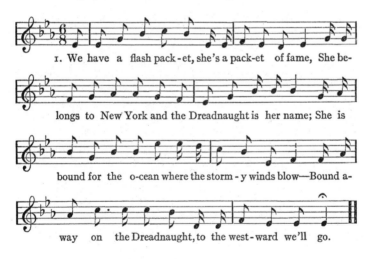

1. We have a flash pack-et, she's a pack-et of fame, She be-longs to New York and the Dreadnaught is her name; She is bound for the o-cean where the storm-y winds blow—Bound a-way on the Dreadnaught, to the west-ward we'll go.

1 We have a flash packet, she's a packet of fame,
 She belongs to New York and the Dreadnaught is her name;
 She is bound for the ocean where the stormy winds blow—
 Bound away on the Dreadnaught to the Westward we'll go.

2 Now we are lying at the Liverpool dock,
   Where the boys and the girls on the pier-heads do flock,
   And they gave us three cheers while their tears down did flow—
   Bound away on the Dreadnaught to the Westward we'll go.

3 The Dreadnaught is lying in the River Mersey,
   Waiting for the tug Constitution to tow us to sea;
   She tows around the Black Rock where the Mersey does flow—
   Bound away on the Dreadnaught to the Westward we'll go.

4 And now we are howling on the wild Irish Sea,
   Where the sailors and passengers together agree,
   For the sailors are perched on the yardarms, you know—
   Bound away on the Dreadnaught to the Westward we'll go.

5 Now we are sailing on the ocean so wide,
   Where the great open billows dash against her black side,
   And the sailors off watch are all sleeping below—
   Bound away on the Dreadnaught to the Westward we'll go.

6 And now we are sailing off the banks of Newfoundland,
   Where the waters are deep and the bottom is sand,
   Where the fish of the ocean they swim to and fro—
   Bound away on the Dreadnaught to the Westward we'll go.

7 And now we are howling off Long Island's green shore,
   Where the pilot he bards [boards] us as he's oft done before,
   Fill away your main topsails, port your main tack also,
   She's a Liverpool packet, Lord God, let her go.

8 And now we are riding in New York Harbor once more,
   I will go and see Nancy, she's the girl I adore,
   To the parson I'll take her, my bride for to be;
   Farewell to the Dreadnaught and the deep stormy sea.

43

Bold Daniel

"Bold Daniel" has some resemblance to "The Saucy Dolphin" (Greig, *Folk-Songs of the North-East*, cxxv), which begins:

> On the fourteenth of June, my boys,
>> In Liverpool where we lay,
> A-waiting for fresh orders,
>> Our anchors for to weigh.

Both songs may be imitated from "Hawke's Engagement" (Firth, *Naval Songs and Ballads*, 217: "The Fourteenth of September, in Torbay as we lay"). The present text is from Dean, 39–40.

Sung by Mr. M. C. DEAN, Virginia, Minnesota

1. On the four-teenth day of Jan-u-a-ry, From Eng-land we set sail. . . . We were bound down to La-guire, With a sweet and pleas-ant gale. The Rov-ing Liz-zie we are call'd; Bold Dan-iel is my name, And we sail'd a-way to Laguire, Just out of the Span-ish main.

1 On the[1] fourteenth day of January
    From England we set sail.
We were bound down to Laguire,
    With a sweet and pleasant gale.
The Roving Lizzie we are called;
    Bold Daniel is my name,
And we sailed away to Laguire,
    Just out of the Spanish main.

2 And we reached Laguire,
    Our orders did read so:
"When you discharge your cargo,
    It's sail for Callao."
Our captain called all hands right aft,
    And unto us did say,
"Here is money for you today, my lads,
    For to-morrow we'll sail away."

3 It was early the next morning,
    As daylight did draw nigh,
The man from at the mast-head
    A stranger sail did espy;
With a black flag under her mizzen peak
    Came bearing down that way;
"I'll be bound she is some pirate,"
    Bold Daniel he did say.

4 In the course of three or four hours,
    The pirate ranged alongside,
And with a speaking trumpet,
    "Where are you from?" he cries.
"The Roving Lizzie we are called,
    Bold Daniel is my name,
And we sailed away from Laguire,
    Just out of the Spanish main."

---

1. Dean (39) prints: "It was on the . . ." But this is as he sang it.

5 "Come, back your topsails to your mast,
   And heave your ship under my lee."
"Oh, no! oh, no!" cried Daniel,
   "I'd rather sink at sea."
They hoisted up their bloody flag,
   Our hearts to terrify;
With their big guns to our small arms
   At us they did let fly.

6 We mounted four six-pounders
   To fight a hundred men,
And when the action did begin,
   It was just about half-past ten.
We mounted four six-pounders,
   Our crew being twenty-two;
In the course of an hour and a quarter
   Those pirates we did subdue.

7 And now our prize we've taken
   Unto Columbia's shore,
To that dear old place in America
   They call sweet Baltimore;
We'll drink success to Daniel,
   Likewise his gallant crew,
That fought and beat that pirate
   With his noble twenty-two.

44

Paul Jones, the Privateer

Colcord, *Roll and Go*, 60–62, prints a text of this vigorous old sea ballad, which is known also as "The Ranger," "The Yankee Man-of-War," and "The Stately Southerner," and which "recounts an exploit of John Paul Jones off the Irish coast in his privateer, the Ranger, which was fitted out in Portsmouth, N. H., in 1777" (61). The melody recorded by Colcord resembles faintly the one given here.

"King Sail": i.e., "Kinsale."

A

Sung by Mr. M. C. DEAN, Virginia, Minnesota

1. It's of a gal-lant south-ern bark that bore the stripes and stars; And the fresh'ning breeze from the west-sou'-west sung through her pitch-pine spars. All with her lar-board tack in-board she hung up-on the gale . . As one autumn's night she rais'd the light under head of old King Sail.

1 It's of a gallant southern bark that bore the stripes and stars,
And the freshening breeze from the west-sou'-west sung through
her pitch-pine spars.
All with her larboard tack inboard she hung upon the gale
As one autumn's night she raised the light under head of old
King Sail.

2 It being a clear and cloudless night, though the wind blew fresh
and strong,
But lightly o'er the channel waves the frigate she rolled on,
And far beyond her foaming bows the dashing waves did spread,
With her bow so low in the drifting spray she buried her lee
cat-head.

3 No thought was there of shortening sail by him who trod her
poop.
And by the weight of her ponderous jib her boom bent like a
hoop,
And her groaning cross-trees told the strain that lay on her stout
main-tack.
But he only laughed as he glanced abaft at her bright and
sparkling track.

4 On Hook Bay Point that starry set four bells had tolled the
hour.
The beacon light shines brightly forth that burns in Wicklow
Tower.
The mist lies heavy along the land and reaches off from shore
To the outer point of Cape Bantra, to the heights of Conamore.

5 What did this daring stranger do when a shot came from ahead?
Hauled up his courses to the wind and his flowing topsails
spread.
With his booms inboard came running down with the white
swell on his bow.
"Fear not, my gallant southern men! Spare not your good ship
now."

B

The Yankee Man-of-War

From *American War Ballads*, (80–82), edited by G. C. Eggleston

1 'Tis of a gallant Yankee ship that flew the stripes and stars,
And the whistling wind from the west-nor'-west blew through
the pitch-pine spars,
With her larboard tacks aboard, my boys, she hung upon the
gale,
On an autumn night we raised the light on the old head of
Kinsale.

2 It was a clear and cloudless night, and the wind blew steady and
strong,
As gaily over the sparkling deep our good ship bowled along;
With the foaming seas beneath her bow the fiery waves she
spread,
And bending low her bosom of snow, she buried her lee
cat-head.

3 There was no talk of short'ning sail by him who walked the
poop,
And under the press of her pond'ring jib, the boom bent like a
hoop!
And the groaning water-ways told the strain that held her stout
main-tack,
But he only laughed as he glanced aloft at a white and silv'ry
track.

4 The mid-tide meets in the channel waves that flow from shore
to shore,
And the mist hung heavy upon the land from Featherstone to
Dunmore,
And that sterling light in Tusker Rock where the old bell tolls
each hour,
And the beacon light that shone so bright was quench'd on
Waterford Tower.

5 The nightly robes our good ship wore were her three topsails
   set,
Her spanker and her standing jib—the courses being fast;
"Now, lay aloft! my heroes bold, let not a moment pass!"
And royals and top-gallant sails were quickly on each mast.

6 What looms upon our starboard bow? What hangs upon the
   breeze?
'Tis time our good ship hauled her wind a-breast the old
   Saltee's,
For by her ponderous press of sail and by her consorts four,
We saw our morning visitor was a British man-of-war.

7 Up spake our noble Captain then, as a shot ahead of us past—
"Haul snug your flowing courses! lay your topsail to the mast!"
Those Englishmen gave three loud hurrahs from the deck of
   their covered ark,
And we answered back by a solid broadside from the decks of
   our patriot bark.

8 "Out booms! out booms!" our skipper cried, "out booms and
   give her sheet";
And the swiftest keel that was ever launched shot ahead of the
   British fleet,
And amidst a thundering shower of shot with stun'-sails
   hoisting away,
Down the North Channel Paul Jones did steer just at the break
   of day.

45

Red Iron Ore

A Great Lakes ballad celebrating the earlier traffic in iron ore from Michigan. It follows perfectly its model, the sea ballad of the "Clipper Ship Dreadnaught" type, a sort of log of the trip. The element of monotony is somewhat relieved in this case by the feat of overhauling the Minch.

This text is printed by Dean, 12–14. The melody given here is a variant of that used for "The Little Brown Bulls" (No. 13). The refrain words are identical.

Sung by Mr. M. C. DEAN, Virginia, Minnesota

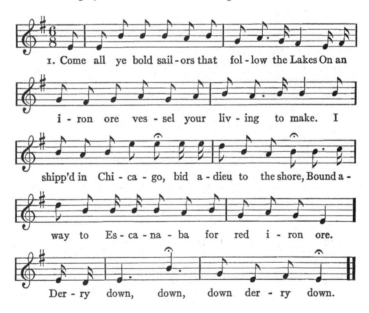

1. Come all ye bold sail-ors that fol-low the Lakes On an i-ron ore ves-sel your liv-ing to make. I shipp'd in Chi-ca-go, bid a-dieu to the shore, Bound a-way to Es-ca-na-ba for red i-ron ore. Der-ry down, down, down der-ry down.

1 Come all you bold sailors that follow the Lakes
 On an iron ore vessel your living to make.
 I shipped in Chicago, bid adieu to the shore,
 Bound away to Escanaba for red iron ore.
  Derry down, down, down derry down.

2 In the month of September, the seventeenth day,
 Two dollars and a quarter is all they would pay,
 And on Monday morning the Bridgeport did take
 The E. C. Roberts out in the Lake.

3 The wind from the south'ard sprang up a fresh breeze,
 And away through Lake Michigan the Roberts did sneeze.
 Down through Lake Michigan the Roberts did roar,
 And on Friday morning we passed through death's door.

4 This packet she howled across the mouth of Green Bay,
 And before her cutwater she dashed the white spray.
 We rounded the sand point, our anchor let go,
 We furled in our canvas and the watch went below.

5 Next morning we hove alongside the Exile,
 And soon was made fast to an iron ore pile,
 They lowered their shutes and like thunder did roar,
 They spouted into us that red iron ore.

6 Some sailors took shovels while others got spades,
 And some took wheelbarrows, each man to his trade.
 We looked like red devils, our fingers got sore,
 We cursed Escanaba and that damned iron ore.

7 The tug Escanaba she towed out the Minch,
 The Roberts she thought she had left in a pinch,
 And as she passed by us she bid us good-bye,
 Saying, "We'll meet you in Cleveland next Fourth of July!"

8 Through Louse Island it blew a fresh breeze;
 We made the Foxes, the Beavers, the Skillagalees;
 We flew by the Minch for to show her the way,
 And she ne'er hove in sight till we were off Thunder Bay.

9 Across Saginaw Bay the Roberts did ride
With the dark and deep water rolling over her side.
And now for Port Huron the Roberts must go,
Where the tug Kate Williams she took us in tow.

10 We went through North Passage—O Lord, how it blew!
And all round the Dummy a large fleet there came too.
The night being dark, Old Nick it would scare.
We hove up next morning and for Cleveland did steer.

11 Now the Roberts is in Cleveland, made fast stem and stern,
And over the bottle we'll spin a big yarn.
But Captain Harvey Shannon had ought to stand treat
For getting into Cleveland ahead of the fleet.

12 Now my song it is ended, I hope you won't laugh.
Our dunnage is packed and all hands are paid off.
Here's a health to the Roberts, she's staunch, strong and true;
Not forgotten the bold boys that comprise her crew.
    Derry down, down, down derry down.

46

The Persian's Crew

An elegiac ballad commemorating a tragedy shrouded in mystery. An instance of how the old singers put themselves into their songs is afforded by Mr. Milloy, the singer of the version of which only the melody is given (B). Instead of singing "they" he sang "we," quite forgetting that no one escaped from the unhappy Persian.

The text of Version A is printed by Dean, 29–30. The melody given for this version is that of Billy Allen's "Driving Saw-logs on the Plover" (No. 20). Colcord also prints the ballad "The Persian's Crew," 111–12, with a melody different from either of those recorded here.

Sung by Mr. M. C. DEAN, Virginia, Minnesota

1. Sad and dis - mal is the sto - ry that I will tell to you, .. A - bout the schoon - er *Per - sian*, her of - fi - cers and crew. They sank be - neath the wa - ters deep, in life to rise no more, Where wind and de so - la - tion sweeps Lake Hu - ron's rock-bound shore.

1 Sad and dismal is the story that I will tell to you,
About the schooner Persian, her officers and crew.
They sank beneath the waters deep, in life to rise no more,
Where wind and desolation sweeps Lake Huron's rock-bound
    shore.

2 They left Chicago on their lee, their songs they did resound;
Their hearts were filled with joy and glee, for they were
    homeward bound.
They little thought the sword of death would meet them on
    their way,
And they so full of joy and life would in Lake Huron lay.

3 In mystery o'er their fate was sealed. They did collide, some say.
And that is all that will be revealed until the Judgement day.
But when the angels take their stand to sweep these waters blue,
They will summon forth at Heaven's command the Persian's
    luckless crew.

4 No mother's hand was there to soothe the brow's distracted
    pain.
No gentle wife for to caress those cold lips once again.
No sister nor a lover dear or little ones to moan,
But in the deep alone they sleep, far from their friends and
    home.

5 Her captain, he is no more; he lost his precious life.
He sank down among Lake Huron's waves, free from all mortal
    strife.
A barren coast now hides from view his manly, lifeless form,
And still in death is the heart so true that weathered many a
    storm.

6 There was Daniel Sullivan, her mate, with a heart as true and
    brave
As ever was compelled by fate to fill a sailor's grave.
Alas! he lost his noble life; poor Daniel is no more.
He met a sad, untimely end upon Lake Huron's shore.

7 O Daniel, Dan, your many friends mourn the fate that has on
  you frowned.
  They look in vain for your return back to Oswego town.
  They miss the love-glance of your eye, your hand they'll clasp
  no more,
  For still in death you now do lie upon Lake Huron's shore.

8 Her sailors' names I do not know, excepting one or two.
  Down in the deep they all did go, they were a luckless crew.
  Not one escaped to land to clear the mystery o'er,
  Or to lie adrift by Heaven's command in lifeless form ashore.

9 Now around Presque Isle the sea birds scream their mournful
  notes along,
  In chanting to the sad requiem, the mournful funeral song,
  They skim along the waters blue and then aloft they soar
  O'er the bodies of the Persian's crew that lie along the shore.

B

Lake Huron's Rock-bound Shore

As sung by Mr. ART C. MILLOY, Omemee, North Dakota

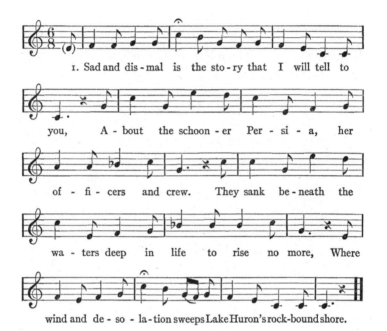

1. Sad and dis-mal is the sto-ry that I will tell to you, A-bout the schoon-er Per-si-a, her of-fi-cers and crew. They sank be-neath the wa-ters deep in life to rise no more, Where wind and de-so-la-tion sweeps Lake Huron's rock-bound shore.

47

The Bigler's Crew

This time from Milwaukee to Buffalo. Otherwise not very different, if one excepts the refrain, which makes the singing of the ballad almost an all-day affair. The various "crew" songs and ballads are parallel to the "shanty-man's life" songs in many respects.

This text is printed by Dean, 19–20. Colcord prints a version ("The Cruise of the Bigler"), 109–11, with a melody which varies very little from the one given here.

Sung by Mr. M. C. DEAN, Virginia, Minnesota

1. Come all my boys and list-en, . . a song I'll sing to you. It's all a-bout the Big-ler . . and of her jol-ly crew. In Mil-wau-kee last Oc-to-ber I chanc'd to get a sight In the schooner call'd the Big-ler be-long-ing to De-troit.

CHORUS

Watch her, catch her, jump up on her jub-er ju. . . Give her the sheet and let her slide, The boys will push her through. You

ought to seen us howl-ing, The winds were blowing free, On our

pas - sage down to Buf-fa - lo . . from Mil - wau - kee.

1 Come all my boys and listen, a song I'll sing to you.
It's all about the Bigler and of her jolly crew.
In Milwaukee last October I chanced to get a sight
In the schooner called the Bigler belonging to Detroit.

Chorus
Watch her, catch her, jump up on her jub er ju.
Give her the sheet and let her slide, the boys will push her
through.
You ought to seen us howling, the winds were blowing free,
On our passage down to Buffalo from Milwaukee.

2 It was on a Sunday morning about the hour of ten,
The Robert Emmet towed us out into Lake Michigan;
We set sail where she left us in the middle of the fleet,
And the wind being from the south'ard, oh, we had to give her
sheet.

3 Then the wind chopped round to the sou'-sou'west and blew
both fresh and strong,
But softly through Lake Michigan the Bigler she rolled on,
And far beyond her foaming bow the dashing waves did fling.
With every inch of canvas set, her course was wing and wing.

4 But the wind it came ahead before we reached the Manitous.
Three dollars and a half a day just suited the Bigler's crew.
From there unto the Beavers we steered her full and by,
And we kept her to the wind, my boys, as close as she would
lie.

5 Through Skillagalee and Wabble Shanks, the entrance to the
      Straits,
   We might have passed the big fleet there if they'd hove to and
      wait;
   But we drove them on before us, the nicest you ever saw,
   Out into Lake Huron from the Straits of Mackinaw.

6 We made Presque Isle Light, and then we boomed away,
   The wind it being fair, for the Isle of Thunder Bay.
   But when the wind it shifted, we hauled her on her starboard
      tack
   With a good lookout ahead for the Light of the Point
      Aubarques.

7 We made the Light and kept in sight of Michigan North Shore,
   A-booming for the river as we'd ofttimes done before.
   When right abreast Port Huron Light, our small anchor we let go
   And the Sweepstakes came alongside and took the Bigler in tow.

8 The Sweepstakes took eight in tow and all of us fore and aft,
   She towed us down to Lake St. Clare and stuck us on the flats.
   She parted the Hunter's tow-line in trying to give relief,
   And stem and stern went the Bigler into the boat called Maple
      Leaf.

9 The Sweepstakes then she towed us outside the River Light,
   Lake Erie for to roam and the blustering winds to fight.
   The wind being from the south'ard, we paddled our own
      canoe,
   With her nose pointed for the Dummy she's hell bent for
      Buffalo.

10 We made the Oh and passed Long Point, the wind was blowing
       free.
    We howled along the Canada shore, Port Colborne on our lee.
    What is it that looms up ahead, so well known as we draw near?
    For like a blazing star shone the light on Buffalo Pier.

11 And now we are safely landed in Buffalo Creek at last,
And under Riggs' elevator the Bigler she's made fast.
And in some lager beer saloon we'll let the bottle pass,
For we are jolly shipmates and we'll drink a social glass.

Chorus
Watch her, catch her, jump up on her juber ju.
Give her the sheet and let her slide, the boys will push her
   through.
You ought to seen us howling, the winds were blowing free,
On our passage down to Buffalo from Milwaukee.

48

Morrissey and the Russian Sailor

This text is printed (without the tune) by Dean, 4–5. A variant may be found in *Delaney's Song Book No. 17*, 21. This puts the fight on the tenth of March, and has one more stanza after the eighth of Mr. Dean's version:

> The Irish offered four to one that day upon the grass,
> No sooner said than taken up, and down they brought the cash.
> They parried away without delay to the 32nd round,
> When Morrissey received a blow that brought him to the
>   ground.

See also Manus O'Conor, *Old Time Songs and Ballads of Ireland*, 30.

The hero of this ballad—John Morrissey (1831–78), pugilist, gambler, M. C. from New York, State Senator—fought many battles—with George Thompson ("Pete Crawley's Big 'Un," whose real name is said to have been Bob M'Laren), on Mare Island, California, in 1852; with James Sullivan (known as Yankee Sullivan) at Boston Corners, New York, in 1853; with Heenan, the Benicia Boy, at Long Point, Canada, in 1858—not to speak of less formal combats like that with Bill Poole celebrated in the ballad of "Rough and Tumble," or "The Amos Street Fight" (Andrews broadside, New York, List 1, No. 91). But no trace of any combat with a Russian sailor has been discovered in Morrissey annals. See *Life of John Morrissey, the Irish Boy Who Fought His Way to Fame and Fortune* (New York, 1878); *The World* (New York), May 2, 1878; *New York Semi-Weekly Tribune*, May 3, 1878, 12; John B. McCormick, *The Square Circle* (New York, 1897), 100–111; "The Great Prize Fight Which Took Place at Boston Corners" (Andrews broadside, List 1, No. 90); "Morrissey and Heenan Fight" (De Marsan broadside, List J, No. 69; cf. O'Conor, *Irish Com-All-Ye's*, 44). (Kittredge.)

Sung by Mr. M. C. DEAN, Virginia, Minnesota

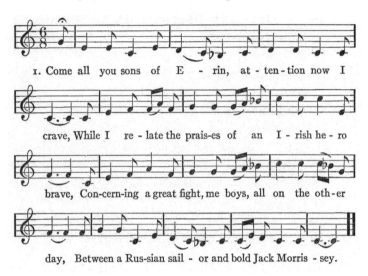

1. Come all you sons of E - rin, at - ten - tion now I crave, While I re - late the prais-es of an I - rish he - ro brave, Con-cern-ing a great fight, me boys, all on the oth-er day, Between a Rus-sian sail - or and bold Jack Morris - sey.

1 Come all you sons of Erin, attention now I crave,
   While I relate the praises of an Irish hero brave,
   Concerning a great fight, me boys, all on the other day,
   Between a Russian sailor and bold Jack Morrissey.

2 It was in Terra del Fuego, in South America,
   The Russian challenged Morrissey and unto him did say,
   "I hear you are a fighting man, and wear a belt I see.
   What do you say, will you consent to have a round with me?"

3 Then up spoke bold Jack Morrissey, with a heart so stout and
        true,
   Saying, "I am a gallant Irishman that never was subdued.
   Oh, I can whale a Yankee, a Saxon bull or bear,
   And in honor of old Paddy's land I'll still those laurels wear."

4 These words enraged the Russian upon that foreign land,
   To think that he would be put down by any Irishman.
   He says, "You are too light for me. On that make no mistake.
   I would have you to resign the belt, or else your life I'll take."

5 To fight upon the tenth of June these heroes did agree,
And thousands came from every part the battle for to see.
The English and the Russians, their hearts were filled with glee;
They swore the Russian sailor boy would kill bold Morrissey.

6 They both stripped off, stepped in the ring, most glorious to be
seen,
And Morrissey put on the belt bound round with shamrocks
green.
Full twenty thousand dollars, as you may plainly see,
That was to be the champion's prize that gained the victory.

7 They both shook hands, walked round the ring, commencing
then to fight.
It filled each Irish heart with joy for to behold the sight.
The Russian he floored Morrissey up to the eleventh round,
With English, Russian, and Saxon cheers the valley did resound.

8 A minute and a half our hero lay before he could rise.
The word went all around the field: "He's dead," were all their
cries.
But Morrissey raised manfully, and raising from the ground,
From that until the twentieth the Russian he put down.

9 Up to the thirty-seventh round 'twas fall and fall about,
Which made the burly sailor to keep a sharp lookout.
The Russian called his second and asked for a glass of wine.
Our Irish hero smiled and said, "The battle will be mine."

10 The thirty-eighth decided all. The Russian felt the smart
When Morrissey, with a fearful blow, he struck him o'er the
heart.
A doctor he was called on to open up a vein.
He said it was quite useless, he would never fight agam.

11 Our hero conquered Thompson, the Yankee Clipper too;
The Benicia boy and Shepherd he nobly did subdue.
So let us fill a flowing bowl and drink a health galore
To brave Jack Morrissey and Paddies evermore.

49

Heenan and Sayers

Professor Kittredge has given me the following note:

This ballad (printed by Dean, 24–25), celebrates the great fight between Tom Sayers (1826–65), then champion of the prize ring, and John C. Heenan (the Benicia Boy), which took place on April 17, 1860, at Farnborough, Hampshire. In the thirty-seventh round, after two hours and six minutes of fighting, the ring was invaded by the mob. The struggle went on, after a fashion, for five rounds more, so that its actual duration was two hours and twenty minutes (see H. D. Miles, *Pugilistica*, Edinburgh, 1906, iii, 427–33; Ed. James, *The Life and Battles of John C. Heenan*, 5–17). The result was declared a draw, but Sayers retired from the championship in the following month. A broadside song of the period (Bebbington, Manchester, No. 495) entitled "Heenan and the Irish Yankee" makes Heenan say:

> "Well! here I am, my lads! your bouncing will not daunt me;
> I am the bold Benicia Boy—the proud Hibernian Yankee;
> I am come to lick your man; right well I begin it,
> Before him I did stand two hours and six minutes."

It is interesting to note the contradiction between the accounts given by two distinguished men who witnessed the fight. According to Locker-Lampson, "The battle ended in a disgraceful scene of riot and blackguardism, especially among the backers of Sayers, who as soon as they saw their money was in extreme peril, broke into the ring" (*My Confidences*, 2nd edition, 1896, 258). Lord Redesdale (then Mr. Mitford) saw with other eyes: "There can be no reasonable doubt that if Heenan's friends, seeing his plight, had not forced their way inside the ropes and broken the ring, five more minutes must inevitably have given Tom Sayers a glorious victory" (*Memories*, 5th edition, 1915, i, 121). John Mackenzie of New York, the author of a broadside ballad on "Heenan and Sayers," of course agrees with Locker-Lampson:

But then the thirty-seventh round came on to be the last;
The Briton's friends they plainly saw their man was failing fast;
When Heenan gave him another blow, which made them feel
    forlorn—
The Briton's friends jumped in the ring and said the fight was
    drawn.

(De Marsan broadside, List II, No. 37; Wehman broadside, No. 690; Henry de Marsan's *Comic and Sentimental Singer's Journal*, ii, 21.)

Frank Leslie's Illustrated Newspaper, May 12, 1860, gives a full account of the fight, with remarkable pictures from ringside sketches by Alfred Berghaus. One of them covers four pages. That which figures Round 37 includes in its legend the statement: "The friends of both parties break into the ring, and the scene becomes one of the wildest excitement, amidst cries of 'Police! police!'"

An English song sounds impartial:

And when the Hampshire bobbies did break into the ring,
There was no doubt tho' both good men were glad for to give in,
Long titling, boxing, fighting, lots of claret they did spill.
Like two game cocks they would have fought till they did each
    other kill.

("Sayers and Heenan's Struggle for the Championship and £400," broadside, Bebbington, No. 475.) The police did, in fact, interfere when the disorder became violent.

Punch (April 28, 1860) published a poetical account of the fight in the style of "Horatius at the Bridge": "The Combat of Sayerius and Heenanus, A Lay of Ancient London" (reprinted in *Pugilistica*, ii, 439–43). This has been ascribed to Thackeray.

There are several other British and American songs on this fight: see De Marsan broadsides, List 10, No. 24; List II, Nos. 22, 25, 34–38, 84; *Arlington's Comic Banjo Songster* (Philadelphia, copyright 1860), 12–14.

A

From Mr. M. C. DEAN, Virginia, Minnesota

1 It was in merry England, the home of Johnnie Bull,
  Where Britons fill their glasses, they fill them brimming full;
  And of the toast they drank, it was to Briton's brave,
  And it is long may our champion bring victories o'er the wave.

2 Then up jumps Uncle Sammy and he looks across the main,
  Saying, "Is that your English bully I hear bellowing again?
  Oh, has he not forgotten the giant o'er the pond
  Who used to juggle cannon-balls when his day's work was
     done?"

3 "Remember, Uncle Johnnie, the giant stronger grows;
  He is always on his muscle and ready for his foes.
  When but a boy at Yorktown I caused you for to sigh,
  So whene'er you boast of fighting, Johnnie Bull, mind your
     eye."

4 It was in merry England all in the blooming spring,
  When this burly English champion he stripped off in the ring.
  He stripped to fight young Heenan, our gallant son of Troy,
  And to try his English muscle on our bold Benicia Boy.

5 There were two brilliant flags, my boys, a-floating o'er the ring.
  The British were a lion all ready for a spring.
  The Yankee was an eagle, and an awful bird she was,
  For she carried a bunch of thunderbolts well fastened in her
     claws.

6 The coppers they were tossed, me boys, the fighting did begin.
  It was two to one on Sayers the bets came rolling in.
  They fought like royal heroes until one received a blow,
  And the red crimson torrent from our Yankee nose did flow.

7 "First blood, first blood, my Tommy boy," the English cried
     with joy.
  The English cheer their hero, while the bold Benicia Boy,

The tiger rose within him, like lightning flared his eye,
Saying, "Mark away, old England; but Tommy, mind your eye."

8 The last grand round of all, my boys, this world has ne'er seen
   the beat,
When the son of Uncle Sammy raised the champion from his
   feet.
His followers did smile while he held him in the air,
And from his grasp he flung him, which caused the English
   men to stare.

9 Come, all you sporting Americans, wherever you have strayed,
Look on this glorious eagle and never be afraid.
May our Union last forever and our flag the world defy,
So whenever you boast of fighting, Johnnie Bull, mind your eye.

B

The Bold Benicia Boy

Printed by R. W. GORDON in *Adventure Magazine*,
September 20, 1923

1 It was down in merrie England
   All in the bloom of spring,
And England filled her glasses,
   She filled them to the brim;
She drank this toast to Englishmen:
   "The bravest of the brave,
Who rule all men or whether it be
   On land or on the wave."

2 Then Uncle Sam put on his specs
   As he looked o'er the main.
"And is this your English bully
   A-bellowin' again?
Oh, doesn't he remember
   Ben Franklin good and strong,

Who used to play with lightning
    When his day's work was done?

3 "Johnny Bull, don't you remember
        Our Washington of old,
    And likewise Lake E-r-i-e,
        With Perry brave and bold?
    It was there you got a lesson
        Which caused you for to sigh;
    So beware of Yankee muscle—
        Johnny Bull, mind yo' eye."

4 It was down in merrie England
        All in the bloom of spring,
    And England's bold champion
        Stood stripped within the ring
    To fight the noble Heenan,
        The valiant son of Troy,
    And to try his British muscles on
        The brave Benicia Boy.

5 Oh the copper was now tossed in air;
        The minutes did begin.
    "It's two to one," said England;
        They both went rushin' in.
    They fought like noble heroes
        Till one received a blow,
    And the red crimson tide
        From the Yankee's nose did flow.

6 "We have got first blood," cried Johnny Bull,
        "Let England shout for joy,"
    Which cheered the British bully.
        And the brave Benicia Boy,
    The tiger rose within him,
        The lightning seized his eye;
    "You may smile away, old England,
        But, Johnny, mind yo' eye."

7 Then the grandest round of all
   That the world has ever seen:
The son of Uncle Sam took up
   The champion off his feet,
And with his grasping withers
   He hurled him in the air,
And over the ropes he knocked him—
   How the Englishmen did stare.

8 Then come all you Yankee heroes
   Whose fame and fortune's made,
Look on that lofty eagle
   And never be afraid!
May the Union last forever!
   The flag is now unfurled
And the Star-Spangled Banner
   Proudly floats o'er the world!

50

The Dying Soldier

An immigrant song growing out of Irish service in the British army in India. "Britannia's Queen," referred to in some versions of the song, became Empress of India in 1876. Dean (5–6) prints a version of this song.

Mr. Ross has sung a great many songs and ballads for me. On one occasion we were sitting at this work, and Mrs. Ross was sewing nearby. Upon hearing her husband state after at least five or six songs that evening, "I learned that one my first winter in the woods," she remarked quietly, "You must have had a lot to do that first winter in the woods!"

Sung by Mr. ANDREW ROSS, Charlevoix, Michigan

1. The sun went down on A - sia's shores when the
dead - ly fight was o'er, . . And thous-ands lay on the
bat - tle - field till it could hold no more. The
pale moon shone on the bat - tle - field where the
dy - ing sol - dier lay, And the shad-ows of death a -
round him crept while his life's blood ebb'd a - way.

1 The sun went down on Asia's shores when the deadly fight
     was o'er,
   And thousands lay on the battlefield till it could hold no more.
   The pale moon shone on the battlefield where the dying soldier
     lay,
   And the shadows of death around him crept while his life's
     blood ebbed away.

2 A passing comrade heard a moan and quickly the sufferer
     found,
   Saying, "Gently lift my aching head from off this cold damp
     ground."
   Saying, "Softly, gently, comrade dear; not long with you I'll
     stay.
   I will no more roam in my childhood's home in old Erin far
     away.

3 "A lock of my hair I'd have you bear to my mother far over the
     sea,
   And every time that she'd look at it she would fondly think of
     me.
   Tell her although on India's shore my mold'ring bones shall lay,
   That my heart still clings to old Ireland, to old Erin far away.

4 "Go tell my sister though years have passed since last I saw her
     face,
   Her form is still present in my mind, her features I can trace;
   Tell her at home I will no more roam where in childhood we oft
     did play,
   In those merry green glades and grassy shades in old Erin far
     away.

5 "Go tell my brother how nobly we fought, and just like our
     fathers, died,
   With bayonets charging on the foe and scabbards by our side.
   It nerves my heart to conquer, these Sepoys for to slay"—
   When a vision so bright rolled over his sight of old Erin far
     away.

6   The dying soldier heaved a sigh as he tried to raise his head.
    His spirit went from this wide, wide world and the soldier he
        lay dead.
    His grave was made and in it laid that doom of a warrior's day,
    Far, far from his home and the friends he loved in old Erin far
        away.

7   His comrades gathered around his grave for to take their last
        farewell.
    'Tis of as brave and true a heart as ever in battle fell.
    And as they lowered him in his grave, his spirit seemed to say,
    "I will no more roam in my childhood's home, in old Erin far
        away."

51

Daniel Monroe

For this song—also known as "Donald Monroe," "Monroe's Tragedy," and "The Sons of North Britain"—see Logan, *A Pedlar's Pack*, 1869, 413–15 (from a Scottish chapbook of about 1778); Mackenzie, *Journal of American Folklore*, xxv, 184–85; Barry, the same, xxvi, 183–84. The two latter variants are from Nova Scotia. (Kittredge.)

This was another ballad that Mr. Ross learned that "first winter in the woods."

Sung by Mr. ANDREW ROSS, Charlevoix, Michigan

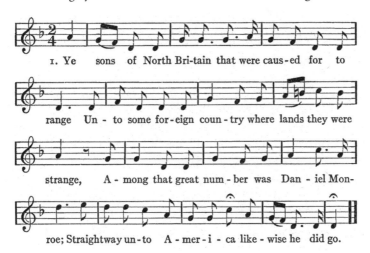

1. Ye sons of North Bri-tain that were caus-ed for to range Un - to some for-eign coun - try where lands they were strange, A - mong that great num - ber was Dan - iel Mon-roe; Straightway un-to A - mer - i - ca like-wise he did go.

1 Ye sons of North Britain that were caused for to range
Unto some foreign country where lands they were strange,
Among that great number was Daniel Monroe;
Straightway unto America likewise he did go.

2 Two sons it was their father advised them to stay.
The price of their passage he could not well pay.

"But be ye contented; stay with your uncle here.
The price of your passage, you know, will be dear."

3 Being discontented, they roamed till they found
Afloat brig-a-mantle to America bound,
In which they enlisted, cross over the main,
In hopes for to meet their parents again.

4 When they landed, America they spied,
Surrounded by ruffians on every side.
With humble submission these two brothers went
Unto their good captain to gain his consent.

5 To which their good captain was pleased for to say
They might go up the country their parents for to see.
And leaving the ship, with a boy for a guide,
To show them the place where their parents reside,

6 They traveled along till they came to a grove.
The leaves and the branches they all seemed to move;
There being two ruffians concealed in the wood,
Presented their pieces where the two brothers stood.

7 Lodging a bullet in each of their breasts,
They rushed on their prey like two ravenous beasts,
To take all their money and rip up their clothes,
And if they're not dead, for to give them some blows.

8 One of them lived. He lifted up his eyes.
As death is approaching, these words he then cries:
"You ravenous villains, you blood thirsty hounds,
You ought not to kill up us until we had found,

9 "Found out our dear parents whom we've sought with care.
We have not seen them for seven long years.
They left us in Scotland, some seven years ago.
Perhaps you might know them; their names were Monroe."

10 The old man astonished with wonder he stood
A-gazing on his sons who lay bleeding in the wood.

"A curse on my hands! I slained my son!
I've blamed my hard fortune for what I have done."

11 "If you be my father," the young man then cries,
"I'm glad for to see you before that I die.
And since it is so, no better it can be,
We'll blame our hard fortune, dear father, not thee."

12 "Oh who is this young man that lies by your side?
Oh who is this young man?" the old man then cried.
"'Tis my only brother, and your youngest son.
The crime would be less had I fallen alone.

13 "There is one advice I'd give you, dear father," he cries,
"To leave off rebellion, and in time to be wise.
And don't tell my mother, if yet she doth live,
That we are both dead, for I fear she would grieve."

14 "I sink beneath sorrow, give way to despair.
I'll linger awhile until death ends my care.
I hope for to meet you on a happier shore
Where I won't be able to kill you any more."

PART THREE

Forgotten Songs from the
Rickaby Manuscripts

By Franz Rickaby and James P. Leary

Introduction

F RANZ RICKABY'S notebooks of "Ballads and Songs"—266 items in fourteen manuscript volumes held in the Wisconsin Music Archives of Mills Music Library at the University of Wisconsin–Madison—reveal an abiding interest in traditional songs of all sorts, encompassing yet extending beyond the realm of Upper Midwestern lumber camps. Throughout his too brief adult life, with characteristic focused frenzy, Rickaby sought songs from women as well as men; from strangers on his treks through Michigan, Wisconsin, and Minnesota; and from students, colleagues, and friends while teaching in North Dakota, Wyoming, and California.

Thanks to a newspaper story in the *Grand Forks Herald*, April 2, 1923, we know that, despite failing health, Rickaby boldly imagined publishing "two books of ballads. One of these books is to be called *Specimens of American Balladry*, and will illustrate the . . . general divisions of the ballad. The other book will be composed of songs of the lumbermen's camps under the title of *Deacon-Seat Ballads*. The book gets its name from the deacon seat, the seat around the lower tier of bunks." *Deacon-Seat Ballads*, the basis of Rickaby's landmark publication, *Ballads and Songs of the Shanty-Boy*, occupies the first of his fourteen volumes. The other ballads and songs, fully listed at the close of this section, were never published.

Setting down lyrics, tunes, and brief notes on singers, songs, and sources, which often included places and dates, Rickaby categorized his hard-won trove of "specimens" in relation to American Wars (from the Revolution through World War I); Cowboys; the Later Frontier (miners and freight haulers); European origin (England, Ireland, Germany); Sailors (chanteys, ballads of the sea, Great Lakes, rivers); Biography and Autobiography (including immigrants' songs); Catastrophe; Lovers and Relatives, Faithful and Faithless; Indians and Dialects (Stage Irish, Stage Dutch); Propaganda and Social Class; Nursery and Games (including a Norwegian song); and Miscellaneous local occurrences. Whether wholly conceived as early as 1919, when he began teaching "The Popular Ballad of England and America" at North Dakota, or influenced by the pioneering publication of *American Ballads and Songs* by Nebraska folklorist Louise Pound in 1922, Rickaby's inclusive classification system, with its emphasis on historical moments and social phenomena in American life, was the most expansive of its era.

The fourteen songs selected here from Rickaby's unpublished volumes, two in multiple versions, numerically extend the sequence of *Ballads and Songs of the Shanty-Boy*, and I have supplemented his notes for each with additional biographical and comparative details. Gathered between 1919 and 1923 from singers living or raised in Michigan, Wisconsin, and Minnesota, most are also set in the region. Representing the full range of folksongs Rickaby encountered in the Upper Midwest, departing from the ethnocentric Anglophile limitations typifying the era's folksong catchers, they chronicle the experiences and perspectives of immigrants, exiles, ditch diggers, deckhands, farmers, miners, soldiers, hunters, rovers, and neighbors; of Anglo-Americans, Canadians, Dakota Sioux, Germans, Ho-Chunk (Winnebago), Irish, Norwegians, Ojibwe (Chippewa), and Swedes; and of ordinary singers and citizens whose voices would otherwise have vanished.

52

Forget Me Not

This is my only attempt (so far) to record a melody sung by an Indian. I heard a young fellow of the Winnebagos sing at a Kiwanis Club luncheon when I was in Eau Claire, and detained him afterward to see what I could do with the melody. He sang so indistinctly and the rhythm and tune were so elusive that I didn't have much luck. I can't believe that he was a very good singer. The young fellow called himself Chief White Eagle.

The title given here is the nearest he could come to giving me a name for the song (in English). The song was that of an Indian lover leaving his sweetheart.

Leary: The young Ho-Chunk (Winnebago) singer self-identified as Chief White Eagle was very likely Winslow White Eagle. Born near La Crosse around 1896, he began performing as early as 1916 for tourists and civic groups under the name Chief White Eagle. In 1919, four years prior to the probable date of Rickaby's presence at the Kiwanis Club program in Eau Claire, Winslow White Eagle had become a regular in the newly launched Stand Rock Indian Ceremonial at Wisconsin Dells.

White Eagle subsequently performed Fish Dance, Green Corn Dance, Horse Dance, War Dance, Women's Dance, Medicine Lodge, Moccasin Game, Night Spirit Bundle, and Peyote Lord's Prayer songs for cylinder recordings made by Frances Densmore in 1928 and 1930, and by Huron Smith in 1928, for the Smithsonian Institution's Bureau of American Ethnology. In 1946 he performed additional songs for Charles Hofmann and Helene Stratman-Thomas, who were making recordings in Wisconsin Dells for the Archive of American Folk Song at the Library of Congress. And he also sang eight songs on March 1, 1958—including "Air Raid on Iwo Jima" and "Korea War Song"—that were issued on a CD in 1996, one hundred years after his birth, as "Winnebago Tribal Songs."

In 1995, Ken Funmaker Sr., a formidable singer who knew more than three hundred traditional songs, remembered White Eagle as an "excellent singer. . . . He could really control his voice. He had that kind of flutter in his voice. He could really sing. He'd go right up to falsetto and right down to a real deep bass. Even in the same song, he could go with that range" (James P. Leary, *Folksongs of Another America: Field Recordings from the Upper Midwest, 1937–1946* [Madison: University of Wisconsin Press: 2015], 217–20).

Rickaby's assessment of singing skill may have stemmed from unfamiliarity with Ho-Chunk vocal style and song structure, combined with the awkwardness of White Eagle's being asked to sing by a stranger in the aftermath of a service club luncheon.

Sung by CHIEF WHITE EAGLE, Eau Claire, Wisconsin

53

Minnehaha, Laughing Water

Words and melody given me by Miss Florence Miller, of Grafton, North Dakota, a member of one of my classes. Date: December 2, 1919. She did not know any name for the song, which was given to her by an aunt, I believe.

The following note was affixed to the manuscript: "As the song indicates, it was written by a man who had lost his mind when his family was killed by the Indians at the New Ulm massacre, in Minnesota."

Leary: In August 1862, starving and goaded by the chicanery of Indian agents, Dakota people attacked farms and settlements in the Minnesota River valley, including the heavily German community of New Ulm. The "Dakota Uprising" was soon quelled by the United States Army, and thirty-eight Dakota men were hanged in December 1862, the largest mass execution in American history.

Florence Miller, Rickaby's song source, was born in 1902 and raised on a farm in Walsh County, North Dakota, just west of the Minnesota border. Her parents had emigrated from Canada in the mid-1860s, shortly after the Dakota Uprising, which also included attacks on Fort Abercrombie, in Dakota Territory, along the Red River just south of present-day Fargo.

In *A Thrilling Narrative of the Minnesota Massacre and the Sioux War of 1862–63* (Chicago: A. P. Connolly, 1896), Alonzo Putnam Connolly attributes "Minnehaha, Laughing Water" to "Captain Chittenden, of Colonel McPhail's command, [who] while sitting a few days after, under the Falls of Minnehaha, embodied in verse this wonderful tragedy" (23–24). *Minnehaha* (waterfall, in Dakota) was the name of Hiawatha's lover in Longfellow's 1855 epic poem, *The Song of Hiawatha*. Chittenden's muse, Minnehaha Falls, is situated in Minneapolis, near the era's major military base, Fort Snelling. His original differs only slightly from Florence Miller's: Fido, the quintessential name for a faithful dog, appears instead of Dido, an ill-fated Carthaginian queen; and Lela, not Lena, is the bereft farmer's wife.

From a manuscript provided by
Miss FLORENCE MILLER, Grafton, North Dakota

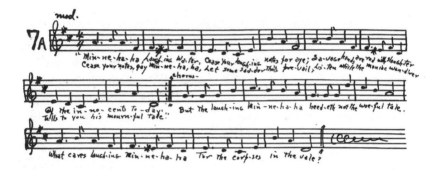

1   Minnehaha, Laughing Water,
    Cease your laughing notes for aye,
    Savage hands are red with slaughter
    Of the innocents today.
    Cease your notes, gay Minnehaha,
    Let some sadder thoughts prevail;
    Listen while the maniac wanderer
    Tells to you his mournful tale.

    Chorus
    But the laughing Minnehaha
    Heedeth not the woeful tale.
    What cares Laughing Minnehaha
    For the corpses in the vale?

2   "Yonder smoke that was my dwelling,
    That is all I've left of home.
    Hark! I hear the fiendish yelling
    As I childless, homeless roam
    Did they slay my Hans and Otto?
    Did they find them in the corn?

Go and tell yond fiendish monster
Not to slay my youngest born!

3 "Bring me back my Lena's tresses,
Let me kiss them once again;
She that blessed me with caresses
Lies unburied on the plain.
Yonder is my new-bought reaper
Standing in the ripening grain;
E'en my cow asks why I leave here
Standing unmilked on the plain.

4 "Oh, my daughter Jennie, darling!
Worse than death was Jennie's fate.
Nelson, as the troupes were leaving,
Turned and closed the garden gate.
Faithful Dido they have left me.
Dido, can you tell me why
That so soon God hast bereft me?
All I ask is here to die."

54

The Indian's Lament

A. Recited for me by Art Alcock, Charlevoix, Michigan, August, 1919. No melody remembered. Had heard the ballad sung a number of years previous, and the singer wrote it down for him. He said he was much moved by the song at the time, and felt keenly the tragedy of the Indian as expressed in the verses, almost to the point of forswearing white society. He added, however, that he had come to feel quite differently about the matter since he had learned more about the Indian as a class!

B. From Mrs. K. C. Mills, Park River, North Dakota. Lived at Dacre, Ontario. A lumbering company on Comstock Creek. Her father a millwright who couldn't read. Mr. Alcock was also a native of Canada (Ontario).

Leary: Arthur "Archie" Alcock (1866–1933) was born in Uxbridge Township, south central Ontario, to an English father, Simon Alcock (1830–1915), and a Canadian mother, Anna Jane Widdifield Alcock (1834–1887). Sometime in the 1880s young Alcock immigrated to Charlevoix, where he was a laborer in 1889 when he married Lydia Shaver, a housemaid. By 1900 Alcock was working as a clerk, and in 1905 he represented Charlevoix's third ward on the city council (http://durancefarm.com/content/charlevoix-history, accessed February 9, 2015). Alcock's Canadian community was also known as Quaker Hill, and perhaps it was through the Society of Friends that he acquired this song, along with youthful sympathy for Native peoples?

Rickaby's note is all we know about "Mrs. K. C. Mills." Census records list many Canadian-born people named Mills in Park River, North Dakota, but none with those initials.

"The Indian's Lament," also known as "The Birchbark Canoe" and "An Old Indian," has been sung throughout eastern Canada, and folklorists have encountered it often. In 1929 Helen Creighton collected a version from Benjamin H. Henneberry of Devils Island, Nova Scotia, publishing it as number 121 in *Songs and Ballads from Nova Scotia* (Toronto and Vancouver: J. M. Dent, 1933). MacEdward Leach's early 1950s field recording from Newfoundland singer Cyril O'Brien can be heard online, thanks to a website launched in 2004 by the Folklore and Language Archive of Memorial University–Newfoundland: *MacEdward Leach and the Songs of Atlantic Canada* (http://www.mun.ca/folklore/ leach/songs/NFLD2/8A-01_51.htm, accessed February 23, 2015). Edith Fowke included a version from Geraldine Sullivan, an Irish Canadian from the Peterborough area, on an LP of field recordings, *Folk Songs of Ontario* (New York: Folkways Records, FW04005, 1958). Yet another version, collected by Kenneth Peacock from Mrs. Thomas Walters of Rocky Harbour, is in *Songs of the Newfoundland Outports* (Ottawa: National Museum of Canada, 1965), 1:157–58.

Earl Clifton Beck included a version from "Mrs. Pringle, of Tawas City" in *Songs of the Michigan Lumberjacks* (Ann Arbor: University of Michigan Press, 1942), 221–22. Beck published the same version subsequently in *Lore of the Lumber Camps* (Ann Arbor: University of Michigan Press, 1948), 281–82; this time stating that "the song was widely sung in the woods of the Great Lakes region" and mentioning other Michigan singers who knew it: "Mrs. Alice Briggs of Birch Run, Bill McBride of Isabella City, Foster Hayward of Maple Rapids, Carl Lathrop of Pleasant Valley, and Bill Ellis of Oscoda."

A

Recited by ART ALCOCK, Charlevoix, Michigan

1 An Indian who sat in his little canoe,
  Sailing along o'er the water so blue.
  He sang of the days when the lands were his own,
  Before the pale-face amongst them were known.

2 "When first the Red Man was lord of the soil
  They lived at their ease and was free from all toil.
  They hunted the beaver, the otter, the deer,
  For they knew in their own woods they had nothing to fear.

3 "When first the White Man came into our land
  We met them like brothers and gave them our hand.
  We knew they were weary; we gave them repose,
  Never thinking those White Men would soon be our foes.

4 "But soon they began to encroach on our rights.
  They increased in their numbers, which caused us to flight.
  They drove us away from our own happy homes,
  Where the smoke of our fires shall rise there no more.

5 "They built their large villages on our rich land,
  And on our high mountains their farm houses stand.
  They own the whole country, from Texas to Maine,
  And the red deer is driven away from the plain.

6 "The graves of our forefathers, where are they now?
  They've been rudely run over and turned by the plow.
  The now wandering children, neglected and poor,
  And the homes of their parents they'll visit no more.

7 "But now we'll go eastward our graves for to find,
  Hoping to meet with the White Man again.
  When our forefathers calls us away from the plain
  In that bright happy world we will meet there again.

8 "And there we shall wander in that happy place,
  And there shall the parents their children embrace.
  No more shall those White Men encroach on our rights
  Nor cause the poor Indian in sorrow to flight."

B

From Mrs. K. C. MILLS, Park River, North Dakota

1 The old Indian he sits in his little canoe
  And he paddles away over the waters so blue,
  And he thinks on the time when the lands were his own,
  Before those pale-faces among them were known.

2 "When first those pale-faces they came to our land,
We met them like brothers and gave them our hand.
We knew they were weary and needed repose,
But we ne'er dreamed those white men would e'er turn foes.

3 "The graves of our forefathers, where are they now?
They've been rudely upturned by the harrow and plow.
They have claimed all our cities from Texas to Maine,
And they've driven the red deer away from the plain.

4 "We have hunted the beaver, the elk, and the roebuck . . .
We knew in the wild wood there was nothing to fear . . ."

55

The Dark British Foes

From Mr. Fred Bainter, Ladysmith, Wisconsin. Learned from his mother when a small boy. He had heard the song as long as he could remember. His mother came from Scotland, first to Indiana, then to Wisconsin. This song was also a great favorite of Mr. Bainter's father.

Leary: Fred Bainter (1856–1927) was born in Baraboo, Wisconsin, the eldest of seven children. His father, Peter Bainter (1823–1895), was a saloonkeeper and soon-to-be Civil War soldier who hailed from Ohio. Fred's singing mother, Martha Jane Cochran (1837–1918), was only thirteen when she married in 1850. Sometime in the 1870s the Bainters moved north to the Bloomer area in Chippewa County. Fred married Deborah Purcell, a widow with three children, in 1880, and made his living as a hired laborer and lumberjack. A widower by the 1890s, he settled near Ladysmith, where he married Frances "Fannie" Gallagher (1856–1929), whose parents had come from Ireland. Both Fred and his youngest brother, Joe, contributed songs to Rickaby's original publication (6A, 13A, 14B).

"The Dark British Foes," also known as "Edwin and Mary," includes sailor/soldier sweethearts, a fair maid left behind, and slow recognition succeeded by joyous reunion, all of which abound in Euro-American balladry, especially in narrative folksongs of English and Irish origin. Emelyon Elizabeth Gardner and Geraldine Jencks Chickering, for example, included five such examples in *Ballads and Songs of Southern Michigan* (Ann Arbor: University of Michigan, 1939), 152–59, 225–26. Yet there are only two other reported instances of Bainter's song: one heard by Virginia folklorist Louis W. Chappell in 1924 and a fourteen-verse nineteenth-century broadside published in Maryland (Chappell, *Folk-Songs of Roanoke and the Albermarle* [Morgantown, WV: Ballad Press, 1939], and http://collections.digitalmaryland.org/cdm/singleitem/collection/mdbv/id/201/rec/1, accessed February 27, 2015). Probably inspired by the War of

1812, when captured American merchant seamen were pressed into service by the British navy, the song is also localized to the Upper Midwest as the sailor lands "at Hudson," a prominent Wisconsin sawmill town in the Saint Croix River valley.

From FRED BAINTER, Ladysmith, Wisconsin

1. The dark British foes was invading our soil And pressing our young men in slavery and war. Young Edwin he bade his fair Mary a-dieu, And they said when they parted their love would prove true.

1 The dark British foes was invading our soil
And pressing our young men in slavery and war.
Young Edwin he bade his fair Mary adieu,
And they said when they parted their love would prove true.

2 Then this young warrior undaunted and brave,
Put on his tarpolian to fight on the waves,
To fight on the deep waters where the loud cannons roar,
To fight for his country and his dear native shore.

3 He had not been gone more than weeks two or three
When Mary no tidings from Edwin could hear.
She asked of each breeze as they below gently by
If they'd brought her no tidings from her sailor boy.

4 To add to her misfortunes, her parents both died,
Which left her abandoned on life's flowing tide.
It seemed her misfortune that caused her to roam
From the scenes of her childhood, her juvenile home.

5 He had not been gone more than two years or three
Until the wars ended and peace smiled again.
He landed at Hudson on the banks of the stream
Where the banks were all covered and clothed in green.

6   The thoughts of his Mary still ran in his mind.
    He says, "I will go and my Mary will find."
    He sought her with love, oh, he sought her with care.
    For it's long had she wandered and no one knew where.

7   One evening on the banks as he strayed
    Where the wild songsters sang and their notes were displayed,
    The sun was declining and the evening drew near,
    When the voice of his Mary enchanted his ear.

8   He saw her declining from the shade of a tree,
    Where the wild branches wove at the sigh of the breeze.
    Her cheeks were growing pale, she was fairer than the sun,
    And those were the accents that fell from her tongue.

9   "Oh pity, kind heavens, and soothe my sad state,
    And why was I doomed from my Edwin to part?
    Oftimes in the shadow of yonder tall pine
    Have I smoothed down his hair with those fingers of mine.

10 "Perhaps he is drowned in some ocean dark wave
    Where thousands have met with their watery grave;
    Perhaps he has died in some far distant land
    Where his death-bed is soothed with no true lover's hand.

11 "I wish he was entombed in some graveyard near home;
    This moment it's I to his grave I would roam.
    With the finest of laurels I'd entwine round his beard [bier],
    And I'd moisten his grave with an affectionate tear."

12 Young Edwin no longer his feelings could contain.
    He rushed from the ambush, he seized her fair hand.
    "Oh Mary, dear Mary, the joys of my heart,
    Through life until death nevermore shall we part."

56

Die Zwei Soldaten

Sung for me by Mrs. I. B. Keeler, Bemidji, Minnesota, March 15, 1923.
Learned from mother 45 years ago (1870–1880). Philadelphia. Mother born in Germany (Pauline Frisk) in 1847. Came to America in 1866. Married Frederick Prinzing of Philadelphia. Prinzing family came to Forest, Minnesota, when Mrs. K was eight years old (1877). Father had been foreman of a tannery in Philadelphia; farmed in Minnesota.

Mrs. Prinzing quit singing this and other songs of the same type when her youngest child (Mrs. K.) became old enough to understand and ask questions about them. Mrs. P. did not admire the style of story; told her little daughter that a great many stories were told in this fashion (i.e., in song) in Germany.

Leary: Louise M. Prinzing married Irvin B. Keeler (1862–1933) sometime prior to 1890, and the couple raised four children in Winona, Minnesota. On October 19, 1920, the *Bemidji Daily Pioneer* reported the couple's move to that city: "Mr. Keeler, who has served many years in the railway mail service, has recently been transferred to the run between Bemidji and Sauk Center. . . . The family has been prominent in Baptist church circles in Winona." Irvin Keeler was likewise a singer, and Rickaby set down a version of "Shanty-man's Life" (9C) from him.

Louise Keeler's *"Die Zwei Soldaten"* is a popular German folksong, with many versions in the Deutsche Volksliederarchiv (http://www.volks liederarchiv.de/volksliedversion-879.html, accessed February 14, 2015). Associated with the Thirty Years' War of the seventeenth century, this particular song is also part of a larger international complex of ballads and legends about disguised or altered soldiers who, upon returning unrecognized to their parents, are sometimes treated kindly and sometimes robbed and murdered. Major sources include: Maria Kosko, *Le fils assassiné (AT 939 A): Étude d'un thème légendaire*, Folklore Fellows Communications, vol. 198 (Helsinki: Academia Scientiarum Fennica, 1966);

Tom Cheesman, "The Return of the Transformed Son," in *The Shocking Ballad Picture Show: German Popular Literature and Cultural History* (Oxford: Berg Publishers, 1994); and David Hopkin, *Soldier and Peasant in French Popular Culture, 1766–1870* (Woodbridge, UK: Royal Historical Society, 2003), 331–38.

Sung by Mrs. I. B. KEELER, Bemidji, Minnesota

1 Es war einmal zwei bauern
Söhn
[Es war'n einmal zwei
Bauernsöhn][1]
Die hatten Lust ins Feld zu
ziehen [ziehn],
Zu einem soldatischen
Leben,
Zu einem soldatischen
Leben.

There once lived two peasant
sons who

Were eager to go to war,

To lead a soldier's life,

To lead a soldier's life.

2 Und als der Krieg vorüber war
De kammen die Burchen
wieder dar,
[Da kamen die Burschen
wieder dar,]
Die Heimat zu besuchen.
Die Heimat zu besuchen.

And when the war was over,
The young lads came back

To visit their home town.
To visit their home town.

3 Sie ritten durch die
Mittelstrasz [Mittelstraß].

They rode down Main Street.

---

1. English translation and standard German corrections [in brackets], Antje Petty, June 2015.

Frau Wirtin an dem Fenster
   sas [saß],
Mit ihren schwartz braunen
   Augen.
Mit ihren schwartz braunen
   Augen.
[Mit ihren schwarzbraunen
   Augen].

The innkeeper's wife sat in her
   window
With her black-brown eyes.

With her black-brown eyes.

4 Frau Wirtin, haben Sie die
      Gewalt
   Zwei Reiter uber [über]
      Nacht zu behalten?
   Zwei Reiter zu lochieren
      [logieren]
   Zwei Reiter zu lochieren
      [logieren]

"Mrs. Innkeeper, is it in your
      power
To host two cavaliers
      overnight?
To provide lodging for two
      cavaliers?
To provide lodging for two
      cavaliers?"

5 Ja, die Gewalt die habe ich
      schon
   Die eine Frau Wirtin haben
      soll,
   Zwei Reiter zu lochieren
      [logieren].
   Zwei Reiter zu lochieren
      [logieren].

"Yes, I have that kind of
      power
That an innkeeper's wife
      should have,
To provide lodging for two
      cavaliers.
To provide lodging for two
      cavaliers."

6 Sie deckte sogleich den
      weisen [weißen] Tisch,
   Unt brachte darauf gebratne
      Fisch,
   [Und brachte darauf
      gebrat'nen Fisch,]
   Unt [und] auch ein Glas mit
      Wein.
   Unt [und] auch ein Glas mit
      Wein.

She quickly set the white table

And served baked fish,

And also a glass of wine.

And also a glass of wine.

7 Frau Wirtin, bringen Sie was
    Sie wollen.
  Wir haben Silber und auch
    Gold,
  Und auch noch Ungarischer
    [ungarische] Thaler.
  Und auch noch Ungarischer
    [ungarische] Thaler.

"Mrs. Innkeeper, bring us
    what you have.
We have silver and also gold,

And Hungarian coins too.

And Hungarian coins too."

8 Und als sie den [dann] im
    Bette war,
  Da sprach die Frau zu ihrem
    Mann,
  Lasz Uns [Laß uns] den
    Reiter töten.
  Lasz Uns [Laß uns] den
    Reiter töten.

And later, when she was lying
    in bed,
The woman said to her
    husband,
"Let's kill the cavalier.

Let's kill the cavalier."

9 Sie machte sogleich das
    Schmalz heis [heiß],
  Und schütz dem Reiter in
    den Halz,
  [Und schütt's dem Reiter in
    den Hals,]
  Daran must' er gleich
    sterben.
  Daran must' er gleich
    sterben.

She immediately boiled some
    lard,
And poured it down the
    cavalier's throat,

So that he died shortly after.

So that he died shortly after.

10 Sie nahmen ihm [ihn] beide
    bei der Hand
  Und gruben ihn in den
    Keller Sand [Kellersand].
  Hier liegst und bleibst
    verschwunden.
  Hier liegst und bleibst
    verschwunden.

They both grabbed him by his
    hand
And buried him in the
    basement dirt.
"Here you will rest and be lost
    forever.
Here you will rest and be lost
    forever."

11 Un als es Morgens vier Uhr
war
[Und als es morgens vier Uhr
war]
Da kam sein anderer Kamerad.
Ach, Gott! Wo ist mein
Bruder?
Ach, Gott! Wo ist mein
Bruder?

And when it was four in the
morning

His comrade came.
"Dear God! Where is my
brother?
Dear God! Where is my
brother?"

12 Ach, Gott! Wo wirt [wird]
dein Bruder sein?

Sein Rösslein steht im Stall
allein,
Sein Rösslein steht and lauert.

Sein Rösslein steht and lauert.

"Dear God! Where do you
think your brother might
be?
His horse is left alone in the
stable.
His horse is left alone and
waits.
His horse is left alone and
waits."

13 Habt Ihr ihm was zu Leid
gethan,
So habt Ihr's eürem [Eurem]
Sohn gethan
Der erst vom Feld is kommen.

Der erst vom Feld is kommen.

"If you did something to him,

you did the same to your son,

Who has just returned from
the field.
Who has just returned from
the field."

14 Der Mann sich in der
Scheune erhinkt [erhängt],
Die Frau sich in dem Wasser
ertrinkt [ertränkt].
Sind das nich drei
Nordthaten?
Sind das nich drei Nordthaten?
[Sind das nicht drei
Mordtaten]?

The husband hanged himself
in the barn,
The wife drowned herself in
the water.
Aren't these three murders?

Aren't these three murders?

57

The Little German Home

Both words and melody sent me by Mr. Ross, August, 1922. This note is appended: "You will notice the fifth and sixth lines of the first verse are missing. That is the way I got it in 1880."

Andy told me once of singing this song at an entertainment in Charlevoix during the War [World War I], and changing the refrain, because of anti-German sentiment, to, "That little Scottish home across the sea."

Leary: Born in Quebec to Scottish immigrant parents, Andrew Ross (1853–1930) crossed the border to Michigan in 1871. By 1893 he was a foreman and [saw] filer for the Charlevoix Lumber Company, before serving as its superintendent, earning "the reputation of being one of the best hardwood mill men in northern Michigan, and one of the most reliable" (http://www.charlevoixlibrary.org/charlevoix-history, accessed February 8, 2015). The mayor of Charlevoix from 1913 to 1914, Ross had been well known as "an entertainer in the early days . . . and even in later years was frequently called upon to display his talents." His obituary tells us that "Mr. Ross carried on the traditions of his Highland Scotch parentage. He had a natural ear for music, an abundance of wit and humor, and his stock of Scotch songs and dances were known to many" (http://obits .charlevoixlibrary.org/articles/article30207.jpg, accessed August 21, 2015).

The source for three songs in the original *Ballads and Songs of the Shanty-Boy*—"Fair Charlotte" (37), "The Dying Soldier" (50), and "Daniel Monroe" (51)—Ross also contributed an additional pair of Irish ballads, "Drummond's Land" and "Hibernia's Lovely Jane," to Rickaby's unpublished collection. Drawing its tune, theme, and rhetoric from Will S. Hays's 1871 minstrel composition "The Little Old Log Cabin in the Lane," "My Little German Home across the Sea" was copyrighted in 1877 by George S. Knight. Folklorists found it as far-flung in oral tradition as Arkansas, California, and Newfoundland, with England replacing Germany in the latter instance. Versions also appeared on Edison and

Columbia 78 rpm records cut by the influential hillbilly performers Ernest Stoneman (1927) and Charlie Poole and the North Carolina Ramblers (1930).

From ANDREW ROSS, Charlevoix, Michigan

1 I love to think about the days so full of joy and glee,
That never will again come back to me,
Where I used to play about all day, and drive the cows and
sheep,
Until I was just as tired as I could be.
. . . .
. . . .
And when my evening prayer was said, I'd lay me down to sleep
In that little German home across the sea.

Chorus
No matter where I roam, I don't forget my home,
My home that was forever dear to me.
And it's many times a day that my thoughts will fly away
To that little German home across the sea.

2   I never shall forget the day I left my fatherland
    For to sail across the stormy ocean foam.
    My friends around they came and took me by the hand
    And softly wished that I'd come back again.
    My father and my mother, oh, they both stood in the door
    And gave their tearful blessings unto me.
    But now they both are dead; I ne'er shall see them more
    In that little German home across the sea.

3   I have traveled many, many weary miles around this dreary
        world,
    And it's many more I yet expect to roam;
    And when I lay me down to sleep, there in my dreams appear
    A vision of my dear old German home.
    And if my days were over here and it was for the best
    'Twould bring much joy and pleasure unto me,
    If I could close my eyelids now and lay me down to rest
    In that little German home across the sea.

58

The Deutscher Volunteer

Leary: Rickaby's notes for this song included only the singer's name, C. C. Talbott, his residence in Forbes, North Dakota, and the date, September 6, 1922.

Charles Clyde Talbott (1877–1937) was raised on an Iowa farm. Like his parents, born in Indiana and Ohio, he and his wife, Mary Emeline, did not stay in one place, living successively in Nebraska and Missouri before settling on a North Dakota farm near Forbes before 1910. An early advocate of farmer-owned cooperative grain elevators and suppliers, and a supporter of the Nonpartisan League, he became renowned as "The Great Organizer." Talbott helped create the North Dakota Farmers Union and served as its first president from 1927 until his death, a decade later.

A feature story, "Northwest's Ballad Collector Will End Search This Summer," in the *Grand Forks Herald* (April 1, 1923) revealed the Talbotts as a singing family: "Last September on a trip to Forbes, N.D., Professor Rickaby found one of the richest 'deposits' in his years of work. He succeeded in getting 25 songs, most of them from the C. C. Talbott family in which three generations sang for him, the grandmother, the mother and father, and the daughter." Likely Rickaby learned of the family through "the only member of the younger generation who knows and sings the songs . . . Mrs. Gerald Edwards (Gladys Talbott) . . . a former student at the state university."

"The Deutscher Volunteer" is a fragment of "The Dutch Volunteer," composed and actively performed in the 1860s by Harry McCarthy (1834–1888), an Ulster Irish immigrant songwriter, comedian, and entertainer best known for "The Bonny Blue Flag," a paean to a popular Confederate battle flag. McCarthy's song commences in New Orleans with its portrayal of a stereotypically frumpy beer-swilling Dutchman (W. L. Fagan, *Southern War Songs: Camp-Fire, Patriotic and Sentimental* [New York: M. T. Richardson, 1892], 10–12).

It vas in Ni Orleans city,
I first heard der drums und fife,
Und I vas so full mit lager,
Dot I care nix for my life.

Mit a schicken tail stuck in mine hat,
I marched up midout fear,
Und joined der Southern Army,
Like a Dutchie—a volunteer.

Three verses on training ensue, followed by the original lines corresponding with Talbott's rendition.

My name iss Yacob Schneider,
Und I yust come here to-night
From Hood's Army up in Georgia,
Ver all de times dey fight.

But, ven I see der Yankee coming,
So mad it makes me feel,
Dot I jumped apoard der steamer cars,
Und come down to Mopeel.

The song concludes with comic advice about provisions and battle behavior.

Take a couble parrels of sauer-kraut,
Und lots of schweitzer kase,
Also, some perloona sausage,
Und everyting else you please

Und ven der pattle commence,
Kill all der Yankees you can,
Und schump perhind some pig-oak-tree,
For dot ish der officer's blan.

Ven der pattle gits vide open,
Und dem palls dey comes so tick,
Oh! you tink you must go somewhere,
Pecause you vas so sick.

Yust lower your knapsack down yer back,
Und cover up your rear,
Den you von't get vounded,
Like dis Dutcher Volunteer.

Germans were numerous combatants on both sides during the American Civil War. Perhaps Talbott encountered the song in Missouri where German Lutherans, whose Missouri Synod ministers were apologists for slavery, sometimes sided with the Confederacy.

Sung by C. C. Talbott, Forbes, North Dakota

My name iss Yacob Schneider en' I yust come here this night
From der army down in Shorgy vhere ye all der times did fight.
Vehn I first seen dem soldiers, how madt id make me feel,
And I yumped aboard der steam-cars and come down to
    Mobile.

59

Three Grains of Corn

Sung for me by Mrs. C. A. Yoder, Bloomington, Indiana. She learned this song in the winter of 1872–73, which she spent in Austin, Minnesota. Two little girls, daughters of a neighboring Catholic family, used to visit the Yoders. Mrs. Yoder thinks she learned this song from them. (Very probable.)

Mrs. Yoder seemed to think there was a part of the song which related that after the little boy had died, three grains of corn were found in his pocket. She never sang it so, but she said she had heard or seen it that way some time or other.

Leary: Catherine Adelaide Van Buskirk (1846–1924) was born in Monroe County, Indiana, where she married William Henry "Bill" Yoder (1845–1921) in 1864. Bill Yoder was a farmer and blacksmith. The couple had five children and, from the 1860s through the early 1890s, they lived successively in Iowa, Minnesota, and South Dakota before returning to Bloomington, Indiana, sometime before 1900. In 1920 Albert Henry Yoder, Catherine's eldest son, was appointed a professor and the Director of Extension at the University of North Dakota in Grand Forks. Recently widowed, she was visiting her son when Rickaby acquired this song. "Three Grains of Corn," concerning a mother and her dying son, was surely poignant for Catherine Yoder. Her second son, Isaac, was only four when he died in Austin, Minnesota, in the winter of 1872–1873 (http://www.yodernewsletter.org/YNCBOOK/Y2JACOB.htm, accessed May 31, 2015).

"Give Me Three Grains of Corn, Mother" was written by Amanda M. Corey Edmond (1824–1862). Born in Brookline, Massachusetts, she married a Boston merchant, James Edmond, and from 1845 until her death she published verses and children's literature. This particular song was issued in sheet music format by Oliver Ditson of Boston in 1848, the first year of the Irish famine. Frequently printed thereafter in newspapers and poetry anthologies (e.g., Bliss Carman et al., eds., *The World's Best Poetry*, vol. 3, *Sorrow and Consolation* [Philadelphia: John D. Morris, 1904]), "Three Grains of Corn" also circulated in oral tradition. In 1951 MacEdward Leach, for example, recorded a version from Paddy Maher, an Irish Canadian in Flatrock, Newfoundland (http://www.mun.ca/folklore/leach/singers/pmaher.htm, accessed May 31, 2015).

Sung by Mrs. C. A. YODER, Bloomington, Indiana,
and Grand Forks, North Dakota

1 Give me three grains of corn, mother,
   Only three grains of corn.
   It will keep what little life I have
   Till the coming of the morn.
   For I'm dying of hunger and cold, mother,
   Dying of hunger and cold,
   And the agony of such a death
   My lips have never told.

2 Oh, what has old Ireland done, mother,
   Oh, what has old Ireland done,
   That the world looks on and sees them starve,
   Perishing one by one?
   There is many a brave heart, mother,
   That is dying of hunger and cold,
   While only acres across the channel, mother,
   Thousands are rolling their gold.

3   Oh, how can I look to you, mother,
    Oh, how can I look to you,
    For bread to feed your starving child
    When you are starving too?
    For when I read the famine on your cheek
    And in your eyes so wild,
    And I felt it in your bony hand
    When you laid it on your child.

4   You are forced to an empty breast
    Your skeleton babe to hold. . . .
    . . . .
    A babe that is dying of want, mother,
    As you are dying now. . . .

5   It has gnawed like a wolf at my heart, mother,
    A wolf that was fierce for blood,
    All the livelong day and the night beside,
    Gnawing for lack of food.
    I dreamed of bread in my sleep, mother,
    The sight was heaven to see.
    I woke with an eager and famishing lip
    And you had no bread for me.

6   Come nearer to my side, mother,
    Come nearer to my side,
    And hold me fondly as you held
    My father when he died.
    Come quick, for I cannot see you, mother,
    My breath is almost gone.
    Mother, dear mother, ere I die,
    Give me three grains of corn.

60

Ned McCabe

From G. M. Hankins, Gordon, Wisconsin. Learned when a small boy. Hankins born in 1849, came to Wisconsin when 12 years of age. Learned this song about that time.

Leary: The source of two other ballads in Rickaby's collection, "James Bird" (38) and "The Hunters of Kaintucky" (40), the Ohio-born Hankins worked in lumber camps on both the Minnesota and Wisconsin sides of the Saint Croix River. He died in 1934 and is buried in Gordon, Wisconsin.

The children of Irish Canadian immigrants likewise flocked to the Saint Croix valley's woods, mills, and farms, very likely bringing "Ned McCabe" with them (Brian Miller, *Northwoods Song Blog,* http://www .evergreentrad.com/ned-mccabe/, accessed February 16, 2015). Unreported in other folksong collections, the song may well have been composed by one of the thousands of Irish laborers who built Canada's Rideau Canal from 1826 to 1832, connecting Ottawa with the port of Kingston on Lake Ontario. Expressing racist sentiments toward Native peoples that, sadly, were common enough, the song also includes several esoteric phrases. "Nary a red at all" refers to a "red cent" or copper penny. "Twenty jiggers a day" perhaps exaggerates a contracted grog ration dispensed by a "jigger boss" for early nineteenth-century canal diggers on both sides of the US-Canadian border:

> In those days laborers could not be secured without a certain allotment of "grog." The men who came for employment first inquired: "How many jiggers do we get?" He was informed and the next query was, "Let's see your jigger!" Nothing was said about the amount of the wages—the size and frequency of the jigger was the prime consideration. There was, however, an established price for wages—fifty cents a day. (F. C. Johnson, ed., *The Historical Record of Wyoming Valley: A Compilation of Matters of Local*

History from the Columns of the Wilkes-Barre Record [Wilkes-Barre, PA: 1899], 8:246)

Being able to hold one's liquor was crucial, however, as stepping "off o' the plank" scaffolding during canal building might result in injury or death.

From G. M. HANKINS, Gordon, Wisconsin

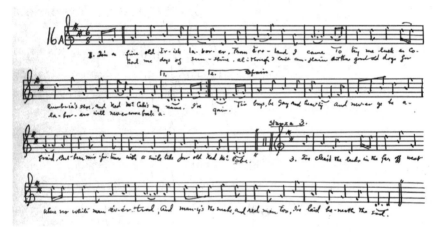

1 I'm a fine old Irish laborer, from Ireland I came
   To try me luck on Columbia's shore, and Ned McCabe's my
      name.
   I've had me days of sunshine, although I can't complain,
   But those good old days for laborers will never come back again.

   Chorus
   'Tis boys, be gay and be hearty, and never ye be afraid,
   But bear misfortune with a smile like poor old Ned McCabe.

2 But when I landed in Quebec, I had nary a red at all.
   I hired out to a contractor, boys, to work upon a canawl.
   I'd be eighty cents a day, me boys, and whiskey too had I,
   But when I think of those good old days, it almost makes me
      cry.

3 I've cleared the lands in the far-off west
Where no white man ever trod,
And many's the snake, and red man too,
I've laid beneath the sod.

4 Now the winter time is coming on, and away down south I'll go
To secure myself a winter's job away from frost and snow.
Old Canady being my favorite whenever there I went,
I could drink my twenty jiggers a day and never step off o' the
plank.

61

The Mines of Carribou

From Mr. Art Milloy, Omemee, North Dakota, June 17, 1923. Learned from a man near Inkster, North Dakota, about 1888, the fall that Harrison was elected president.

The Carribou Mines, according to Milloy, were in a bunch of hills near the Black Hills. He also said that a woman wrote this ballad and "The Dreary Black Hills" to discourage people from going to hunt gold in the Black Hills country.

Milloy got his information, he said, from an old pioneer and Indian scout down in the Wisconsin woods.

Leary: "Carribou" was Rickaby's spelling.

Arthur Milloy (1864–1944) is the source of seven songs in Rickaby's 1926 publication: "The Flat River Girl" (1B), "The Foreman Monroe" (2D), "Shanty-man's Alphabet" (6B), "Save Your Money When You're Young" (7), "Michigan-I-O" (8), "The Flying Cloud" (41), and "Lake Huron's Rock-Bound Shore" (46B). Thanks to Brian Miller's research, we know Milloy was born to Irish immigrant parents in Emily, Ontario, an area settled in the 1820s by Irish from Fermanagh and Cork who typically farmed and worked in the woods. The Milloys were a singing family, and the popular Irish Canadian family band Leahy is descended from Arthur's sister Ann and her husband, John "Black Jack" Leahy. Milloy went into the woods as a teenager and, after marrying Elizabeth Farrell in 1894, he left Canada to work in lumber camps and as a harvest hand in Michigan and North Dakota before settling on a North Dakota farm near Omemee, a community established by Irish Canadians (Brian Miller, "History," *Minnesota Lumberjack Songs* [St. Paul: Two Tap Music, 2011], 10–11, compact disc). Active in the Democratic Party, Milloy decried "socialists" in the Nonpartisan League in 1917 through letters to the editor and at a mass meeting in Bottineau in opposition to the league-controlled state government (*Grand Forks Herald*, February 21 and 27,

1917). In 1918 Milloy placed third in a field of six in the Democratic primary for a seat in the state's House of Representatives; in 1930 he won the Democratic primary but was defeated in the general election.

Although Milloy's source attributed this composition to a woman and situated it in the Dakotas, there is contrary evidence on both counts. In *Ho! for the Black Hills: Captain Jack Crawford Reports the Black Hills Gold Rush and Great Sioux War* (Pierre: South Dakota State Historical Society Press, 2012), a collection of 1874–1877 letters to the *Omaha Bee*, historian Paul L. Hedren includes an 1870s broadside of "The Dreary Black Hills" attributed to "Banjo Dick" Brown, "one of Jack Crawford's closest associates during his Black Hills adventure." Brown was a veteran gold camp entertainer in California, Colorado, and Dakota Territory who eventually departed for Australia in 1879. Intriguingly, Crawford "bounded off for the Cariboo Region of British Columbia" in 1878 (chapter 2). Canada's "Cariboo Gold Rush" commenced in 1858, and as a roving "gold camp entertainer" Brown may well have brought "The Mines of Carribou" to the Dakota Territory. The song's sea voyage and long inland trek correspond with the Canadian experience, and the only other reported versions are from British Columbia. To confuse matters, however, there was a gold mining camp called Caribou (sometimes Cariboo) in the Black Hills, as well as a Great Cariboo Gold Company formed in South Dakota in 1908.

Sung by ART MILLOY, Omemee, North Dakota

1 On the banks of the Mississippi my parents reared me well,
There was nothing for to hinder me along with them to dwell.
But I got discontented, I bid my friends adieu,
So I left them all behind me for the mines of Carribou.

2 With an aching heart I trod the ship that bore me far from
home,
And upon the crowded deck I found myself alone,
With strangers all around me, not one of them I know.
But I kept up my courage for the mines of Carribou.

3 At length our ship she anchored. We landed safe ashore.
I thought my troubles ended, but disappointed sore.
Five hundred miles to travel where none but mosses grew,
And that's the kind of roads we had to the mines of Carribou.

4 There was no way to carry our provisions, or to mount the hills
and plains,
Or nothing for to shelter us from the cutting winds and rain;
Hungry wolves all round us, and tigers in full view,
To ease the lonesome pilgrims on the road to Carribou.

5 But hungry, weak, and weary at length we did arrive,
In the mines of Carribou, half dead and half alive.
For nine long years I toiled and stroved, in search of gold
pursued,
Till I got broken-hearted in the mines of Carribou.

6 So come all you single young men, wherever that you be,
Never leave your happy home for gold or misery.
For every man that makes a strike, misfortune follows two;
So never go a-rambling to the mines of Carribou.

62

The Selkirk

Given me by Mrs. G. H. Walsh, 615 N. 3rd Street, Grand Forks, and her daughter, Gertrude, August 9, 1922. They remembered only one stanza and chorus.

She remembered her brother, William Griggs, a pilot on the Red River, singing it accompanying himself with a banjo. A general favorite (the song). William Griggs served in the Indian Wars, stationed at Fort Abercrombie. Died in 1914 at the Soldier's Home in Minnehaha Falls, Minnesota.

Mrs. Walsh (born Griggs, Laura) born in Cassville, Wisconsin, 1850. Moved to St. Paul, 1852. Married there in September 1868. Moved to Grand Forks in 1875.

Mrs. Walsh's brother, Alexander Griggs, was a captain on the Red. Captain of the Selkirk. Both brothers had been pilots on the Mississippi before coming to the Red. The reference to the Louisiana as "down" in the chorus suggests that the song might have been adapted to the Red River and the Selkirk. Mrs. Walsh said there was no such boat on the Mississippi.

Boats on the Red River: The International; Pluck; Minnesota; Manitoba; Selkirk; Alpha; Cheyenne; Alsip. The Alsip the last one sailing. Most of these owned sooner or later by the local firm of Hill, Griggs, and Kittson.

Leary: When visited by Rickaby in 1922, Laura Griggs Walsh (1850–1937), a widow, was living with her daughter Gertrude Walsh (1877–1958). George H. Walsh (1845–1913), her Canadian-born husband, had been a prominent banker, land speculator, and North Dakota's railroad commissioner (*Bismarck Daily Tribune*, April 8, 1891). Alexander Griggs (1838–1903), Laura's brother and captain of the steamboat *Selkirk*, founded Grand Forks in 1875 and eventually served as mayor, postmaster, and city council member (http://en.wikipedia.org/wiki/Alexander_Griggs, accessed

February 14, 2015). His fellow firm member, James J. Hill, is best known as the chief executive of the Great Northern Railway.

Launched in 1871 to haul freight and passengers, the *Selkirk* was named for Thomas Douglas, the fifth Earl of Selkirk, who presided over the Red River Colony, encompassing parts of Manitoba, Minnesota, and North Dakota in the early nineteenth century (Donald Lilleboe, "Grand Forks and the Steamboat," *Red River Historian* 10 [Winter 1975–1976]: 3–14). Griggs's associated ditty, as Rickaby speculated, was indeed adapted from a prior song, "The Glendy Burk," composed in 1860 by renowned minstrel show songwriter Stephen C. Foster concerning a steamboat that worked the Ohio and Mississippi rivers until hitting a snag and sinking in 1855 near Cairo, Illinois. Unable to discover "versions collected anywhere along the Mississippi itself," Robert Waltz rightly figured it was known on the Upper Mississippi and included "The Glendy Burk" in *The Minnesota Heritage Songbook* (Minneapolis: Fort Snelling Park Association, 2008, 25, 28). Singing banjoist William Griggs, perhaps responsible for substituting the *Selkirk* for the *Glendy Burk*, had indeed piloted steamboats on the Upper Mississippi and Red Rivers. His version makes over only the first verse and chorus of Foster's eight-verse original about a discontented upriver farmhand who joins the *Glendy Burk*'s crew, vowing to bring his sweetheart to New Orleans's "sunny old south."

Sung and played by Miss GERTRUDE WALSH,
Grand Forks, North Dakota

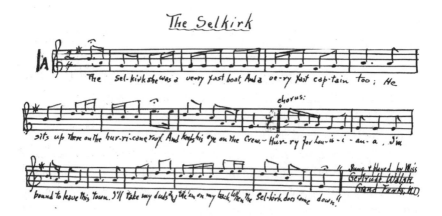

The Selkirk she was a very fast boat,
And a very fast captain too;
He sits up there on the hurricane roof
And keeps his eye on the crew.

   Chorus
Hurry for Louisiana!
I'm bound to leave this town.
I'll take my duds and tote 'em on my back
When the Selkirk does come down.

63

The Song of Mrs. Shattuck

Manuscript sent me by Glennie Todd, Eau Claire, Wisconsin. This note attended it:

"We have come into possession of another song which I am sure you will be interested in. We are sending it to you with a bit of information concerning the setting. It is known as 'The Shattuck Song,' and took place sometime between fifty and fifty-two years ago, 1873–1875. It happened between Jug Creek and Bear Creek as the people were going down Jug Creek hill early in the morning on their way to a Fourth of July celebration at Rockton, Vernon County. A tree was blown onto their wagon, killing Mrs. Shattuck and seriously injuring Mr. Shattuck and their son and daughter. It has been sung. Mrs. Elva Long, Bloom City, Wisconsin, can sing it.

Both of the songs, 'The Fatal Oak' and 'The Shattuck Song,' were written by Mrs. Abbie Payne, a past resident of North Bear Creek, Wisconsin."

—Note date October 5, 1923

Leary: Rickaby's correspondent, Elene "Glennie" Gladys Todd (1906–1986), was born on a farm near Bloom City, Richland County, Wisconsin. She taught school from the mid-1920s through the 1930s prior to marrying Henry Ziemann and settling on a Burnett County farm near Siren. Todd was a student at the Eau Claire State Normal School where Rickaby "delighted a large audience of students and faculty" with a presentation on folksongs. "Listeners were urged to preserve whatever of such material might come their way" ("Ballads of Old Days Delight Normal School," *Eau Claire Leader*, July 13, 1923). The "we" in Ms. Todd's message is her first cousin Lee Todd, a fellow schoolteacher likewise raised in Bloom City, whom Rickaby credits as having sent him a copy of Abbie Payne's "The Fatal Oak" (29). Regarding "The Song of Mrs. Shattuck," Beatrix Marie Larson, the great-granddaughter of the fatally injured Eliza Little Shattuck, reported that her mother, Roberta Larson, came by a "copy of that ballad written on a paper flour sack," thanks to Lee Todd's mother, Alta, whose husband's family had preserved it for several generations (*Looking at Bear Creek* [Richland County, WI, 1995], 370). Both Glennie and Lee Todd were neighbors of the singer Elva Mae Kidd Long (1878–1944), who farmed with her husband, Orville Long, in the Town of Bloom.

The song's composer, Abigail Jane Ingraham Harness Payne (1833–1921) was the youngest of seven children born in Carmichaels, Pennsylvania, to John and Tamara (Potts) Ingraham. In 1849 she traveled with a married older sister, Massie Cumly, to Green County, Wisconsin. There she married Levi Harness, a farmer, in 1853 and the couple had six children. Levi died in 1866, and two years later Abigail married another farmer, Truman Payne, with whom she had three children before divorcing him in 1884 (Larson, *Looking at Bear Creek*, 329–31).

Abbie Payne did not write music but set some of her poems to the era's hymn tunes. "The Song of Mrs. Shattuck" concerns a friend and neighbor, Eliza (Little) Shattuck, the wife of George Washington Shattuck, who died seventeen days after being struck by a windfall on July 4, 1873. A native of Northern Ireland, the wife of a much admired Civil War veteran, and the mother of five children, Eliza Shattuck had been farming with her husband in Vernon County for less than a year (*History of Vernon County, Wisconsin* [Springfield, IL: Union, 1884], 641–42; Earl M. Rogers, ed., *Memoirs of Vernon County* [Madison, WI: Western Historical Association, 1907]).

From GLENNIE TODD, Eau Claire, Wisconsin

1 Farewell, my dear husband and children, farewell.
  How I feel to leave you, there is no one can tell.
  We've enjoyed all the pleasure this life can afford,
  And now I must leave you and dwell with my Lord.

2 In my richest attire on the Fourth of July,
  How little we knew that death was so nigh!
  My whole family circle, my husband and me,
  Came nigh getting killed by a limb from a tree.

3 While passing through the green woods and down a long hill,
A storm was fast approaching, my blood seemed to chill.
My soul was filled with horror, but all did no good.
It was bound to overtake us while passing through the wood.

4 The storm came on quickly, the wind it did blow.
The lightning did flash and the thunder did roll.
The trees were fast a-falling, the limbs all around.
One fell on our wagon and swept us to the ground.

5 We were picked up insensible, all of our sad fate,
And carried to the neighbor's our destiny to wait.
But when I survived from the wounds I received
The state of my family my spirit did grieve.

6 But I have no time to murmur, for soon I must go
To leave my dear family and friends here below.
But your Master has told you that you can come to me,
For I must go forever and cannot come to thee.

7 My thanks to the Grangers for this kindness to me.
There's a lodge up in heaven for thee and for me.
The Savior is our President, our password is prayer.
We will gain the lost victory when we get up there.

8 Farewell, Christian friends this whole world around.
I shall sleep in the grave till the trumpet shall sound.
Then my Master will call me and bid me arise
To meet you in glory in yonder bright skies.

9 Farewell, my dear husband, for you I do love.
Prepare for to meet me in heaven above.
We will celebrate a day far better than this.
Where the storm and the tempest of this life is past.

10 Farewell, my dear children, I bid you adieu.
This time is fast approaching when I must leave you.
But your father will love you as he has done before.
Prepare for to meet me on Canaan's bright shore.

11 My family is surviving and free from all pain.
They all have got better and gone home again.
But oh, how lonesome and lonely it will be,
For that bright and happy home is no longer for me.

12 Farewell, my dear mother, I can no longer wait.
You will come to see me, but will be too late,
For I will be buried beneath the cold clay.
Come visit the spot and see where I lay.

13 She claps her bright wings and we see her no more.
We think we now see her on Canaan's bright shore,
Where the angels are waiting to welcome her home,
Where the storm and the tempest never can come.

64

Paul and His Chickens

From Miss Huldah Listug, Roseau, Minnesota, a student who I met in one of the Minnesota Normal Schools, 1923.

Leary: Huldah C. Listug (1897–1982) was born in Roseau, the daughter of Norwegian immigrants, Thore Listug (1847–1919) and Sigrid Listug (1855–1909). She is mentioned as a teacher in the *Bemidji Daily Pioneer*, September 7, 1922. At some point she acquired training in nursing and moved to Minneapolis, where she is listed in the 1940 census as a "practical nurse" seeking rest home work, while living in a boardinghouse with mostly Scandinavian women. She is buried in the Lakewood Cemetery, Minneapolis.

The song Listug sang for Rickaby is an artful English translation of a Norwegian folksong, "Pål på Haugen" (Paul on the Hill), that has been widely sung in the United States for more than a century. After emigrating from Norway in 1913, Carsten Woll (1885–1962) popularized the song through concert appearances, recordings for Columbia in 1915 (E2540) and Victor in 1917 (72581) and including it as "Paal paa Haugen" in his influential *Sangbog for Sönner af Norge* (Minneapolis: Supreme Lodge of Sons of Norway, 1926, 106). An English translation, quite different from Listug's, was subsequently published in the bilingual *Sons of Norway Songbook* (Minneapolis: Supreme Lodge of the Sons of Norway, 1948, 112–13). The standard-setting Woll version, in both Norwegian and English, has only three verses, however, matching the first, second, and fourth in Listug's rendition. A Norwegian equivalent of Listug's third verse may be found in the *Slim Jim and the Vagabond Kid Song Collection* (Minneapolis: Ernest and Clarence Iverson, 1939), published by the Iverson brothers, radio entertainers who barnstormed throughout Minnesota in the 1930s.

"Hadd' eg no nebb, og hadd' eg no klo,
og visste eg berre kvar revane låg,
skull' eg dei både rispa og klora
framantil nakken og bak over lår.
 Skam få alle revane raude!
 Skam få alle revane raude!
 Gud han gjeve dei alle var daude,
 Så skull' eg trygt koma heim åt ho mor!"

From Miss HULDAH LISTUG, Roseau, Minnesota

1 Paul let his chickens run down from the hillside,
 They o'er the hill went tripping along.
 Paul understood by the way they were acting,
 Reynard was out with his red tail so long.

 Chorus
 Chuck, chuck, chuck
 Chuck, chuck, chuck,
 The chickens were sighing
 Chuck, chuck, chuck,
 The chickens were sighing,
 Paul was making such faces and crying,
 "Now I'm afraid to go home to my ma."

2 Paul then did go further up on the hillside,
 There he saw Reynard on a hen lie and gnaw.
 Paul a big stone did pick up with his hand and
 Finally he threw at the Reynard's old jaw.
 Reynard he ran and
 His tail kept shaking.
 Reynard he ran and
 His tail kept shaking.
 Paul's poor old heart for his chickens was breaking—
 "Now I'm afraid to go home to my ma."

3 "Had I now jaws and had I now claws, and
 If I but knew where old Reynard lay,

How I would bite him and how I would scratch him.
I off his body his hide would soon flay.
Shame on all the
Red-haired foxes.
Shame on all the
Red-haired foxes!
Oh, how I wish they were dead in their boxes,
Then I'd not fear to go home to my home."

4 Paul took some corn to the mill and he ground it,
So that it echoed forth far and wide.
Dust and the chaffs were flying around him.
There stood the meal in a bag by his side.
Paul now roared and
Laughed till the tears came.
Paul now roared and
Laughed till the tears came.
"Now I have paid for my eggs and my chickens.
Now I can safely go home to my ma!"

65

Hunting Deer (Air: Casey Jones)

Miss McGrady taught at Becida, Minnesota, in which community this song was made and sung. Becida was a Scandinavian community, rather backward and isolated. Some of the children had never been to town in their lives. The community was heavily intermarried, and very fond of self-entertainment. This song, probably written by Gettsmer, a German there, was sung over and over. Not all the song is given here. The object was probably not so much to record actual incidents of the hunt as to "guy" certain members of the community.

Leary: The singer is likely Irene C. McGrady, a schoolteacher born in 1904, in the Park Rapids area of Hubbard County, Minnesota, not far south from Becida and Bemidji. Becida's surroundings were heavily timbered, and its settlers worked in the woods, established small farms, fished, and hunted. Census records suggest the song's composer was a bachelor farmer, German-born Fred C. Gutzmer or Getsmer (1847–1950), who immigrated to the United States ca. 1880, turning up in Hubbard County before 1905. The song mentions two local hunters, both bachelors born in 1866 and perhaps Gutzmer's hunting companions: Anton O. Hanson (1866–1931), born in Minnesota to Norwegian immigrant parents, and Swedish-born Martin B. Matson.

Deer-hunting poetry is a longstanding tradition in the Upper Midwest, frequently celebrating and satirizing local characters and incidents, as suggested by Rickaby's use of "guy" ("to tease, kid, josh," *Dictionary of American Regional English*, ed. Frederic G. Cassidy and Joan Houston Hall [Cambridge, MA: Harvard University Press, 1991], 2:857). The Becida song's borrowed tune, "Casey Jones," began circulating in popular culture and oral tradition in the first decade of the twentieth century. Its opening lines—"Come all you rounders if you want to hear / The story of a brave engineer"—commemorate the death of a railroad engineer, John Luther "Casey" Jones, and are echoed by Gutzmer (Norm Cohen,

Long Steel Rail: The Railroad in American Folksong, 2nd ed. [Urbana: University of Illinois Press, 2000], 132–65). The phrase "shipping tag" seems to indicate market rather than subsistence hunting, further suggesting that the memorialized incident may have happened in the 1890s or very early twentieth century. In 1895 Minnesota's hunters were restricted to five deer; the limit dropped to three in 1901, to two in 1905, and to one in 1915.

From IRENE MCGRADY, Bemidji, Minnesota

1 Come on, ye hunters, if ye want to hear
   That famous story of hunting deer.
   A deer in the woods and not a deer in the bag,
   And it isn't quite ready for the shipping tag.

2 Away last fall a-hunting I went,
   The ammunition wasted and the time I spent.
   And when I returned all tired and sore
   I vowed I'd never go a-hunting any more.

   Chorus
   Don't skin your deer before you kill it,
   Don't hang it up before it's dead.
   Don't have its hide tanned into buckskin,
   Nor a taxidermist mount its head.

3 There's Martin Mattson, a big tall Swede,
   He said, "Bring 'em round and I'll give 'em what they need."
   A deer he saw, and a deer he shot.
   Did that deer drop? Well, I guess not.

4 There's Anton Hanson, he's six foot tall,
   He went hunting a way last fall.
   The stag went round, so some people say.
   He could kill a deer half a mile away.

An Inventory of
Franz Rickaby's Notebooks

Compiled by MATT APPLEBY, Mills Music Library,
University of Wisconsin–Madison

VOLUME 1: BALLADS AND SONGS
OF THE SHANTY-BOY

1. Gerry's Rocks
2. Jack Haggerty
3. Jim Whalen
4. The Banks of the Little Eau Pleine
5. The Shanty-man's Alphabet
6. Save Your Money When You're Young
7. Michigan-I-O
8. The Shanty-man's Life
9. The Shanty-boy and the Farmer's Son
10. The Shanty-boy on the Big Eau Claire
11. Ye Noble Big Pine Tree
12. The Little Brown Bulls
13. Jim Porter's Shanty Song
14. The Three McFarlands
15. Ye Maidens of Ontario
16. The Falling of the Pine
17. The Pinery Boy
18. The Maine-ite in Pennsylvania
19. Driving Saw-logs on the Plover
20. Fred Sargent's Shanty Song
21. On the Lac San Pierre
22. The Festive Lumberjack
23. The Crow Wing Drive
24. The M. and I. Goo-goo Eyes
25. Harry Dunn
26. Harry Bail
27. Shanty Teamster's Marseillaise
28. The Fatal Oak
29. Bung Yer Eye
30. The Backwoodsman
31. The River in the Pines
32. Silver Jack
33. Ole from Norway
34. The Lost Jimmie Whalen
35. Kenneth Cameron
36. A-lumbering We Go (The Logger's Boast)
37. 'Way Down Near Alpena

VOLUME 2: BALLADS AND SONGS OF THE AMERICAN WARS

A. *Colonial (Indian) and Revolutionary Wars*

1. The Battle of Point Pleasant

B. *War of 1812*

1. James Bird
2. The Hunters of Kaintucky

C. *The Mexican War*

1. The Texas Rangers
2. The Battle of Buena Vista
3. My Pretty Little Pink
4. Jackson

D. *The Civil War*

1. The Charge at Fredericksburg
2. The Monitor and the Merrimac
3. The Cumberland's Crew
4. Colonel Ellsworth
5. Libby Prison
6. The Faded Coat of Blue
7. The Drummer Boy of Shiloh
8. The Soldier Boy at Gettysburg
9. Sherman's March to the Sea
10. Richmond on the James
11. Old Governor Jackson
12. The Deutscher Volunteer
13. The Bounty-jumper
14. The Wisconsin Soldier-boy (The Dying Soldier)

15. 'Way Down in the Cane-brake
16. Hold My Shoulder, Faithful Pompey
17. Just Before the Battle
18. Just After the Battle
19. Soldier's Return
20. You Said Last Night, Dear Reuben
21. Glory, Glory, Hallelujah (John Brown's Body)
22. The Guerillas (A Southern War Song)

E. *The Spanish-American War*

1. In the Land of the Philippines
2. The Battle of Bungou
3. Ain't It Nice to Be a Soldier
4. [Comrades Dear and Did You Hear]
5. Just As the Sun Went Down
6. The Blue and the Gray
7. The Dewey Far Away
8. Down in the Harbor of Havana
9. I'm Called Away

F. *The World War*

1. Hinky Dinky, Parlez Vous
2. Ashes to Ashes
3. *Pas de Cogniac*
4. *Apres la Guerre*

VOLUME 3: BALLADS AND SONGS OF THE COWBOY

1. The Dying Cowboy (The Cowboy's Lament)
2. The Cowboy's Lament (The Dying Cowboy)
3. Round-up Lullaby
4. Whoopee ti yi yo, Git Along Little Dogies
5. The Dreary, Dreary Life

6. The Old Chisholm Trail
7. The Easy Rider
8. Punching Cows

9. The Texas Kid
10. The Cowboy's Dream

VOLUME 4: BALLADS AND SONGS OF THE LATER FRONTIER

1. A Home on the Range
2. The Stone That Keeps Rolling
3. The Mines of Caribou
4. The Little Old Sod Shanty on My Claim
5. The Dreary Black Hills
6. The Little Old Log Cabin in the Lane

7. California Joe
8. The Buffalo Skinners (Range of the Buffalo)
9. The Dying Ranger
10. Joe Bowers
11. Dakota Land
12. The Old Sod Shack
13. A Packer's Wooing

VOLUME 5: BALLADS AND SONGS TRANSPLANTED TO AMERICA

1. The House Carpenter (The Daemon Lover)
2. The Brown Girl (Lord Thomas and Fair Ellinor)
3. Barbary Allen (Barbara Allen)
4. Mary Across the Wild Moor
5. On the Banks of the Clyde
6. The Battle of Harlaw
7. The Rich Merchant's Daughter (Constant Farmer's Son)
8. Drummond's Land
9. Van Dieman's Shore
10. The Dying Soldier (In Old Erin Far Away)
11. Hibernia's Lovely Jane
12. Peggy Walker

13. The Silver Dagger (The Drowsy Sleeper)
14. Old Crumny
15. Three Loving Brothers
16. The Wild Shore
17. The Noble Skew Bald
18. The Heights of Alma
19. Brennan on the Moor
20. Rosalie, the Prairie Flower
21. They Say I May Marry a Laird
22. The Old Miller
23. My Willie's on the Dark Blue Sea
24. The Old Virginia Lowlands
25. *Die zwei Soldaten*
26. Lady Leroy
27. Young Sandy

VOLUME 6: SEA CHANTEYS AND LAKE SONGS

A. Hoisting and Other Chanteys

1. Sally Brown
2. Blow the Man down

3. *Vidi Vidi Vik*
4. Were You Ever in Rio Grand?
5. Blow, Boys, Blow

6. Haul on the Bow-lin'
7. English Chantey
8. We'll Pay Paddy Doyle
9. A Long Time Ago

B. Sea Ballads

1. The Flying Cloud
2. The Clipper Ship Dreadnaught
3. Bold Daniel
4. The Demon of the Sea
5. Paul Jones, the Privateer

C. Lake Ballads

1. Persian's Crew
2. Red Iron Ore
3. The Bigler's Crew
4. Samuel Hall (Samuel Small)

D. River Ballads and Songs

1. The Selkirk
2. The Raging Canawl

VOLUME 7: BIOGRAPHY AND AUTOBIOGRAPHY

1. McAfee's Confession
2. The Wild Colonial Boy
3. Jim Fiske
4. The Boston Burglar
5. Morrisey and the Russian Sailor
6. Heenan and Sayers
7. The Little German Home
8. Jesse James
9. The Beggar Maid
10. In Springfield Town (Springfield Mountain)
11. Sam Bass
12. Charles Guiteau
13. The Emigrants' Lament (Scotch)
14. S. D. Knowles (The Ballad of a Blowhard)
15. The Dying Nun
16. Ned McCabe
17. The Roving Irishman
18. Heroic Dick
19. The Village Blacksmith
20. We Have Been Friends Together
21. Poor Little Joe
22. The Soldier's Poor Little Boy
23. The Wild Rover
24. The Fatal Hiss
25. Wisconsin Again
26. The Old Musician and His Harp
27. The Deep, Deep Sea (Sea Burial)
28. Hard Up

VOLUME 8: CATASTROPHE

1. The Chatsworth Wreck (Chatsworth Bridge)
2. The Two Orphans
3. Lost on the Lady Elgin
4. The Boston Fire
5. Jim Blake
6. Old Ninety-seven
7. Minnehaha, Laughing Water (New Ulm Massacre)
8. Late Shooting
9. Dublin Bay
10. Song of Mrs. Shattuck
11. Fair Charlotte (Young Charlotte)
12. Naragansett Bay

VOLUME 9: LOVERS AND RELATIVES, FAITHFUL AND FAITHLESS

1. The Fatal Wedding
2. Drifting Apart
3. Edwin and Mary (The Dark British Foes)
4. The Creole Girl on Lake Ponchartrain
5. Come Home, Father
6. Red River Valley
7. Johanna Shay
8. Grandfather's Story
9. The Stepmother
10. Johnny Sands
11. Over the Hills to the Poorhouse
12. The Gipsy's Warning
13. The Sick Husband
14. Will and Kate
15. Fuller and Warren
16. Daniel Monroe
17. Brown Girl
18. The Beautiful Christine Leroy (Christine Leroy)
19. Rosabelle
20. Liziany Quirl
21. My Darling Irish Boy
22. Twilight on a May Morning
23. Young Henry Green
24. Young Betsy
25. Fair Fanny Moor
26. Weeping Willows
27. Sweet William, the Sailor Boy [fragment]

VOLUME 10: INDIAN AND DIALECT

1. Falling Leaf
2. The Indian's Lament
3. White Man, Let Me Go
4. Niagara Falls
5. The Pale-faces
6. The Blue Juniata
7. The Indian Maid
8. Indian Death Song
9. Amanda, the Captive
10. Forget Me Not
11. A Norwegian Folksong Melody
12. The Deutscher Volunteer
13. The Wild Irishman
14. The Irish Barber
15. Dan McGinty
16. The O'Kelly Brothers
17. Lannigan's Ball
18. A True Paddy's song
19. Oh! Susanna
20. Every Day'll Be Sunday
21. If My Father Should Ask for Me

VOLUME 11: PROPAGANDA AND SOCIAL CLASS

1. Three Grains of Corn

VOLUME 12: DIALOG, NURSERY AND GAME SONGS

1. So We Hunted and We Hallooed
2. Father Sent Me Here A-courting
   (The Quaker's Courtship)
3. The Paper of Pins
4. The Seven Days of Christmas
5. Paul and His Chickens
6. The Man Who Wouldn't Hoe
   Corn

VOLUME 13: UNCLASSIFIED

1. Hunting Deer
2. The Blackberry Girl
3. Mother Shipman's Prophecy
4. The King and His Three Sons
5. A Motto for Every Man
6. Wait for the Wagon
7. Behind the Times

VOLUME 14: ADDENDUM

1. Jane and Lucy
2. The Dumb Wife
3. By the Side of the River So Clear
4. The Lament of the Sailor's Wife
   (The Sailor Boy)
5. Timo'ra
6. Sam Bass
7. The London Boy
8. The Sabbath Day Was Ending in
   a Village by the Sea
9. Chisholm Trail
10. I'm a Bold, Bad Man
11. It's Hard for to Love
12. I'm Bound to Follow the Long
    Horn Cow
13. O Bury Me Not on the Lone
    Prairie
14. The Irish Wake
15. The Roving Boy
16. Sid Mason's Waltz
17. *Saeterjentens Sondag*
18. *Den Store, Hvide Flok Vise*

Glossary

The following definitions are those of a few of the terms and expressions found in the shanty-boy's vocabulary.

Bateau. A flat-bottomed but not ungraceful boat of the skiff variety, varying somewhat in pattern in different localities, used on the waters of the logging country.

Birl. To revolve or whirl. Specifically applied to revolving a log in the water while standing on it; "rolling it squirrel fashion with the feet" (White). Broadly it came to mean to handle or manipulate skillfully, as applied to anything. "To birl the crooked steel" ("The Festive Lumberjack") meant to handle the cant-hook or peavy skillfully.

Birler. One skilled in birling or rolling. A "white water birler" meant a skillful and daring riverman generally. Paul Bunyan was said to be able to "birl a log till the bark came off and then run ashore on the bubbles." The "broncho busting" of the riverman was the "log rolling," a birling contest between two men on the same log, the object of each being to dislodge the other.

Boom. An enclosure formed by logs chained end to end, in which other logs were gathered and held—corralled, the cowboy would say. When different owners had logs driven down the same stream at the same time, the logs were thus separated at their destination. Such enclosures, filled with logs and secured by chains and lines, were often towed long distances, as across lakes, to the mills.

Boot-pack. A heavy and roomy foot-wear, usually of rubber, somewhat higher than a shoe, buckled or laced. Its roominess allowed the wearing of several pairs of thick woolen socks. This was worn mainly in the winter or cutting period, giving way to the corked, or calked, shoe or boot on the drive.

Cant-hook. An implement consisting of a strong handle perhaps five feet in length, from about the lower third of which swings a large steel hook. Used in rolling or moving logs, as in loading and unloading, decking, or piling, the logs at the roll-ways. Although simple in design and principle, a difficult instrument to learn to use efficiently.

Centre jam. A log jam that forms free of the banks of the stream, usually upon some rock or obstruction amid stream.

Corks (calks). Sharp spikes screwed or driven into the soles of the riverman's boots. They were indispensable in driving logs, as they alone guaranteed sureness of footing on floating logs.

Crib. A raft.

Cross-haul. A line (chain) used in the early days in loading logs. Cross-haul loading, in spite of the fact that it has been superseded by the modern (but less romantic) steam loaders, served the shanty-boy long and well. The process required four men: a loader, or top-loader, whose position was on the sled; two cant-hook men, who controlled the progress of the log up the incline; and the cross-haul man, who drove the animal by which the log was drawn up. The cant-hook men, having put a log in position at the base of the pieces inclined from the ground against the sled, or the load, at whatever stage it might be, a line was passed across the load from the side opposite the log to be loaded, over and under the log, and the end hooked firmly to the sled bunk or the load. When this was done, the cross-haul man hooked his animal to the other end of the line and drove forward, rolling the log up the incline. The two cant-hook men saw to it that the log went up evenly. At the psychological moment the loader shouted the cross-haul man a halting signal, and putting his cant-hook to the log, dropped it squarely where it was needed on the load. This makes clear the degree of the lumberjack's boasting when he intimates that his "peakers" rise so high that his cross-haul man has to work by a code of signals, as the loader's "Whoa!" could not be heard so far below! (See "The Festive Lumberjack.")

Cruiser. A "land-looker." "The cruiser's duty is to establish definitely the company's boundary lines and to estimate the amount of lumber that can be obtained from the land within these confines. Using his compass, the cruiser paces off the boundaries of an acre of land. Though going through thick underbrush, often having to chop his way through, or clambering up a steep hillside covered by a slippery carpet of pine needles, the cruiser will not miss his paced measurement by as much as a foot. After measuring off the acre, he looks at the trees and estimates the exact size of each one large enough for cutting, the amount of lumber obtainable from each such tree in the acre, and thus how much there will be to the acre. It is uncanny to see an old cruiser at work. A mere glance at a tree tells him its circumference in inches, another its height in feet; and almost as by magic he sets down the amount of linear feet of lumber which, with the most economical cutting and sawing, can be had from that tree." (Miss Helen Blymyer, Pomona College, student essay on logging.)

Deacon seat. A bench, or more properly a shelf, consisting usually of a single wide board, projecting from the lower tier of berths or bunks in the bunk-shanty or sleeping quarters. This seat extended thus practically entirely around the room. In the center stood the stove. The deacon seat was the only seating facility offered by the ordinary camp, if one excepts the floor. It was the shanty-boy's throne, where of olden days he sat after supper and smoked and talked, told stories, or sang. See illustration, page 176.

Drive. The shanty-boy's "round-up." The floating of the winter's cut down the stream to market when the ice went out in the spring. It was the climax of the year's work, significant somewhat for its many dangers, but mainly for the fact that it immediately preceded the shanty-boy's annual celebration: the spending of his stake.

Driver. A man employed on the drive. A riverman.

Fleet. A group of rafts under the command of a pilot.

Go-devil. A stubby, sled-like affair, three or four feet in length, shaped like the letter A with the point turned up. Used in skidding logs, especially large ones. The front end of the log was hauled up on the go-devil and secured by a single wrap of chain. The skidding team, or yoke of oxen, was hitched to the point of the diminutive sled and the log half-sledded, half-dragged to the skidways. See illustration, page 171.

Jam. A congestion and piling-up of logs on the drive. Preventing jams, or breaking them if they formed in spite of him, was the principal care of the driver. Some logging rivers were famous, or notorious, for their jams, literally dozens of them occurring on every drive. Jams were variously caused: by a sharp turn in the channel of the stream, by obstruction amid stream, by the confluence of two streams, or by any condition which interrupted the straight flow of the current and set the logs to swirling, or as the cowboy might say, "milling."

Jam-pike. An implement consisting of a pole or shaft twelve or fifteen feet long, with a combined spike and hook at one end. The point of the spike had a slight spiral twist, so that, when once struck forcibly into a log, it stuck fast until the pole was given a turn backwards—unscrewed, as it were. The jam-pike was used in "punching" logs—handling and guiding them, especially in still water. Also called a pike-pole.

Jobber. One who takes a contract to get out the timber in a certain territory for a company.

Landing. A place along the stream where the winter's cut of logs is piled on the bank, and even down onto the ice. The logs are piled parallel to the stream, and when the ice goes out in the spring, the landings are "broken down" into the swollen river, inaugurating the drive.

Loader. Specifically, the man who stands on the sled and receives and guides into place the logs drawn up by the cross-haul. Sometimes called the top-loader. A position requiring skill with the cant-hook, and considerable agility and presence of mind.

Mossback. A farmer. Sometimes spelled "mothback."

Peavy. A tool exactly like the cant-hook except that the handle ends in a spike. The peavy is the driver's constant companion and is indispensable to him.

Pike-pole. See *jam-pike.*

Pilot. A man in charge of a fleet of rafts. He is, of course, a skilled riverman and thoroughly familiar not only with the river on which he is rafting but also with rivers and their ways generally. The Ross Gamble mentioned in "On the Banks of the Little Eau Pleine" and the "Sailor Jack" O'Brien mentioned in "The Shanty-boy on the Big Eau Claire" were such pilots.

Raft. Logs or lumber banded together for floating down the larger rivers. See also *rapids piece.*

Raftsman. One employed in managing rafts, as against driving loose logs.

Rapids piece. A section of a raft. So called because when approaching a dangerous rapids the raft was divided for easier handling in the passage.

Riverman. A shanty-boy employed on the drive. A driver.

Roll-way. Logs or trimmed trunks laid down, twelve or fifteen feet apart, to receive the logs piled at the landings. They facilitated piling or decking the logs through the winter and breaking them out and rolling them into the river in the spring.

Scaler. The man who computed the amount of lumber in the logs cut. He computed this by a mathematical process based on the diameter of the log at the smaller end. As he scaled each log, he marked it. He usually worked at the landings.

Shanty. Any of the several buildings comprising a logging camp. In the plural, means a camp. Thus: "To the shanties he will not go—"

Shanty-boy. A member of a logging crew. A lumberjack. In the golden days of logging the woodsman evidently preferred the name "shanty-boy." At least it is the word he uses most generally in referring to himself. Probably owes its prevalence to the Irish.

Shingle-bolt. A short billet of wood, usually cedar, from which shingles were hewn or sawed.

Skidding. The process of drawing the saw-log from where the tree was felled to the skidway. The log was dragged by oxen or horses. The skidding of larger logs was facilitated by the use of a go-devil. See illustration, page 171.

Skidway. The point to which the logs were skidded, and where they were piled convenient for loading on sleighs for hauling to the landings. The skidways were at points along the prepared roads from the river back into the timber.

Stake. Specifically, the collective term for the shanty-boy's earnings for a season, which he drew in a lump after the drive, or when he quit the camp for any reason. The amount of a full year's stake varied between two hundred and six hundred dollars, depending upon the rate of pay. More generally, a "stake" was any considerable sum of money in the shanty-boy's possession and at his disposal.

Sucker. A derisive term applied to the new man in the shanties, or more particularly on the river, as in rafting.

Swamper. A man whose work was that of clearing the fallen tree of limbs, knots, etc., and preparing the way generally for the sawyers, who cut the trunks into logs. Also worked at cutting and clearing the roads. The swamper stood on the first and lowest rung of the shanty-boy ladder.

Switch-hog. A small engine used on log trains. A switch engine.

Tote team. The team used in bringing supplies overland by sled from the trading centers to the camps. In early days these hauls were scores of miles. Horses were used, even in the days of oxen, because of their superior speed and endurance. The sled was the tote sled.

Wanigan (also *wangan* and *wanagan*). (1) The store or canteen in the camp, maintained by the company, where the shanty-boy obtained what he needed or wanted in the way of clothing, tobacco, etc. (2) A large, heavy boat or scow, generally enclosed, in the charge of the cook and his helpers, which followed the drive down and was the base of provisions and supplies and the general headquarters on the drive. See illustration, page 149.

White water. The riverman's highly descriptive name for rapids or any rough passage in a river. "Paul Bunyan was a 'white water bucko' and rode water so rough it would tear an ordinary man in two even to drink out of the river." (W. B. Laughead, *Paul Bunyan and his Big Blue Ox.*) See illustration, page 149.

Index of Titles

349

Index of First Lines

Index of Singers and Song Sources

This index includes people who sang or recited songs for Rickaby, as well as those who provided him with unpublished manuscript copies of songs and those who offered accounts of singers and songs.

FRANZ RICKABY (1889–1925) was born in Arkansas, educated at
Knox College and Harvard University, and taught at the University of
North Dakota. GRETCHEN DYKSTRA was the founding president of the
National 9/11 Memorial Foundation, commissioner of the New York City
Department of Consumer Affairs, and president of the Times Square Alliance.
JAMES P. LEARY is professor emeritus of folklore and Scandinavian studies
at the University of Wisconsin–Madison. His publications include the
Grammy-nominated multimedia production *Folksongs of Another America.*